Praise for *Employee Benefits and*

"When Alan Cohen opened the doors at Liazon in 2007, he revolutionized the way insurance was sold. Though the idea was simple, it was also ahead of its time. Liazon was among the first companies to establish a private health insurance exchange, a trend that has since exploded. *Employee Benefits and the New Health Care Landscape* gives us a rare, inside look into the mind that created 'the exchange wave' ten years ago."

—**Kathryn Mayer**, Editor-in-Chief, *Employee Benefit News*

"Regardless of your political affiliation, sitting out the current debate on health care and benefits is no longer an option. Private exchanges offer one solution to one part of the problem; this book explains why."

—**Christopher E. Condeluci**, CC Law & Policy PLLC, ACA expert

"It has been my pleasure to work with Alan Cohen over the years and observe the private exchange evolution firsthand. The industry has been in need of a book like this for a very long time."

—**Rhonda Marcucci**, Vice President, HR & Benefits Technology
Consulting Practice at Gruppo Marcucci, a division of
Gallagher Benefit Services, Inc.

EMPLOYEE BENEFITS AND THE NEW HEALTH CARE LANDSCAPE

EMPLOYEE BENEFITS AND THE NEW HEALTH CARE LANDSCAPE

How Private Exchanges Are Bringing Choice and Consumerism to America's Workforce

ALAN COHEN

With

JAMI KELMENSON

For information about buying this title in bulk quantities, or for special sales opportunities (which may include electronic versions; custom cover designs; and content particular to your business, training goals, marketing focus, or branding interests), please contact our corporate sales department at corpsales@pearsoned.com or (800) 382-3419.

For government sales inquiries, please contact governmentsales@pearsoned.com.

For questions about sales outside the U.S., please contact intlcs@pearson.com.

Company and product names mentioned herein are the trademarks or registered trademarks of their respective owners.

The health care landscape is changing rapidly. As a result, we have made every effort to keep the information and resources in this book as up to date as possible. All the opinions of the author and individuals and third-party sources quoted are accurate as of the time they were obtained, and like health care and benefits, are subject to evolve over time.

ISBN-10: 0-13-466530-9
ISBN-13: 978-0-13-466530-6

Pearson Education LTD.
Pearson Education Australia PTY, Limited
Pearson Education Singapore, Pte. Ltd.
Pearson Education Asia, Ltd.
Pearson Education Canada, Ltd.
Pearson Educación de Mexico, S.A. de C.V. Pearson Education—Japan
Pearson Education Malaysia, Pte. Ltd.

Library of Congress Control Number: 2017946910

1 17

Editor-in-Chief
Greg Wiegand

Associate Editor
Kim Spencely

Senior Marketing Manager
Stephane Nakib

Editorial Assistant
Cindy Teeters

Managing Editor
Sandra Schroder

Senior Project Editor
Lori Lyons

Cover Designer
Chuti Prasertsith

Project Manager
Dhayanidhi

Copy Editor
Kitty Wilson

Proofreader
Rupa H S

Indexer
Erika Millen

Compositor
codeMantra

CONTENTS AT A GLANCE

TABLE OF CONTENTS

Acknowledgments

Throughout this book you will often see the words *we* and *our* rather than *I* and *my*. It's not because the ideas and concepts explained are not my own point of view; they are. But it's a point of view I cultivated and honed with the help of many people over the years—and a few select people from the beginning. The concepts highlighted in this book were formed largely in concert with Ashok Subramanian, with whom I cofounded Liazon, one of the industry's first private exchanges, in 2007. Also included in the use of *we* are the numerous conversations I've had with various brokers, consultants, insurers, technologists, vendors, professors and economists, and many others over the past decade, who have helped me to shape my view that employees (and their employers) are better off when they get to choose their own benefits.

Particular thanks for turning "a good idea" into this book—hopefully one that will serve as an educational tool for the HR pros, CFOs, CEOs, brokers, consultants, and insurers of the future as well as a business handbook for anyone in the benefits industry today—go to Jami Kelmenson, Liazon's "editor-in-chief," for taking complicated and often misunderstood concepts and turning them into cohesive marketing materials and, in this case, chapters. Thanks also to Chuck Green of GreenHouse Marketing Consulting, who brought 30 years of industry experience to serving as Liazon's guiding hand in all things benefits related, for being an "early and often" reader of preliminary chapters to help whip them into shape; Herb Schaffner of Big Fish Media, who saw the value in this concept early on and lent his expert publishing guidance, thorough research skills, and adept storytelling abilities to give us a compelling storyline; Jeanne Glasser Levine, former executive editor at Pearson, who immediately "got" why our story should be told; and Kim Spencely and her top notch staff at Pearson's IT Professional Group, including Lori Lyons, Production Editor, and countless others behind the scenes, for picking up the reins midstream to lead us through the process of turning a manuscript into a published book.

Two long-time colleagues who served as readers and contributors to this book, and who have supported our efforts at Liazon since the beginning, warrant special mention: Rhonda Marcucci, vice president, HR & Benefits Technology Consulting Practice at Gruppo Marcucci, a division of Gallagher Benefit Services, Inc.; and Christopher E. Condeluci, principal, CC Law & Policy PLLC. Their benefits guidance and expertise have been invaluable to me throughout my career.

Finally, complicated stories need more than words to be effective. We hope you enjoy the illustrations in this book, most of which were designed by Meredith Rund, an extraordinary resource to us in giving a visual edge to all of our communications.

About the Author

Alan Cohen co-founded Liazon, operator of one of the industry's leading private benefits exchanges for businesses of all sizes, in 2007. Liazon was acquired by Towers Watson, now Willis Towers Watson, in 2013.

Alan has been a leader in the benefits space for over two decades. Prior to cofounding Liazon, he was CEO and cofounder of Online Benefits, one of the first web-based benefits technology companies in the United States. He led the company through its sale to A.D.A.M, a global provider of consumer health information and benefits technology solutions, and later served as president of A.D.A.M. Prior to cofounding Online Benefits, he worked in the insurance industry for Prudential, Mass Mutual, and Cigna and served as managing director for a division of Northwestern Mutual Life.

Alan is often sought out for his insights on private exchanges, their role in the new health care landscape, and their effect on businesses. His expert commentary has appeared in *Bloomberg Businessweek*, *Forbes*, *The New York Times*, *USA Today*, *The Washington Post*, Yahoo! Finance, CNBC.com, and numerous benefits publications, including *Employee Benefit News* and *Benefits Pro*. In 2016, Alan was a recipient of an "Industry Innovator" award by the Institute for HealthCare Consumerism (IHC). IHC's 11th annual "HealthCare Consumerism Superstars and Industry Innovator Awards" recognized the year's top executives for their work in transforming the landscape of corporate health and benefits.

In this book, Alan draws on his in-depth experience in the benefits industry to share how the key principles he used to create one of the first private exchange platforms over 10 years ago is still relevant to anyone interested in forging a better system for all.

Alan holds a BA from Cornell University, an MBA from Columbia Business School, and an MBA from London Business School, where he won the Award for Academic Excellence.

Alan resides in Westchester, New York, with his family and spends summer weekends in Woodstock, New York. The Cohens are avid skiers and outdoors people.

How to Read This Book

Like any other written account, this story is meant to be read through from the beginning to the end. But we recognize that many of you who are drawn to this subject matter will have other pressing engagements to deal with—such as making sure employees and employers get the most bang for their benefits buck. So we've taken great care in designing this book in a modular fashion so that you—a CFO or CEO, an insurance broker, an insurer, an HR professional, a health care reform advocate, or even an employee who gets that things could be better—can find valuable grains within individual chapters to help you make sense of the current environment and give you the information you need to find a better way when it comes to benefits.

What might seem repetitive at times is merely our way of intentionally stressing the key points we'd like you to take away from our discussion, expressed in slightly different ways in varying contexts to help drive the points home. We recognize that, just as with benefits, what resonates with one reader in one section might not be the same for another.

To help guide you through our benefits story, the following sections explain how this book is organized.

Introduction

If you're anything like me, you may be prone to skipping the Introduction of any business book. I hope you won't in this book. It lays the groundwork for the entire conversation to come in terms of why benefits are important (something that those of us in the industry often lose sight of day to day), why choice matters, and what the new paradigm shift in benefits is all about.

Part I: The Changing Benefits Landscape

Before we tackle the new benefits landscape, we have to understand the old one, as well as where things stand today. **Chapter 1, "Building a Better Benefits System,"** lays out what we mean by the concept of a "benefits store" (also known as a "benefits marketplace" or "private exchange") and the seven key principles that my early colleagues and I believe define one. And while I promise not to bore you with pages and pages on the history of insurance (okay maybe just a few pages in **Chapter 2, "Benefits: The Accidental Entitlement"**), knowing the historical context behind benefits will help you understand exactly how we got into our current situation—which encompasses much more than legislative infighting, premium rate hikes, and the prices of prescription drugs.

Throughout this book, you'll find references to the "status quo." You'll find a full explanation of what we mean by the status quo in benefits in **Chapter 3, "They Don't Know What They're Missing: Flipping the Status Quo on Its Head,"** as well as why it has to go. And if you read only one chapter in this book, make it **Chapter 4, "Making Sense of Benefits Solutions: Public Exchanges and Private Exchanges."** With the help of industry veteran Rhonda Marcucci, Chapter 4 provides an overview of today's benefits solution landscape—everything from the public exchanges for individual and retiree benefits to the various types of commercial offerings for the group exchange market, including benefits administration systems, insurer- and consultant-sponsored platforms, systems that started out as "pure play" technologies, and more. This discussion wouldn't be complete without references to the types of products available through these solutions, as well as the features that distinguish them from one another and make today's benefits ecosystem one of the most competitive and exciting fields to examine.

Part II: Stakeholders: Making the Move from "One Size Fits All"

Various stakeholders have interests in employer-sponsored benefits, and Part II provides firsthand insights from each of them. In **Chapter 5, "Employers Find Skin in the Game,"** we hear from two human resources managers about why they decided to adopt a private exchange for their company's benefits delivery and how it worked out for them. **Chapter 6, "Six Questions to Ask Before You Choose a Private Exchange,"** provides information and key questions to ask any exchange provider so that you feel more comfortable about the prospect of moving to a private exchange at your company or recommending one to your clients. **Chapter 7, "Brokers and Exchanges: Better Together,"** focuses on the role of insurance brokers in today's evolving benefits landscape, and **Chapter 8, "Insurers Find a New Way to Move Product,"** looks at how insurers are viewing the landscape as fertile ground for innovation.

Part III: Future Vision

Armed with the necessary background and information to make sense of employee benefits and the new health care landscape, in **Chapter 9, "Innovation in Benefits (Yes, Benefits)"** we look to the future to see where the next great innovation in benefits might come from. **Chapter 10, "The 'Law of the Land,' Insurance Tax Reform, and the November Surprise,"** covers how recent legislation, including the contentious debate over the future of the Affordable Care Act (ACA), has and will continue to impact employer-sponsored benefits. In this chapter, we also hope to plant a few seeds in terms of what's next for benefits and why focusing on the consumer will take on even more importance. **Chapter 11, "Who's Afraid of the**

American Consumer?" takes a look at how the consumer can and should impact the future of health care and benefits.

Part IV: Appendixes: A Practical Guide to Private Exchanges

In Part IV we move from the philosophical to the practical in terms of how to bring choice and consumerism to America's workforce. We start off with an infographic that answers the key questions most people have when they first hear about private exchanges in **Appendix A, "Private Exchanges 101."** While we are far from the ultimate authority on benefits lexicon, for the purposes of this reading, in **Appendix B, "Making Sense of Benefits Terms,"** we've defined certain key words and phrases to help illuminate the discussion throughout the book. We've also included a product guide that explains some of the different types of offerings that might be found in a benefits store. **Appendix C, "Real-World Data and Applications,"** highlights findings from the most recent data analyzed by Liazon and the Private Exchange Research Council (PERC) concerning behavior patterns on private exchanges. This section also provides a glimpse into what an exchange marketplace experience looks like from the user's perspective. And if you've made it this far, you might find the "Health Care Timeline" we've included, courtesy of Annenberg Classroom, of interest.

But for now, it's time for that can't-miss Introduction mentioned earlier.

 Note

The health care landscape is changing rapidly. As a result, we have made every effort to keep the information and resources in this book as up to date as possible. All of the opinions of the author, and people and third-party sources quoted, are accurate as of the time they were obtained—and like health care and benefits, are subject to evolve over time.

Introduction

If you are reading this book, you likely have a vested interest in the future of health insurance and, by association, health care, in America.

Health care is about the prevention and treatment of disease. There are lots of great books out there about fixing the U.S. health care system (*Who Killed Health Care?* by Regina Herzlinger and *Redefining Health Care* by Michael E. Porter come to mind). This book limits the conversation primarily to *how we pay for and receive these and other crucial services in an employer-sponsored environment*—not how we improve the services themselves.

Health insurance in the United States has long been inextricably linked to employment, with companies typically offering limited choices in plans. In fact, estimates indicate that in the late 1990s, 38% of employees had no choice of health plans, and 62% of employees had a choice of only two plans (see Figure I.1).[1]

Surprisingly, with just about every product from laundry detergent to cars offering an abundance (some would argue overabundance) of options for consumers over the past 20 years, choice in health insurance has lagged significantly behind. While employers are starting to recognize the value of offering more choice in health plans, the growth in the number of companies offering multiple plans has been slow until very recently. Between 2010 and 2015, the number of firms offering two or more plan choices grew by about 9 percentage points, but nearly half of that growth took place between 2014 and 2015.[2]

Recent research from PwC indicates that 40% of private sector firms across all industries still offer only one or two plans. In addition, the average number of medical plans offered among all companies actually decreased from 4.1 plans in 2015 to 3.6

1. Center for Studying Health System Change. Community Tracking Study Household Survey, 1996–1997; [United States]. ICPSR02524–v5. Ann Arbor, MI: Inter-university Consortium for Political and Social Research [distributor], 2009–10–27. https://doi.org/10.3886/ICPSR02524.v5 and Center for Studying Health System Change. Community Tracking Study Physician Survey, 1998–1999: [United States]. ICPSR03267–v2. Ann Arbor, MI: Inter-university Consortium for Political and Social Research [distributor], 2009-02-02. https://doi.org/10.3886/ICPSR03267.v2.

2. U.S. Department of Health and Human Services, Agency for Healthcare Research and Quality, Center for Financing, "Access and Cost Trends. 2010–2015," Medical Expenditure Panel Survey Insurance Component, https://meps.ahrq.gov/mepsweb/.

Choice of Health Plans for Families Offered and Eligible for Employer-Sponsored Insurance

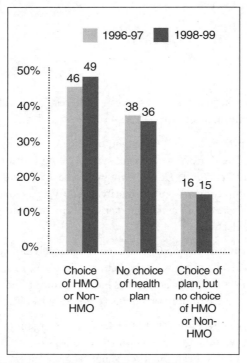

HSC Community Tracking Study Household Survey, 1996-1997 and 1998-1999.

Figure I.1 *Choice of Health Plans for Families Offered and Eligible for Employer-Sponsored Insurance, Late 1990s.*

plans in 2016 (see Figure I.2).[3] In my opinion, this is moving in the wrong direction, for reasons that will be discussed throughout this book.

Employer-sponsored health insurance is the primary source of coverage for individuals under age 65 in the United States. According to the most recent estimates from the Medical Expenditure Panel Survey Insurance Component (MEPS-IC), 57.3 million employees were enrolled in employer-sponsored health insurance in 2015, an increase of 1.5 million workers from 2014.[4]

Why does it matter how many insurance choices an employer offers?

---

3. PwC, "Health and Well-Being Touchstone Survey Results," June 2016, www.pwc.com/us/touchstone2016.

4. *Medical Expenditure Panel Survey Insurance Component Chartbook 2015*. AHRQ Publication No. 16-0045-EF. Rockville, MD: Agency for Healthcare Research and Quality, August 2016, https://meps.ahrq.gov/mepsweb/survey_comp/MEPSICChartbook.pdf.

Medical plan options

Number of medical plan options	<1,000 employees	1,000–4,999 employees	5,000+ employees	All participants
1	26%	9%	6%	15%
2	28%	28%	19%	25%
3	25%	30%	24%	27%
4	11%	18%	13%	14%
5	4%	5%	9%	5%
6	2%	4%	7%	4%
7	1%	1%	7%	3%
8	2%	1%	3%	2%
9	0%	1%	3%	1%
10+	1%	3%	9%	4%
2016 average	2.7 plans	3.2 plans	5.1 plans	3.6 plans
2015 average	3.0 plans	4.2 plans	5.7 plans	4.1 plans

Shaded most frequent

Source: 2016 Health and Well-being Touchstone Survey results / PwC.

Figure I.2 *Number of Medical Plans Offered, 2015–2016.*

Attracting and Retaining Employees

In the aftermath of World War II, employee health insurance was broadly introduced in response to wartime wage freezes. Since that time, employers have offered health care and retirement benefits as part of the employment compact with their workforce. Recent estimates from the Bureau of Labor Statistics indicate that benefits comprise over 30% of the total compensation for employees.[5]

> Employers always anticipate yearly increases in their benefits costs and generally have three options to weigh...None are desirable options.

Employers always anticipate yearly increases in their benefits costs and generally have three options to weigh: absorb these costs themselves, pass them on to their employees, or offer less coverage (see Figure I.3). None are desirable options, especially if the goal is to use benefits as a means of attracting and retaining the best employees.

---

5. U.S. Department of Labor, U.S. Bureau of Labor Statistics, "Employer Costs for Employee Compensation," June 2016, www.bls.gov/news.release/pdf/ecec.pdf.

Consumer-driven health care
The percentage of companies making changes to their benefits programs

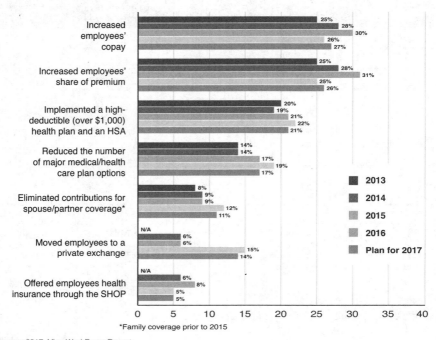

*Family coverage prior to 2015

Source: 2017 Aflac WorkForce Report

Figure I.3 *How Companies Deal with Benefits Cost Increases.*

Employers have historically known that benefits are a crucial part of an employee's total compensation, and now employees are starting to pay more attention to their value as well. Findings from the 2015/2016 Willis Towers Watson Global Benefit Attitudes Survey indicate that 8 out of 10 employees who are happy with their health care and retirement benefits are also highly engaged at work.[6] Further, the most recent findings from Mercer indicate that 9 in 10 employees agree with the statement "My health benefits are as important as my salary" and 63% of employees say benefits are a major factor in choosing where they work.[7]

---

6. Willis Towers Watson, "2015/2016 Global Benefit Attitudes Survey," www.willistowerswatson.com/en/insights/2016/02/global-benefit-attitudes-survey-2015-16.

7. Mercer, "Mercer Survey Finds US Workers Satisfied with Benefits, but Fears of Future Affordability Rise Dramatically," *Inside Employees Minds Survey*, November 5, 2015, www.mercer.com/newsroom/mercer-survey-finds-us-workers-satisfied-with-retirement-and-health-benefits-but-fears-of-future-affordability-rise-dramatically.html.

Thanks to new innovations, legislative measures, and technological advances in the way employees purchase their benefits and use their health care, employee awareness of the value of benefits is only expected to grow. This means employers have an even greater responsibility in ensuring that their benefits packages are competitive and that the value of those benefits is communicated to current and prospective employees so that they can realize a return on their investment.

> Thanks to...technological advances in the way employees purchase their benefits and use their health care, employee awareness of the value of benefits is only expected to grow.

What is being done to help employers make more efficient use of their benefits dollars to ensure and maintain employee satisfaction over the long term?

A New Paradigm Shift for Benefits

Ten years ago, my partners and I had a crazy idea that was simple yet powerful: Let people choose the benefits they want rather than having their employer do it for them. We envisioned an online benefits marketplace, or store (known as a *private exchange*), that would enable and empower employees (or *benefits consumers*), to create a collection of different types of benefits (or *portfolio*), based on their own particular needs and preferences (see Appendix B, "Making Sense of Benefits Terms"). This portfolio would include products such as health insurance and dental and vision benefits; financial vehicles such as HSAs or FSAs; benefits to protect assets and income, such as life and disability insurance; and much more. Instead of offering one or two standard options, employers would allocate a set amount of money to workers to spend in the marketplace as they chose (see Figure I.4).

> Ten years ago, my partners and I had a crazy idea...Let people choose the benefits they want rather than having their employer do it for them.

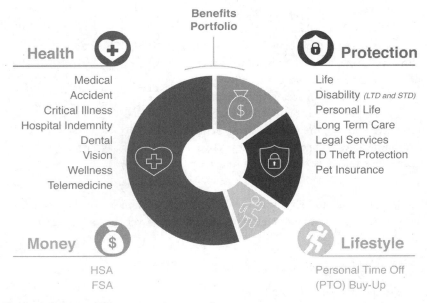

Figure I.4 *A Portfolio Approach to Benefits.*

Our philosophy stemmed from the belief that different people want and need different things when it comes to a matter as personal as their own financial protection, and those same people are the ones best equipped to make these important decisions, based on their family's needs and goals. Employers, quite simply, cannot know all the private information, plans, and dreams of their employees. As with their personal finances, an employee may want to consult an advisor for guidance, but their requirements for health and financial protection are personal and should remain so. That's the concept on which we founded our company, Liazon, and it remains our North Star to this day.

Long before the arrival of *private exchanges* (online benefits marketplaces through which employees can choose their own benefits), it was widely acknowledged that employees given a choice are more satisfied with their health plan, regardless of the type of plan.[8] With their share of the cost of the plans rising, the case for choice becomes even stronger.

In 2016, the average total premium for family medical coverage for employees who receive health insurance through their employers was over $18,000, with employees contributing about 30% of that amount out of their own pockets. While the average annual total premium for family coverage has increased by 58% in the past 10 years, the

---

8. Atul A. Gawande et al., "Does Dissatisfaction with Health Plans Stem from Having No Choices?" *Health Affairs*, 17(3):184–194, September/October 1998; Karen Davis et al., "Choice Matters: Enrollees' Views of Their Health Plans," *Health Affairs*, 14(2):99–112, Summer 1995, as reported by Sally Trude, "Who Has a Choice of Health Plans?" Center for Studying Health System Change Issue Brief No. 27, February 2000.

employee share has increased by 78% (see Figure I.5).[9] People tend to be more discerning in terms of what they buy when they are spending their own money, and this is one of the economic principles in support of a private exchange model.

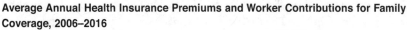

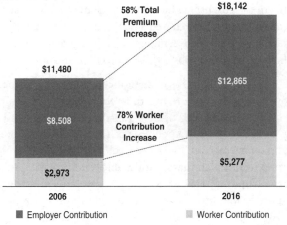

SOURCE: Kaiser/HRET Survey of Employer-Sponsored Health Benefits, 2006–2016.

Figure I.5 *Average Annual Health Insurance Premiums and Worker Contributions for Family Coverage, 2006–2016.*

My cofounders and I did not set out to solve America's flawed health care system with our "crazy idea." There are myriad other books and experts attempting to do that, many of them referenced throughout this book. Our company, like this book, is about solving the specific problem of how to make the employer-sponsored system work more efficiently by changing fundamental perceptions around who is best equipped to make the choices regarding what benefits employees should get. True private exchanges have the potential to upend the negative perceptions surrounding employer-sponsored benefits and greatly improve how people feel about their companies, their careers, and their financial futures.

...this book is about solving the specific problem of how to make the employer-sponsored system work more efficiently by changing fundamental perceptions around who is best equipped to make the choices regarding what benefits employees should get.

9. Kaiser Family Foundation, "2016 Employer Health Benefits Survey," http://kff.org/report-section/ehbs-2016-summary-of-findings/.

The Exchange Evolution

For people of every political affiliation, the passage of the Affordable Care Act (ACA) in 2010 brought the issue of access to health insurance to the forefront of the national dialogue when it required every individual in the United States to obtain health insurance or pay a penalty tax. The ACA created *public exchanges*, or marketplaces, as an enrollment platform for purchasing health coverage in the fully-insured individual market. Some consumers who purchased a qualifying health plan through a public exchange could be eligible for a government subsidy or credit (for example, premium subsidy, cost–sharing reduction subsidy) based on their income.

The key point for employer-sponsored insurance resulting from the ACA is that it required employers with 50 or more full-time-equivalent (FTE) employees to offer a group health plan to at least 95% of their full-time employees and their child dependents (up to age 26) or pay a penalty tax. (A *full-time* employee is defined as someone working on average 30 hours per week.) The ACA also required employers to offer a group health plan that is "affordable" and provides "minimum value," or the employer must pay a penalty tax. The penalty tax is also triggered for an employer if a full-time employee opts out of the employer's group health plan, purchases an individual market plan through an ACA exchange, and qualifies for a premium tax credit.

To ensure that the Internal Revenue Service (IRS) could enforce these penalty taxes (commonly referred to as the "employer mandate"), Congress subjected employers with 50 or more FTEs to a new reporting requirement. Under this reporting requirement, these employers must send a notice to all of their full-time employees, and also to the IRS, detailing information about the health coverage offered.

While private exchanges had existed years before the ACA went into effect, the debate spurred by the ACA, and the additional attention from employers who wished to comply with its employer mandate, brought the concept of shopping for insurance online to a wider population. According to a 2016 study by Accenture, about 8 million people enrolled in benefits on a private exchange for the 2016 plan year, an expansion of 35% over the previous year.[10] In addition, a 2017 report by the Private Exchange Evaluation Collaborative indicates that several employers are leveraging private exchanges for certain employee cohorts: 23% have implemented them for part-time employees, 19% have made them available for pre-retirees, and 33% have implemented them for COBRA-eligible employees.[11]

---

10. Accenture, "Private HIX Enrollment up 35 Percent in 2016," January 2016, www.accenture.com/us-en/insight-new-private-enrollment.

11. Private Exchange Evaluation Collaborative, "What Happened to Private Exchanges?" February 27, 2017, http://nebgh.org/wp-content/uploads/2017/03/FINAL-2016-PEEC-webinar-v8.pdf.pdf.

Another factor playing into the exchange evolution is *health care consumerism*, a movement that puts economic purchasing power and decision making regarding benefits in the hands of consumers. Employers that recognize the value of employees' personal involvement in changing their health and health care purchasing behaviors, and that empower employees with the tools

> When employees start to spend their own money, they pay more attention to what they're spending it on...

and resources to do so, will be able to reap benefits in terms of more satisfied employees and better health outcomes. When employees start to spend their own money, they pay more attention to what they're spending it on, and this leads to less waste in the system—which is what will ultimately lead to controlled costs for employers.

"Try It, You'll Like It"

As of this writing, we estimate that there are approximately 150 private exchange operators in the United States. Liazon was one of the pioneers of a smart idea that caught on, and as of 2016, as part of Willis Towers Watson, it serves more than 1,000 employers, offering coverage to nearly 500,000 active employees, available in all 50 states. Liazon has learned a thing or two along the way, but in an industry still in its infancy, our greatest advances are still ahead.

Our experience at Liazon shows that people who use private exchanges have higher levels of satisfaction and engagement than do people who obtain benefits through traditional distribution methods. Of the employees Liazon surveyed, 94% said they were satisfied with their experience, 85% said they became more engaged in their health care decisions, and 75% said they were more likely to stay with their current employer as a result of using a private exchange to choose their benefits. In addition, 87% of employees said they were more aware of their employer's contribution to their benefits, and 83% said they valued their company's contribution more.[12]

In the past few years, companies such as Starbucks, UPS, Hallmark, 1-800-Flowers, and Bed, Bath & Beyond have decided to move to a private exchange, and many more are considering making the move. Insurers are clamoring to be included in the best exchanges as additional distribution mechanisms. In general, the more people experience private exchanges, the more they like them.

This book shares the principles Liazon has refined in creating private exchanges that leverage and implement the online store concept, which is already business as usual to consumers in the digital age. A great deal of time, effort, and resources go into giving consumers the most meaningful choices, and by providing a glimpse into what's behind the curtain, we hope to assuage some of the confusion or misunderstanding regarding how private exchanges work.

> ...by providing a glimpse into what's behind the curtain, we hope to assuage some of the confusion or misunderstanding regarding how private exchanges work.

The expansion of private exchanges not only can transform the benefits industry but may potentially bring some much-needed innovation to the U.S. health care system overall. An improved health care system can in turn lead to less waste, more productivity, more jobs, and overall economic growth.

This book presents a blueprint for an optimal private exchange built on the pillars of *meaningful choice* (with effective merchandising), price transparency (within a *defined contribution* model), and sophisticated *decision support*. Drawing on Liazon's successes, learnings, and client experiences, as well as those of other innovators in the benefits industry, this book shows how the economics of

> ...this book shows how the economics of informed choice is transforming the industry, employee well-being, and the health care economy as a whole.

informed choice is transforming the industry, employee well-being, and the health care economy as a whole. As more companies look to enter this market, an analysis

---

12. Liazon, "Liazon's 2017 Employee Survey Report: Health Care Consumerism in a Marketplace Environment," March 2017 http://liazon.hs-sites.com/liazon/employeesurvey-1-0.

of the best practices of the companies already using private exchanges is essential. It's imperative that we help employers, as well as their employees, understand this burgeoning industry in order to create value for all stakeholders. This book provides firsthand insights from many of those stakeholders, including companies large and small that have already made the switch to a private exchange, such as:

- HR visionaries who understand that change management is attainable and well worth the effort

- Insurance brokers who realize that having exchanges in their solutions toolkit is in their own best interest and is also beneficial to their clients and their employees

- Insurers who have seen an opportunity for greater distribution of their products, as well as a road toward innovation

- Industry consultants who see the market potential and have put a stake in the ground toward claiming their share

- Policymakers who are committed to the early strides made by the ACA but know there's much more work to be done

When it comes down to it, this whole conversation is about individuals, so in this book we always circle back to what it means for them. This is how we've built our company, and we don't know how to look at it any other way.

Overcoming the "Wait and See" Mindset

It's not that companies are reticent to explore ways to make their benefits more meaningful to employees. It's that they aren't aware that they have options or how the options work or can save them money. With the private exchange option, in particular, companies have largely adopted a "wait and see" approach—to see how it all shakes out before they dive in.

When it comes to the "wait and see" approach, Liazon cofounder and former CEO Ashok Subramanian summed it up adeptly:

> I think people need to trust their gut more often. If something sounds good, if it sounds like it is better for the employer, it is better for employees, and there are somewhat obvious negatives in other parts of the ecosystem, then I think a lot of times people spend time looking for the catch. They ask: "how can this be? There can't be win–wins in life. Someone has got to lose."

> They may be rare, but there are opportunities for win–win.[13]

---

13. Personal interview with Ashok Subramanian, November 24, 2015.

Part I

The Changing Benefits Landscape

Building a Better Benefits System

Access to health care has long been an emotionally and socially charged issue. During the Progressive Era of the early 1900s, President Theodore Roosevelt believed that "no country can be strong whose people are sick and poor." Such beliefs gave rise to much of the activism and political mayhem over health care and health insurance we see today.

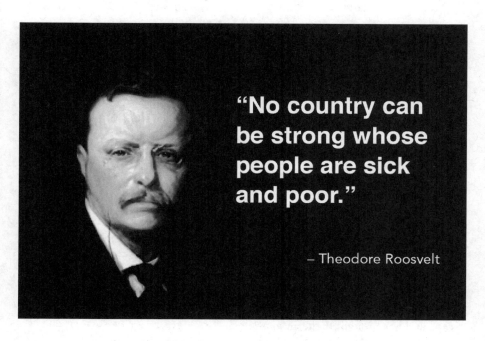

"No country can be strong whose people are sick and poor."

– Theodore Roosvelt

One recent action that has riled public opinion on both sides of the health care debate is the Patient Protection and Affordable Care Act (PPACA), typically called the Affordable Care Act (ACA) or my least favorite term, "Obamacare," which

President Obama signed into law in 2010. By 2014, the first coverage year for which it was implemented, the ACA succeeded in its mission of getting millions of previously uninsured Americans enrolled in some form of health coverage, such as private insurance or Medicaid (see Figure 1.1).

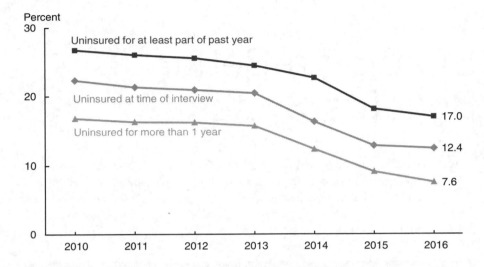

Notes: In 2016, answer categories for those who are currently uninsured concerning the length of noncoverage were modified. Therefore, 2016 estimates of "uninsured for at least part of the past year" and "uninsured for more than a year" may not be completely comparable with previous years. For more information on this change, see Technical Notes. Data are based on household interviews of a sample of the civilian noninstitutionalized population.
Source: NCHS, National Health Interview Survey, 2010–2016, Family Core component.

Figure 1.1 *Percentage of Uninsured U.S. Adults, 2010–2016.*

Other than the burden of increased reporting requirements and headaches about which employees need to be covered by an employer's health insurance, the hoopla surrounding the ACA and its attempted repeal has very little to do with employer-sponsored group insurance. Still, the steam rising from President Obama's pen since the signing of the ACA has served to increase consumer awareness and engagement in the overall benefits land-scape and has brought the term *marketplace* into the mainstream when it comes to purchasing *individual* health insurance.

...the steam rising from President Obama's pen since the signing of the ACA...has brought the term *marketplace* into the mainstream when it comes to purchasing *individual* health insurance.

In contrast to the individual market, *private* benefits marketplaces, also known as *private exchanges*, enable people who receive insurance from their employers to tailor-make their coverage portfolios, just as they would select their 401(k) portfolio, as well as access advice and tools that can help them feel more confident about these types of transactions. Giving the American people the freedom to shop online for the coverage they want and need has opened opportunities for innovation and market growth for insurers, human capital experts, consultants, and employers themselves. Indeed, we are actualizing the potential of private exchanges forecast by experts such as Dr. Paul Fronstin of the nonpartisan Employee Benefit Research Institute (EBRI), who said in 2012:

> Through these exchanges, in tandem with a defined contribution funding approach, employers can accelerate the drive toward a more mass, consumer-driven insurance market and gain more control over their health care contribution costs, capping their own contributions, and shifting to workers the authority to control the terms (and to some extent, the costs) of their own health insurance.[1]

Using the sound principles of variety, quality, and transparency that have guided effective marketplaces throughout time, private exchanges are poised to empower more people to make personalized, informed choices about their health and well-being in an environment in which the health care conversation is front and center—and this is where it gets really exciting.

> Using the sound principles of variety, quality, and transparency,...private exchanges are poised to empower more people to make personalized, informed choices about their health and well-being...

The success of our company Liazon, one of the first private exchange operators, and some of its competitors, demonstrates that private exchanges are becoming a sustainable fit for employers and their employees. A recent press release from Frost and Sullivan, titled "Private Health Insurance Exchanges Solutions Primed for Robust Growth Among U.S. Employers as Vendors Differentiate to Meet Evolving Consumer Expectations," notes "employers' growing need to reduce the costs, complexities, and back–office administrative burdens" and consumer "expectations derived from shopping experiences with online retailers."[2] With Liazon-powered exchanges, companies can adopt prestocked, "ready to go" online stores for buying benefits, or they can design their own custom stores that provide their employees with meaningful choices in medical, dental, and vision insurance, along with protection benefits like life and disability insurance, identity theft protection, and much more (see Figure 1.2).

---

1. Paul Fronstin, "Private Health Insurance Exchanges and Defined Contribution Plans: Is It Déjà vu All over Again?" *EBRI Issue Brief*, 373, July 2012. https://www.ebri.org/pdf/briefspdf/EBRI_IB_07-2012_No373_Exchgs2.pdf

2. "Private Health Insurance Exchanges Solutions Primed for Robust Growth Among U.S. Employers as Vendors Differentiate to Meet Evolving Consumer Expectations," Frost & Sullivan Press Release, April 11, 2017, ww2.frost.com/news/press-releases/private-health-insurance-exchanges-solutions-primed-robust-growth-among-us-employers-vendors-differentiate-meet-evolving-consume/.

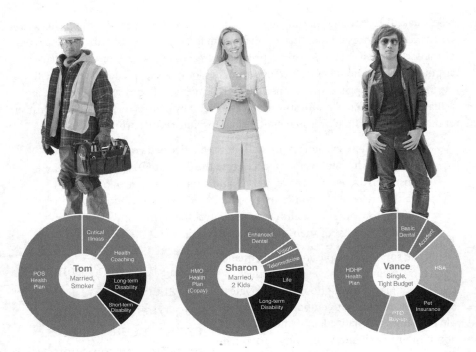

Figure 1.2 *Different Benefits Portfolios for Different Folks.*

Until recently, most people had limited health insurance choices. Employers typically contracted with an insurer to offer one or two plans that people either signed up for or waived in lieu of paying out-of-pocket for their own care. As discussed in this book's Introduction, the average number of medical plans offered actually decreased from 4.1 plans in 2015 to 3.6 plans in 2016.[3] In contrast, the average number of medical plans offered on Liazon private exchanges in 2016 was 7.2, in line with the previous year.[4] With private exchanges, also known as benefits marketplaces, people have more choices and can select the specific plans to create a unique portfolio that satisfies their personal and family needs.

> With private exchanges... people have more choices and can select the specific plans to create a unique portfolio that satisfies their personal and family needs.

The following sections dig a little deeper into some essential principles from economics and other disciplines and show how they are at play in a benefits marketplace.

3. PwC, "2016 Health and Well-Being Touchstone Survey," June 2016, www.pwc.com/us/en/hr-management/publications/health-well-being-touchstone-survey-2016.html.

4. Private Exchange Research Council (PERC), 2017 data analysis based on offerings and enrollment on Liazon-powered exchanges from 2013–2017.

Principle #1: Give Them Money and Let Them Shop

By offering employees control over and accountability for their money, the defined contribution model is one cornerstone of an efficient market. With a defined contribution model, an employer allocates a certain amount of money to each employee, who then decides what combination of benefits they'd like to purchase. Each employee can choose from a variety of plan designs for health insurance, for example, and decide how much he or she is comfortable paying for monthly premiums now versus how much may have to be paid later—in the form of deductibles, coinsurance, and so on. The employee can also allocate dollars from his or her paycheck toward additional benefits to help round out any gaps that may be missing from their medical coverage.

The defined contribution model became commonplace in retirement benefits planning decades ago. Employers and employees embraced the concept of people managing their own IRAs and 401(k)s, combining personal savings with designated annual employer contributions, with caps and floors based on an employee's salary. From the employer's perspective, 401(k)s saved money, compared to a pension plan. These vehicles contributed to a vast portion of individuals' savings for a number of reasons: the psychological appeal of controlling one's own retirement dollars, defaults on private pension plans (which scared employees and employers alike), fairly robust public confidence in rising stock and bond markets, and the role of many federal policies (including adjusting interest rates) in influencing returns. Viewed in this context, the concept of defined contribution is fairly simple to understand and often used as an analogy for how it works for employer-sponsored benefits.

By offering workers a defined, or fixed, contribution as part of their compensation to purchase health insurance and other benefits, employers cut through the murkiness that has long been associated with the cash value of employer-sponsored benefits. Employees would never accept not knowing how much salary a prospective employer is offering, and the same should be true for the compensation that comes in the form of benefits—which on average account for nearly one-third of the total employer costs of employee compensation.[5] Giving employees cash to spend in a store instead of a predetermined insurance policy makes it clear how much the benefit contribution adds to a person's total pay (a far bigger chunk than they may realize). When people understand that they're spending their own money, they can make smarter, more personalized, decisions than their employers did on their behalf in the past. Liazon's data show that with private exchanges, the value equation works better all around: Employees are more satisfied and engaged with benefits, and employers save money or control costs.[6]

> Employees would never accept not knowing how much salary a prospective employer is offering, and the same should be true...for...benefits...

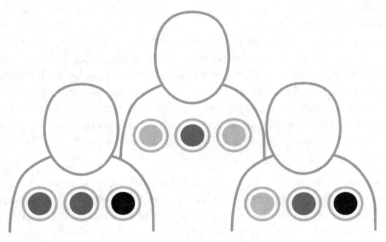

Different employees make
different choices, optimizing
for their individual needs

Writing in the 2014 *New England Journal of Medicine* with Barak Richman and Kevin Shulman, Harvard Business School professor and consumer-driven health care trailblazer Regina Herzlinger summarized the defined contribution difference:

> In rigid sectors of the economy, defined-contribution strategies could burden employees disproportionately with the weight of medical

5. Bureau of Labor Statistics, "Employer Costs for Employee Compensation," June 9, 2017 https://www.bls.gov/news.release/pdf/ecec.pdf.

6. Liazon, "Liazon 2017 Employer Survey Report: Employer Satisfaction with Private Exchanges," May 2017 http://liazon.hs-sites.com/liazon/employeesurvey-1-0.

inflation. Yet the appeal of defined-contribution plans—whether as part of Medicare reform or in the form of changing benefits for retirees and workers—remains potent. Defined-contribution strategies reveal to employees and health insurance customers any cost increases that exceed the growth of wages, and individuals purchasing insurance on exchanges have shown a growing preference for lower-priced plans that increase cost sharing for health expenditures.[7]

With control of these dollars turned over to them, consumers are using private exchanges to foster the market-based competition many analysts have sought for years. They're deciding how much to allocate to certain benefits, based on the perceived value of those benefits to their lives.

Professor Mark Hall, director of the Health Law and Policy Program at Wake Forest University, put it this way:

> In the past with traditional plans, the employer picked up the whole or most of the cost. People had to decide whether they wanted single or spousal coverage and the differences between the various options they had were quite small. The key to defined contribution and employee control is how we make cost decisions at the margin.
>
> Under defined contribution, we see the cost of what we're adding to our basic package. This means paying a great deal of attention to what the added value will be of more generous coverage that comes at a higher cost. That kind of focus on the marginal cost is critical and helps drive value-based competition. It makes the consumer think hard: is it really worth it for me to opt into a plan that has a broader network or that frees me from certain restrictions? We're asking ourselves not only about whether a benefit fits our needs—but is that extra cost worth it? That is the critical piece that the exchange concept brings.[8]

There are many advantages resulting from people spending their money more thoughtfully in private exchanges. Consumers are more aware of overall plan costs, as well as their share of them, because of true price transparency. They, in

> We're asking ourselves not only about whether a benefit fits our needs—but is that extra cost worth it? That is the critical piece that the exchange concept brings.
>
> —*Professor Mark Hall*

---

7. Kevin A. Schulman, Barak D. Richman, & Regina E. Herzlinger, "Shifting Toward Defined Contributions—Predicting the Effects," *New England Journal of Medicine*, 370:2462–2465, June 26, 2014. http://www.nejm.org/doi/full/10.1056/NEJMp1314391#t=article.

8. Personal interview with Mark Hall, director of the Health Law and Policy Program at Wake Forest University, November 9, 2015.

effect, demand their own cost controls through benefits selection, with guidance in the form of decision support. Thanks in part to the private exchange paradigm, more people (particularly single and younger workers) are choosing high-deductible health plans, narrower provider networks are becoming more popular, and nonmedical products from critical illness insurance to telemedicine are finally getting their due.

SHINING A LIGHT ON SOME SKELETONS IN THE CLOSETS OF TRADITIONAL BENEFITS OFFERINGS

Ever wonder why so many companies unwittingly hand out marriage or child bonuses to employees?

If you asked executives whether they give a bonus to their employees when they get married or have a child, they'd say "No, of course not." But in fact they do by paying the additional benefit costs of spousal and dependent coverage. For many employees, this is the biggest annual cash bonus they receive—though they rarely look at it this way.

A company might spend $5,000 a year on medical insurance for a single employee and $12,500 a year for an employee who needs family coverage. If an employee gets married in year two, has a child, and stays at the company for 10 more years, he or she will likely never think about the compensation value of the *tax-free* gift he or she receives over a decade of service—to the tune of $75,000.

According to recent estimates from the Kaiser Family Foundation, the average annual premiums in 2016 were $6,435 for single coverage and $18,142 for family coverage (see Figure 1.3). The same report found that employers contribute on average $5,306 toward annual coverage for their single employees and more than twice that amount, $12,865, for their employees with family coverage.[9] So one way to reduce benefits costs is to just hire single employees, right? Of course not. Employers hire the best employees for the job, regardless of whether they have families. But employees with families often overlook this approximately $7,500 annual bonus their employer is providing. If you are the employer paying out this "bonus" to a good portion of your employees, wouldn't you want them to know about it?

---

9. Kaiser Family Foundation, "2016 Employer Health Benefits Survey," http://kff.org/report-section/ehbs-2016-summary-of-findings/.

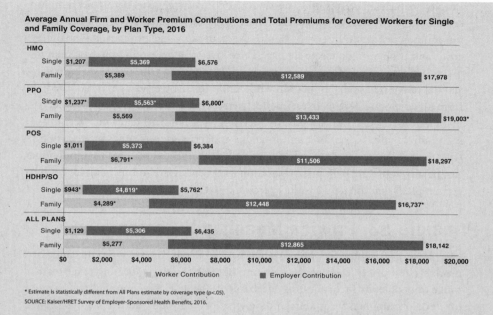

Average Annual Firm and Worker Premium Contributions and Total Premiums for Covered Workers for Single and Family Coverage, by Plan Type, 2016

HMO
- Single: $1,207 | $5,369 | $6,576
- Family: $5,389 | $12,589 | $17,978

PPO
- Single: $1,237* | $5,563* | $6,800*
- Family: $5,569 | $13,433 | $19,003*

POS
- Single: $1,011 | $5,373 | $6,384
- Family: $6,791* | $11,506 | $18,297

HDHP/SO
- Single: $943* | $4,819* | $5,762*
- Family: $4,289* | $12,448 | $16,737*

ALL PLANS
- Single: $1,129 | $5,306 | $6,435
- Family: $5,277 | $12,865 | $18,142

$0 $2,000 $4,000 $6,000 $8,000 $10,000 $12,000 $14,000 $16,000 $18,000 $20,000

▨ Worker Contribution   ■ Employer Contribution

* Estimate is statistically different from All Plans estimate by coverage type (p<.05).
SOURCE: Kaiser/HRET Survey of Employer-Sponsored Health Benefits, 2016.

Figure 1.3 *Single Versus Family Premium Contributions by Plan Type.*

Requiring more transparency around benefits contributions forces employers to clarify their own strategies. When employers spend more on family benefits, are they consciously giving a break to some employees over others? Is there a way to manage these distributions to achieve workforce goals? Employers need to determine what they want to achieve and determine how to manage their allocation of benefits dollars to maximize that result.

The same sort of issue arises with employer-paid benefits like life or disability insurance, wellness incentives, and any other "freebies" an employer may choose to offer. Such bonuses mean a lot more when employees are aware of them.

Principle #2: Provide True Price Transparency

As with any other true "exchange" of goods and services, benefits marketplaces have to ensure that participants receive unbiased, credible market information in order for a free market to thrive. When consumers log on to a benefits exchange, they must rely on the true pricing and coverage information for comparison shopping. Sellers must understand that if they misrepresent their policies or pricing, the system cannot work efficiently.

Employers have a responsibility here, too: For a true free market to work, employers shouldn't be steering employees to any plans they deem "better" for them (or for the company's bottom line) but should offer a broad range of plans, transparency in costs, and proper guidance so that each employee can determine the best plan for his or her situation. This is how inefficiencies associated with overinsuring a substantial portion of your population while underinsuring others gets smoothed out from an economic perspective. An effective recommendation engine (the mechanism that drives decision support in a technology platform) takes into account each individual's risk outlook and financial concerns, among other factors, along with the true prices of plans, when suggesting the optimal plan for that individual. Artificially adjusting plan prices based on a current desire to push employees into certain plans is ultimately a futile exercise.

Principle #3: Provide Meaningful Choice

Just like any other store, an online benefits store needs to have the right range of products and prices, the right brands, and options that are appealing to a broad range of people. By incorporating mechanisms (such as a recommendation engine for decision support) for understanding what people want and need, a marketplace can provide the appropriate levels of customization, information, and choice. The resulting buying patterns can yield much more effective information over time than the annual "guess the spread" exercise so many brokers undertake with their spreadsheets each year, which ultimately is like trying to guess the stock market. When you continually refine and hone your store offerings based on actual usage patterns, you operate more like Amazon and Zappos in stocking inventory than you do a financial advisor trying to predict the market.

When consumers are given the right amount of choice and can spend their own allocation of money, they seek the best value for their dollars. This economic principle works for both the supply- and demand-side actors in the health care benefits transaction. Employers can save time because they make one big decision—how much money to allocate to employees—and then let their employees do the rest. Companies do this in other ways; for example, they pay their employees a salary, which the employees may use to buy their own homes, cars, and TVs as well as choose their own investments, including complicated financial products such as 401(k)s. Employees make big decisions with high price tags every day, and no one says they're not qualified to make these decisions if that's what they choose to do with their money.

> Employees make big decisions with high price tags every day, and no one says they're not qualified to make these decisions...

By having employees self-select their own insurance and other products, the supply side is incentivized to become more competitive and agile to adapt to these preferences and encourage higher adoption by offering more of what people want. Because employees can use any remaining funds from their employer's defined contribution or supplement with their own money to ensure that they have the right protection in place for their needs, insurance carriers can create innovative products, such as hospital indemnity insurance or accident insurance, to meet particular needs. And it stands to reason that in spending these dollars, people are going to be very smart because they're not only allocating a fixed amount from their employer but potentially spending their own money. They're going to ask questions and make decisions that work for them, and they're going to be more engaged in these decisions.

For example, a young, single shopper may choose a health plan with a lower premium and higher deductible, along with a health savings account (HSA) to help save for qualifying expenses with tax-free funds. (Data based on actual usage from Liazon exchanges show that 4% more Generation Xers and 8% more Millennials buy HSA-qualified plans than Baby Boomers.)[10] Those who are healthy and free of chronic medical conditions are more likely to choose a narrower network of doctors. A married employee with four children may choose a dental plan that covers orthodontia. Another employee may need a personal health coach to help him quit smoking. This variety of needs calls for a store that presents a number of different options.

MORE CHOICE = MORE HAPPINESS

Employees are gravitating toward high-deductible health plans (HDHPs) as they better understand their roles as consumers and the ability of these new options to help them control costs. Findings from the Kaiser Family Foundation indicate a 25% increase in high-deductible plans from 2006 to 2016 (see Figure 1.4).[11] Liazon's own data have shown that, on average, 46% of employees choose an HSA-qualified HDHP[12]; recent industry averages from United Benefits Advisors place this figure at 17%.[13]

Employees are also showing higher satisfaction with making their own choices over benefits. Nearly all employees Liazon surveyed (94%) reported overall satisfaction with their exchange experience. When we dug a little deeper to determine what specific factors delighted employees, we discovered that 96% of employees found the extensive education and decision support tools to be an important part of the marketplace, and 84% found the recommendation they received from the system to be helpful. In addition, 92% of employees said they were satisfied with the benefits choices available.[14] These findings are especially impressive given the distrust and confusion surrounding health care and health care reform in recent years.

10. Private Exchange Research Council (PERC) analysis, 2017, www.percinsights.com. Information here based on groups enrolling in benefits on Liazon exchanges with a benefits effective date of January 1, 2017. Data representative of all employees in the study sample who were at a company and eligible to purchase an HSA-qualified plan.

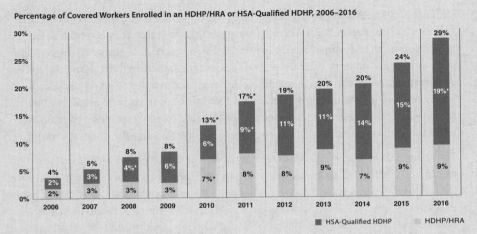

Percentage of Covered Workers Enrolled in an HDHP/HRA or HSA-Qualified HDHP, 2006–2016

*Estimate is statistically different from estimate for the previous year shown (p<.05).

NOTE: Covered Workers enrolled in an HDHP/SO are enrolled in either an HDHP/HRA or a HSA-Qualified HDHP. For more information see the Survey Methodology Section. The percentages of covered workers enrolled in an HDHP/SO may not equal the sum of HDHP/HRA and HSA-Qualified HDHP enrollment estimates due to rounding.

SOURCE: Kaiser/HRET Survey of Employer-Sponsored Health Benefits, 2006-2016.

Figure 1.4 *Enrollment in High-Deductible Health Plans, 2006–2016.*

Liazon also found that 97% of employers are satisfied with their exchange experience,[15] and they are making considerable strides in understanding how important it is for their employees to be in the driver's seat about these decisions; 98% of employees believe it's important to be able to choose their own benefits rather than have their employers choose for them. This is a meaningful finding when evaluating benefits as a retention tool because various studies,[16] in addition to Liazon's own research, have found that the quality of benefits offerings are increasingly affecting employees' intention

11. Kaiser Family Foundation, "2016 Employer Health Benefits Survey," http://kff.org/report-section/ehbs-2016-summary-of-findings/.

12. Private Exchange Research Council (PERC) analysis, 2017, www.percinsights.com. Information here based on groups enrolling in benefits on Liazon exchanges with a benefits effective date of January 1, 2017. Data representative of all employees in the study sample who were at a company and eligible to purchase an HSA-qualified plan.

13. United Benefits Advisors, "UBA Special Report: How Health Savings Accounts Measure Up," May 10, 2017, http://blog.ubabenefits.com/news/uba-special-report-how-health-savings-accounts-measure-up.

14. Liazon, "Liazon's 2017 Employee Survey Report: Health Care Consumerism in a Marketplace Environment," March 2017, http://liazon.hs-sites.com/liazon/employeesurvey-1.

15. Liazon, op. cit.

16. Various industry sources, as cited by Access Perks Blog, "Benefits and Employee Engagement/Retention/Recruitment Stats," February 28, 2017, http://blog.accessperks.com/employee-benefits-perks-statistics#engagement.

to stay with their employer. Further, Liazon's research indicates that 92% of individuals who choose their benefits through an exchange are satisfied with the benefits they chose one year later.[17]

A year later,
9 out of **10**
employees are
satisfied with
the benefits they
purchased.

Source: 2016 Liazon Employee Survey

17 Liazon, op. cit.

Principle #4: Offer Guidance in the Form of Decision Support

When employees are empowered to choose their own combination of plans and products to create a portfolio of benefits that fit their needs and their budget, how can they go about making the right decisions for their individual situations? Decision support provides guidance for these important choices, and can take many forms.

Decision support can be as simple as access to a live advisor who gathers information about each person's unique situation. Liazon uses an online questionnaire to ask an employee a series of questions related to, among other things, the employee's expectations of care usage (such as pregnancy or prescription drug use), risk tolerance, financial position, and health status. The tool predicts a

The [decision support] tool predicts a full range of possible health care expense outcomes to determine the package of plans that best fits the employee's needs.

full range of possible health care expense outcomes to determine the package of plans that best fits the employee's needs.

Liazon also makes information available in the form of plan summaries and detailed plan overviews, along with plan comparison tools, for more analytics-oriented employees who need to see and compare the numbers in order to understand their options. An employee might consider a recommendation for a medical plan as a base and then choose a plan that is a step up or step down from the recommended plan (in terms of price and plan design), based on the information obtained through deeper research into the options.

Other forms of support might be offered, such as online "avatars," which use a search functionality to serve up answers to users' particular questions. Decision support can be as basic as setting up kiosks for live on-site Q&A support, holding traditional meetings in which employees can get their questions answered by HR or brokers, or making brokers or other service representatives available on the phone or via web chat to address employee concerns.

Finally, decision support may include interactive education tools. An employee may, for example, review informational material or watch an educational video explaining the benefits and services offered. With information available at the point of purchase, the employee can better understand why the particular product or plan was recommended, step up or down from that option, or shop for a different offering within the exchange.

Different types of employees will respond to different support avenues, and the key is to offer a range of informative options that allow an employee to make meaningful choices (see Figure 1.5).

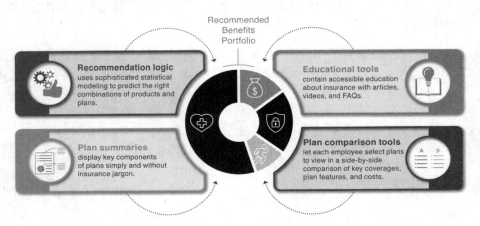

Figure 1.5 *Liazon's Decision Support Model.*

If you were providing decision support for individuals to buy cars rather than bene-fits, you could assume a general baseline knowledge of cars among members of the group. All will know cars are a means of transport, have four wheels, run on gas, and so on. The more you can find out from individuals how they plan to use their vehicles, the more apparent it becomes which vehicle best suits each person's needs. For some individuals, a pickup truck might make the most sense, whereas for oth-ers, a convertible or a sedan or a jeep might be the best fit.

Choice can be overwhelming. Decision support makes it not only manageable but optimal. Is Amazon overwhelming? Not when it helps you narrow down the choices and suggests what products you might like, based on what it knows about you. In the case of benefits choices, it's not about the size of the portfolio or the tier of the plan; it's about the right fit for each individual. And when employees are guided by robust decision support, employers don't have to worry that they are not capable of choosing their own plans.

> In the case of benefits choices, it's not about the size of the portfolio or the tier of the plan; it's about the right fit for each individual.

Principle #5: Optimize the Shopping Experience

In addition to having the right products and the right guidance, a benefits market-place should have an optimal design to make it easy and familiar for people to shop for and buy products. What optimizes shopping in a store? For one thing, support. Zappos offers free returns on all shoe purchases, so users are free to try a few dif-ferent sizes, knowing they can send back whatever doesn't fit. Trader Joe's has plenty of "crew members" around its grocery stores to return something to the shelf while you're shopping or get something you may have forgotten in a different aisle. Hav-ing a sharp focus on the customer experience in a benefits marketplace is essential because the process is new, and product knowledge is often limited.

Just as in a retail environment, optimal experiences in an online benefits market-place can be made smart, simple, and relevant when the needs of the customer (or employee) are prioritized.

Whether your favorite store is Trader Joe's, Zappos, or Home Depot, you know what a great customer and transactional experience feels like. These markets work because their fundamentals are sound. Private exchanges have the potential to pro-vide such experiences as well.

ENSURING A GREAT SHOPPING EXPERIENCE IN AN EXCHANGE ENVIRONMENT: A GLIMPSE BEHIND LIAZON'S CURTAIN

Liazon's principles for enabling an optimal shopping experience include universal design, metrics-based iteration, and a climate of innovation.

Universal Design

Liazon's process for creating the optimal experience starts with understanding people. Everyone, regardless of ability, should experience our interface in a way that is engaging, simple, and intuitive (see Figure 1.6). Our research indicates that people have varied experiences buying benefits and shopping online. Some people are familiar with benefits, while others need more guidance. Some are frequent online shoppers, while others may face technical challenges or shop using screen readers or other assistive devices. Understanding the specific users is the basis of Liazon's "user personas," or representations, of both novice and experienced shoppers. Using personas, Liazon can outline the various paths a person might take toward purchase, using a "journey map." User personas and journey maps are tools Liazon uses to empathize, streamline complex tasks, and seek areas to create delight. These tools are the foundation for an inclusive experience.

Universal design also involves considering a multitude of devices and technologies. People often switch between devices, choosing to start an experience on a smartphone, for instance, and then switch to a tablet or another device. It's important for familiarity and consistency to be maintained across devices to ground people in their experience. Liazon ensures that the benefits shopping experience is not only consistent, but exceptional, across devices.

Choosing benefits is an important decision that takes time and careful consideration. However, people want to move through the process quickly. The complexities of benefits and insurance shouldn't hinder the shopping process. We constantly strive to offer a streamlined experience, with helpful information and engaging interactions to guide customers through the process. The experience is reminiscent of other online shopping experiences, down to the universal shopping cart icon and an easy way to review what's in the cart.

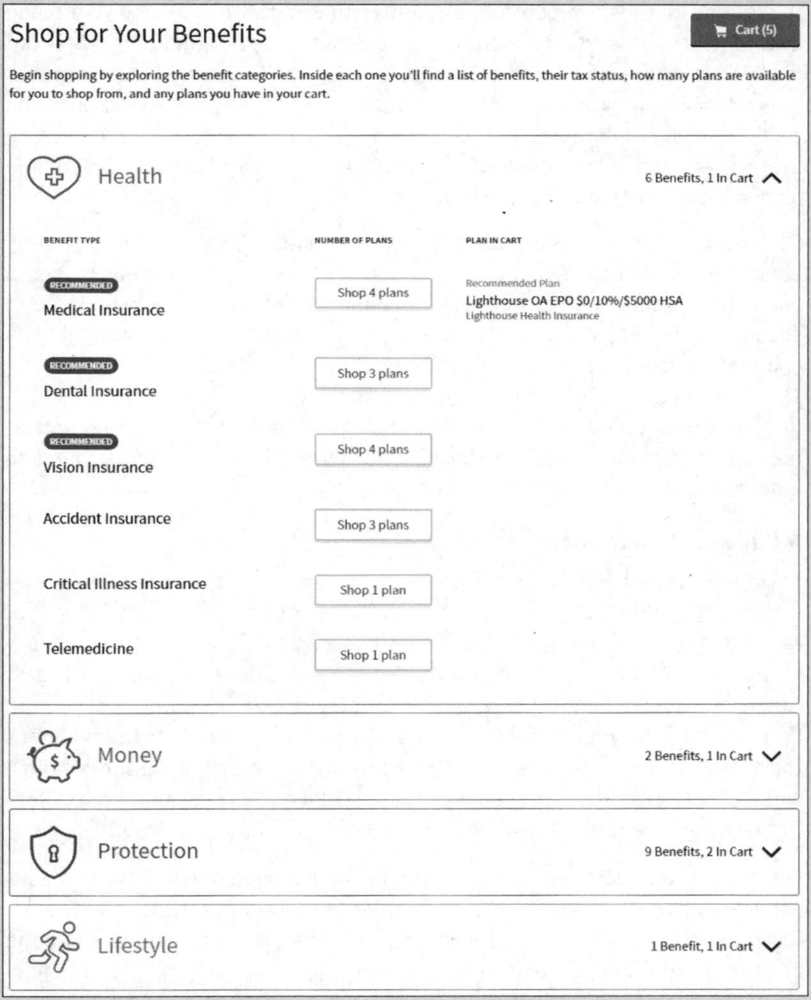

Figure 1.6 *The Simplified User Interface on Liazon Exchanges.*

Metrics-Based Iteration

Liazon's user personas are created based on quantitative and qualitative metrics that are also the driving force behind continuous improvements to the shopping experience. These metrics provide a complete understanding of customer interactions and help us identify possibilities for product innovation. For example, we observed users interacting with the Liazon system and noted that username recovery and password resetting was a pain point for consumers. Liazon combined this observation with support call data received from the employee service center to create and implement a new workflow to simplify the login process and improve the overall experience. We made usernames unique yet memorable for users and redesigned the password reset process to show and hide the password, which helps to reduce errors. This improved workflow also presented an opportunity for us to enhance the security of user information. These small innovations led to a more positive user experience and decreased the number of support calls for username recovery and password reset assistance.

System analytics, employer surveys, service center call logs, online polling, benchmark studies, and one-on-one user interviews are all collected and compared against key performance indicators (KPIs) to track and report successes. If data indicate, for example, that customers are struggling to complete a task, we see an opportunity to revisit the shopping experience. This may mean reducing the number of clicks to add products to the shopping cart or simplifying complex terminology to help customers understand medical deductibles. Data are critical to understanding customers and to innovating, reviewing, and testing progress.

A Climate of Innovation

Liazon's internal teams challenge themselves to create new experiences through usability best practices and iterative design, understanding that technology is just one part of the user experience. Innovation is a collaborative effort, and insights from the entire team drive the best changes. Client Service, Operations, and the Employee Service Center at Liazon help define customer support needs and issues. The Product team shapes the business requirements and strategy (the *value* of the features built), whereas the Development team outlines the best way to implement features within the system (*feasibility*).

Ultimately, the best user experience is one in which people can easily achieve their goals. Simple factors, such as content that's difficult to read or icons that people don't easily recognize, can affect how users understand the choices in front of them and can negatively impact the shopping experience. Usability best practices, combined with multiple data sources and collaboration among teams, is essential in creating an optimal benefits enrollment experience.

Principle #6: Ensure a Cultural Fit Within the Organization

Just as individuals are on their own curves of knowledge and needs in terms of what their portfolios will look like, each employer is on its own glide path toward having its benefits marketplace make sense for the company and its users. From the company point of view, one element of readiness might be the degree to which the company recognizes and understands the employee experience and culture within the organization; for example, the type of employees attracted to their industry and business, employee education levels, as well as the company mindset and leadership style. Overcoming barriers such as resistance to cultural change is therefore another essential element in the success of private benefits exchanges.

For some organizations, such as unions or small, family-owned businesses, replacing the traditional benefits program may be nearly impossible. For larger organizations, each group and every person in each group will have different levels of familiarity with decision making in an e-commerce environment. Therefore, an effective benefits marketplace requires an intuitive user design and a learning curve that adapts to where people are in their level of understanding benefits as well as technology. It requires a willingness to build different levels of customization and complexity into an exchange so that it is appropriate to the culture of the particular workplace. Chapter 5, "Employers Find Skin in the Game," takes a look at the educational approaches that have worked for actual employers, given that some employees are more comfortable in an online shopping environment than others.

Principle #7: Refine, Iterate, and Improve

Analysis and data refinement are an essential part of organizing an exchange and maximizing its potential, but when an industry is in its infancy, information can be scarce. Early in 2015, together with leading brokers, consultants, and private exchange experts, Liazon began a major industry initiative called the Private

Exchange Research Council (PERC). The goal of this initiative is to assemble an analytic storehouse based on user preference and satisfaction data gleaned from Liazon exchanges over time to further the industry at large. (For the latest data from PERC, see Appendix C or visit www.percinsights.com.)

> Benefits aren't a "set it and forget it" proposition, and neither is building an exchange or measuring its success.

Benefits aren't a "set it and forget it" proposition, and neither is building an exchange or measuring its success. The more data that can be uncovered about a company, the more refinements can be made to its systems based on actual user interaction.

Summary

This chapter examines the seven principles that make up an efficient benefits system: defined contribution, price transparency, meaningful choice, decision support, an optimized shopping experience, organizational fit, and iteration and improvement. Could it be we're on the verge of a new Progressive Era when it comes to employee benefits? Following this blueprint for an efficient system could be a catalyst.

Throughout this book, we will delve more deeply into these seven principles as a foundation for fixing the broken benefits system in the United States. But first, Chapter 2, "Benefits: The Accidental Entitlement," discusses how we got to where we are in order to help shed light on where we're going.

2

Benefits: The Accidental Entitlement

When running a marathon, you don't begin at the starting line. You begin when you decide to enter the race. Then you focus on your physical fitness, your diet, your clothing and gear, and a host of other factors before actually starting to run. Similarly, we can't simply look at the private exchange marathon from this point forward; rather, we need to consider the history of benefits and health insurance in the United States—and elsewhere—as a reality check on the complexity and consequences of providing improved access to health care and the need to proceed carefully.

Private exchanges work by fostering efficient markets for benefits with the right balance of supply- and demand-side incentives. Indeed, health care analysts borrowed the concept of an insurance exchange from the marketplaces that have existed for many centuries, where goods were traded, bought, and sold at public prices with accurate transactions documented by public accounts. (If this is your cue to skip to the next chapter, we suggest that before you move to Chapter 3, "They Don't Know What They're Missing: Flipping the Status Quo on Its Head," take a look at the health care timeline in Appendix C, "Real-World Data and Applications," for a visual journey through the past 100+ years in health care. However, if your daily life is somehow impacted by the health insurance and benefits industry, it may behoove you to trace the roots of your livelihood in the pages that follow.)

Health Care Timeline

New Focus With Hard Economic Times	**FDR Proposes 'Economic Bill of Rights'**	**National Health Insurance Condemned**
➤ 1934	➤ 1944	➤ 1945

The Depression shifts attention to unemployment insurance and "old age" benefits. President Franklin Roosevelt creates the Committee on Economic Security to address these issues as well as medical care and insurance. But when the Social Security Act is passed, health insurance is omitted. The American Medical Association strongly opposes a national health insurance program, saying it would increase bureaucracy, limit doctors' freedom and interfere with the doctor-patient relationship.

A family affected by the Depression, 1936.
Photo: Wikimedia Commons

In his State of the Union address, President Franklin Roosevelt outlines an "economic bill of rights" that includes the right to adequate medical care and the opportunity to achieve and enjoy good health. During World War II, U.S. businesses begin to offer health benefits as they compete for workers, giving rise to the employer-based system in place today.

Shortly after becoming president, Harry Truman proposes a broad health care restructuring that includes mandatory coverage, more hospitals, and double the number of nurses and doctors. Denounced by the American Medical Association and other critics as "socialized medicine," his plan goes nowhere in Congress.

Harry Truman
Photo: Wikimedia Commons

Source: AnnenbergClassroom.org

The term *exchange* conjures images of an organized center for trading—as in exchanges for securities or commodities, like gold or soybeans. When we talk about a benefits exchange, we are talking about an exchange in its simplest context: a store specializing in a particular type of merchandise—in this case, benefits products. To simplify the communication with employees who use the Liazon technology platform to choose their benefits, we prefer the terms *marketplace* and *store* over *exchange*.

The term *exchange* as it relates to health care entered the mainstream with the introduction of the Affordable Care Act (ACA), which borrowed the term to describe the establishment of online marketplaces that enable individuals to buy medical insurance. These are referred to as *public exchanges*. In contrast, *private exchanges* enable employees to choose from a variety of employer-sponsored benefit offerings, typically anchored by medical insurance. The vision of a private exchange stems more from the forces driving a free market economy, in which prices are set freely by the forces of supply and demand, and not by an outside authority, such as the government, or carriers, or even employers.

> To simplify the communication with employees who use the Liazon technology platform to choose their benefits, we prefer the terms *marketplace* and *store* over *exchange*.

Credit: E.Walker/AMP/Getty Images

Marketplaces can be traced back to the Sumerian civilization of ancient Mesopotamia, in which literacy and accurate bookkeeping facilitated open-air markets typically located near religious temples. Lowland farmers bartered surplus produce for stone, wood, and metals such as copper mined in the mountains or shipped by boat. If money had to be used, it was usually in the form of small silver disks. Sumerians benefited from a free economy that allowed ordinary people to access goods according to their needs. Scribes kept strict records of all business transactions and checked written contracts when there were disputes. These receipts and contracts became the first written artifacts recovered by archaeologists and helped contribute to Sumer also being known as "the birthplace of economics."

Ancient Rome was a cosmopolitan city with a thriving urban retail economy. Traders and street sellers would congregate in central areas around temples, bathhouses, and theatres—an early prototype for a modern–day mall, where shoppers could efficiently find all the goods they needed in one place. These central markets are precursors to what we know of as competing stores today; consumers could evaluate a range of goods in one walkable location to determine how to budget their spending. If the fish stand was too far from the grain stand, a shopper might be busy evaluating sardines and discover later that the wheat prices he had seen earlier had gone up by the time he returned to the grain stand. This same enduring principle may be at work in an online "store," such as the airline marketplace, where products can easily be compared and prices can fluctuate rapidly.

Ancient Roman marketplace

Credit: jpa1999/E+/Getty Images

Holland's medieval commodity markets during the thirteenth and fourteenth centuries also operated free from undue influence of the ruling classes (which was a far bigger problem in England), thereby allowing buyers and sellers in urban and rural areas access to markets with uniform pricing, stimulating agricultural production and economic growth.[1] The rise of modern commodities markets in the United States was similarly enabled by rules and laws which ensured that traders could make informed choices in a market with consistent rules and pricing.

Not Really an "Exchange"

Specialized marketplaces have a history of improving conditions for sellers and buyers and have informed the development of benefits exchanges. Efficient and fair markets operate by informed choice, with buyers knowing and trusting the rules and enabling consumers to compare and evaluate multiple options.

The term *exchange* doesn't fully capture the range of supply and demand interactions in benefits marketplaces. Pure commodity exchanges focus more on suppliers, requiring them to sell their undifferentiated produce, goods, or materials in one place and by the same pricing rules. The buyer benefits from commodity markets because he or

---

1. J. E. C. Dijkman, "Medieval Market Institutions. The Organization of Commodity Markets in Holland, c. 1200–c. 1450," www.researchgate.net/publication/44387727_%27Medieval_market_institutions_The_organization_of_commodity_markets_in_Holland_c_1200-c_1450%27.

she doesn't suffer geographic arbitrage (that is, if someone in Chicago was selling soybeans a lot cheaper than someone else in St. Louis, or if the price of gold in New York was more than in San Francisco). Efficient markets that remove geographic price arbitrage also foster better choices in how people buy health insurance.

SUPPLY- VERSUS DEMAND-SIDE ECONOMICS IN BENEFITS

In a commodity exchange, everyone buys and sells at the same price, which is determined by the market, and there is no differentiation in product. The marketplace determines exactly what the product is, according to accepted specifications; for example, in a gold exchange, gold has to be 99.9% pure to be 24 karat, 75% pure to be 18 karat, and so on. In a store like Amazon, the marketplace doesn't define what it means to be a TV set or what is the value of a TV set; the consumers decide, based on what they like, so that if everyone likes Panasonic or Samsung, the demand side will determine the prices for these TV sets that the market will bear. Certain farmers complain about their food products being a commodity, like soybeans, because they feel their cultivation should merit more of a demand-side pricing so they can see more profits.

A few private exchanges in the health care industry operate like commodity markets in that they offer a menu of similar health plan designs from different suppliers at relatively the same prices. Other private exchanges concentrate more on the demand side. At Liazon, for example, the consumer has a greater variety of quality choices than in a pure commodity exchange. In fact, Liazon's approach is more like a free market system, in which there is open competition among the designated merchants, and private transactions between buyers and sellers may occur without the intervention of a regulator (in this case, the employer).

Think of it this way: When you walk into Best Buy to buy a television, you first enter the store (marketplace), then find your way to the aisle where the home entertainment systems are displayed, and then find the shelf or two with the 40-inch televisions you're looking for. You may see some TVs with slightly different features, from different manufacturers, and perhaps most importantly, at different prices. You use the knowledge you have about what it is you're looking for, coupled with the perceived value of each offering, to weigh your options and make a decision. When suppliers understand that this is how consumers make their choices, they're cognizant of their price points vis-á-vis their competition. That's the store concept, and it can work the same way for purchases of benefits products as well. Benefits exchanges facilitate this type of shopping experience by creating these marketplaces online.

"Modern-Day" Insurance

Insurance made its earliest appearance in the late 1800s, in various forms that led to the health and nonmedical offerings we know today. In one example, railroads and mining companies deducted small amounts of employees' wages and, in return, provided doctors and medical services. Other insurance plans simply covered compensation for lost wages due to illness—but not medical services and fees. The first group insurance plan originated with teachers at the Dallas, Texas, public schools; in exchange for monthly payments to Baylor University Hospital, the teachers were guaranteed some hospitalization services, if needed. During the 1930s, several hospitals modeled their own insurance plans on the Dallas teachers' plan, and these were eventually brought together under the framework of the American Hospital Association (AHA) and given the name Blue Cross. Even at this early stage of modern medicine, the AHA recognized the importance of patient choice.

Melissa Thomasson, an economics historian at Miami University, wrote,

> The AHA designed the Blue Cross guidelines so as to reduce price competition among hospitals. Prepayment plans seeking the Blue Cross designation had to provide subscribers with free choice of physician and hospital, a requirement that eliminated single–hospital plans from consideration. Blue Cross plans also benefited from special state–level legislation allowing them to act as non–profit corporations, enjoy tax–exempt status, and be free from the usual insurance regulations.

Originally, the reason for this exemption was that Blue Cross plans were considered to be in society's best interest since they often provided benefits to low–income individuals.[2]

In the wake of Blue Cross, physicians initially resisted accepting any form of insurance, fearing that they would have to give up setting their own fees and choosing their own patients. They eventually relented out of fear that hospitals would bring general medical practices under their roofs. The first of what became known as Blue Shield plans originated in California in 1939. State laws granted these Blue Shield companies nonprofit, tax-exempt status and freedom from regulations imposed on other insurance firms. It wasn't until 1982 that the two "Blues" merged into the Blue Cross Blue Shield Association that exists to the present day.[3]

Benefits as Compensation

As discussed in this book's Introduction, health insurance provided by employers is a legacy of World War II. As Thomasson writes, "wage and price controls prevented employers from using wages to compete for scarce labor." However, Congress wrote the legislation in such a way that it "permitted the adoption of employee insurance plans. In this way, health benefit packages offered one means of securing workers."[4] Interestingly, the attraction and retention of employees remains the sole reason most companies offer employer–paid benefits as part of total compensation.

> Interestingly, the attraction and retention of employees remains the sole reason most companies offer employer-paid benefits as part of total compensation.

Essentially, employee benefits were conceived as compensation to get around legislative hurdles and attract workers during wartime, when labor was in high demand. After World War II, two decisions reinforced this pact between management and workers. First, the National Labor Relations Board ruled that unions could bargain on behalf of their workers for benefits as well as wages. Second, the IRS in 1954 codified a wartime rule that "payments made by the employer directly to commercial insurance companies for group medical and hospitalization premiums of employees were not taxable as employee income."[5]

---

2. Melissa Thomasson, "Health Insurance in the United States," Economic History Association, https://eh.net/encyclopedia/health-insurance-in-the-united-states/.

3. Ibid.

4. Ibid.

5. Ibid.

Taken together, these two decisions meant that management and labor could negotiate contracts that made trade–offs between taxable wages and nontaxable benefits as part of a worker's compensation package. Once this arrangement was in place, it spread rapidly and eventually became codified as part of U.S. workforce culture, although the vast majority of people who use this system today likely don't know the origins, nor do they generally have much indication of what their premiums are and how much their employers contribute. (It was this lack of transparency that led, in part, to the development of private exchanges, as discussed in Chapter 1, "Building a Better Benefits System.")

HISTORY OF HEALTH INSURANCE BENEFITS[6]

Employment–based health benefit programs have existed in the United States for more than 100 years. In the 1870s, for example, railroad, mining, and other industries began to provide the services of company doctors to workers. In 1910, Montgomery Ward entered into one of the earliest group insurance contracts. Prior to World War II, few Americans had health insurance, and most policies covered only hospital room, board, and ancillary services. During World War II, the number of persons with employment–based health insurance coverage started to increase for several reasons. When wages were frozen by the National War Labor Board and a shortage of workers occurred, employers sought ways to get around the wage controls in order to attract scarce workers; offering health insurance was one option. Health insurance was an attractive means to recruit and retain workers during a labor shortage for two reasons: Unions supported employment–based health insurance, and workers' health benefits were not subject to income tax or Social Security payroll taxes, as were cash wages. Under the current tax code, health insurance premiums paid by employers are deductible for employers as a business expense and are excluded, without limit, from workers' taxable income.

6. Employee Benefit Research Institute, "History of Health Insurance Benefits," 1999; and Marilyn J. Field and Harold T. Shapiro, eds., *Employment and Health Benefits: A Connection at Risk*, Washington, DC: National Academy Press, 1993.

Efforts to rescind the tax exemption in the 1940s failed, and by the 1960s, nearly three in four Americans had some form of private health insurance coverage, and employer–provided health care in the form of "major medical" or "catastrophic" insurance was almost universal.[7] However, over the next two decades, health cost

7. Rosemary Stevens, "Health Care in the Early 1960s," *Medicare and Medicaid Research Review*, Winter 1996, p. 11–22, www.ncbi.nlm.nih.gov/pmc/articles/PMC4193636/.

inflation took hold, and corporations began seeking ways to reduce, limit, and cut the cost of employer–sponsored health coverage.

Though the Health Maintenance Organization (HMO) Act was signed by President Richard Nixon in 1972 by as part of a national strategy to reduce health care costs, the system failed to take hold for a few more decades. The HMO Act provided millions of dollars in start-up funding for HMOs and required employers with 25 or more employees to offer an HMO option.[8] While HMOs later fell into disfavor due to mismanagement and restrictions that consumers found onerous, their original design was still used in later iterations of the system, and HMOs are still considered a viable option as part of a larger set of choices for health insurance plan types.

Well into the 1980s, most insurance plans were indemnity plans. Through an indemnity plan, an insurer (or a self-insured employer) reimburses employees for medical expenses without much restriction on the services or health care providers (that is, within the limitations placed by a certain network), although in some cases the amount of the reimbursement may be limited. The patient bore only a small percentage of the costs and therefore had no incentive to be cost conscious. Insurers paid health care providers for all covered administered procedures. Therefore, the physician benefited financially from any service the patient selected while advising patients on what procedures to undertake. As noted in the book *Work in America*, "With these conflicting interests, physicians had an incentive to go in for expensive procedures, even if they were not absolutely essential. Such an incentive system led to an annual growth rate of 13.5 percent in per capita health expenditures"[9] [between 1966 and 1982].

Managed care plans—typically referred to as health maintenance organizations (HMOs), preferred provider organizations (PPOs), or point-of-service (POS) plans—became an integral part of the health insurance landscape throughout the 1990s. These plans, which involve an arrangement between the insurer and a "network" of providers (physicians, hospitals, and other care providers) selected by the insurer, offer greater incentives to physicians who are part of the insurer's network, and patients, who receive care from providers in that network for a prepaid fee rather than paying per visit.

Rather than figure out how to manage someone's care when they got sick, medical insurance started to focus on how to keep them well in the first place, which meant coordinating care among physicians while a person is healthy to hopefully reduce

---

8. "Health Maintenance Organization Act of 1973," *Social Security Administration Bulletin*, U.S. government report, www.ssa.gov/policy/docs/ssb/v37n3/v37n3p35.pdf; and Peter R. Kongstvedt, *The Essentials of Managed Health Care*, Sudbury, MA: Jones and Bartlett Publishers, 2007.

9. Herbert Schaffner & Carl Van Horn, *Work in America: An Encyclopedia of History, Policy, and Society*, Santa Barbara, CA: ABC-CLIO, 2003.

excessive treatments and testing when he or she gets sick. These innovations were retained in later consumer-driven reforms such as accountable care organizations (ACOs), in which groups of doctors, hospitals, and other providers come together to coordinate patient care. ACOs took hold, and a number of managed care organizations, such as Kaiser Permanente, continue to thrive today.

> Rather than figure out how to manage someone's care when they got sick, medical insurance started to focus on how to keep them well in the first place...

The managed care model opened the door to new ideas—and also criticism. A notable voice was Alain Enthoven of Stanford University in the *New England Journal of Medicine* in 1978. Enthoven's articles, primarily "Consumer-Choice Health Plan— Inflation and Inequity in Health Care Today: Alternatives for Cost Control and an Analysis of Proposals for National Health Insurance," received wide notice. Enthoven critiqued rising medical costs and recommended "that the government change financial incentives by creating a system of competing health plans in which physicians and consumers can benefit from using resources wisely."[10] He called for need-based subsidies, open enrollment, community ratings, and limits on patient out-of-pocket costs. At the core of his proposals: that efficient systems pass their savings on to consumers and that freedom of choice for consumers and patients be preserved.

Regina Herzlinger of Harvard Business School, along with other proponents of consumer choice, became an intellectual pioneer for market-based reforms. The 1990s saw the early roots of consumer–driven health care as the next solution to keep costs and usage in check. Through high–deductible health plans and corresponding health savings accounts (HSAs), individuals could effectively set up a safety net against the potential need to pay the deductible and any associated coinsurance or copayments that might arise. (For more about health savings accounts, see Appendix B, "Making Sense of Benefits Terms.")

Herzlinger's landmark 2002 *Harvard Business Review* article, "Let's Put Consumers in Charge of Health Care," laid out the failures of managed care and made a formidable case for the growing momentum of consumerism:

> About 20 years ago, managed care was widely viewed as the silver bullet that would curb cost increases while ensuring patients good and convenient treatment. But managed care has been a bust. The original HMO models—vertically integrated systems for managing care or those that use gatekeepers to impose stringent controls on care—were resisted by patients and physicians. In response, the managed care organizations

10. Alain C. Enthoven, "Consumer-Choice Health Plan—Inflation and Inequity in Health Care Today: Alternatives for Cost Control and an Analysis of Proposals for National Health Insurance," *New England Journal of Medicine*, 298:650–658, March 23, 1978.

began relaxing their controls, allowing patients more freedom to see specialists and out-of-network doctors. Costs began to climb again, yet patients and providers continued to feel constrained. Now, no one's happy—not the insurers, not the patients, not the doctors and nurses, not the hospitals, and certainly not the companies that are footing the bill.

The situation is dire, but there is a way out of the mess—and the key lies with the business community. If companies are willing to embrace a new model of health coverage—one that places control over costs and care directly in the hands of employees—the competitive forces that spur productivity and innovation in consumer markets can be let loose upon the inefficient, tradition-bound health care system.[11]

To say that managed care "has been a bust" does not tell the full story. The 1990s did see rampant dissatisfaction on the consumer side, with individuals seeing their freedoms being taken away as they were forced into restrictive plans, and frustrations on the employer side due to failures of the promised cost containment. Managed care had failed to live up to expectations. But all health insurance as we know it today is still considered "managed" care, with more of a "consumer-driven" focus, in an attempt to recover from the backlash of the late 1990s in response to the "dire" situation Professor Herzlinger references.

> ...all health insurance as we know it today is still considered "managed" care, with more of a "consumer-driven" focus...

Still, consumer–driven models had not yet won favor by the mid-2000s, in large part because employers and employees didn't want to take a chance on fundamental changes in what, for most people, is an essential safety net. As a result, employers were inevitably left with three undesirable options when it came to the yearly benefits cost conundrum: (1) eat the cost increases themselves, (2) shift the cost to employees, or (3) reduce the value they provide to employees by eliminating certain benefits or reducing the amount of coverage. Something had to be done to help employers out of this decidedly unhealthy situation.

---

11. Regina Herzlinger, "Let's Put Consumers in Charge of Health Care," *Harvard Business Review*, July 2002, https://hbr.org/2002/07/lets-put-consumers-in-charge-of-health-care.

So Where Does This Leave Us?

Passage of the ACA in 2010 had a striking impact in bringing the exchange conversation front and center, but consumer–driven health plans and private exchanges as a way to deliver these types of plans, and others, were already gaining steam in the market. While providing needed coverage for many, the public exchanges were not seen as a way of deflecting employers' responsibilities to their employees, as had been originally feared by some early opponents of the ACA. On the contrary, many employers doubled down on their commitment, viewing the offering of health insurance and other benefits as critical to attracting and retaining talent and building a competitive workforce. The visibility of the ACA, with all its controversy and publicity, made millions of Americans familiar with the exchange model and its benefits, lowering the bar to adoption of private exchanges. Plus, the law required employers with 50 or more "full-time equivalent employees" to offer an "affordable/minimum value plan" or pay a penalty tax. Hence, a greater market of employers looking for new options opened new doors for private exchange adoption.

Lost in the noise over health care reform politics, however, was the fact that the U.S. government had already successfully deployed a health benefits exchange that is used by millions of people today. The Medicare Part D program uses an exchange-like mechanism for offering prescription drug coverage in a range of 15 to 20 plans, with total enrollment close to 20 million in 2017.[12] The Federal Employees Health Benefit (FEHB) program, created in 1960 and currently operated by the U.S. Office of Personnel Management, is the most successful model of a health care exchange to date. Original plans for the federal government to create its own self–insured system met resistance from unions and employee associations that had already sponsored their own plans. Congress decided to grandfather all the existing plans into one program for employees of the U.S. government, thereby creating a marketplace of fully-insured health plans driven by consumer choice.

So why is the time now ripe for private exchanges, considering the historical record? Many industry panels and journals regularly revisit the question. Our view is that until the mid-2000s, we didn't have the technology to deliver the usability and decision support required for a system to be able to compete with the status quo. Customers also didn't have the familiarity with online shopping that they do today. Millennials are getting older, moving up in their careers, and gaining more influence as sophisticated users of digital, co–created services from iTunes to Netflix. Many professionals, no matter their ages, are looking for savvy alternatives to legacy systems that are out of step with today's digital sophistication in design, navigation, and, quite simply, what it means to shop.

> Many professionals, no matter their ages, are looking for savvy alternatives to legacy systems that are out of step with today's digital sophistication...

In the spirit of co–creation, exchanges work much like actual stores, in which manufacturers of different products can offer their wares to the public, and the public can decide which ones offer the best value for the dollar. Then the manufacturers can modify their strategies and offerings in accordance with the demand they see. This marketplace design optimizes the benefits of market competition by giving multiple vendors access to the marketplace and arming shoppers with good information and support to make smart purchases. Private exchanges make insurance policies readily comparable, giving shoppers a financial stake in their choice, and offering quality measures that can be used to make informed decisions.[13]

12. Centers for Medicare & Medicaid Services, "Medicare Advantage, Cost, PACE, Demo, and Prescription Drug Plan Contract Report Monthly Summary Report (Data as of June 2017)," https://www.cms.gov/Research-Statistics-Data-and-Systems/Statistics-Trends-and-Reports/MCRAdvPartDEnrolData/Monthly-Contract-and-Enrollment-Summary-Report-Items/Contract-Summary-2017-06.html?DLPage=1&DLEntries=10&DLSort=1&DLSortDir=descending.

13. Paul Fronstin, "Private Health Insurance Exchanges and Defined Contribution Plans: Is It Déjà vu All over Again?" *EBRI Issue Brief*, 373, July 2012.

Successful private exchanges have more variety, quality, and transparent pricing options than traditional commodity exchanges. They stimulate manufacturers—in this case, insurers—to innovate products that people will buy, and use, as opposed to selling to employers who select products on their employees' behalf. While opening a store to buy health insurance or life insurance is somewhat new, shopping at a store—be it online or brick-and-mortar—is a deeply engrained consumer behavior. We know what good-functioning stores are and do not have to blindly go down a path that we hope will work. We know what makes Amazon, Walmart, and Best Buy successful. And we are learning more about how to adopt best-in-class retailing practices to make private exchanges more productive and usable.

As the private exchange industry continues to grow, the most successful benefits stores will optimize informed choice by (1) expanding the quality and variety of options available to shoppers in terms of products and prices and (2) making the historic shift in terms of who gets to make the benefits choice (that is, the employee, not the employer). After all, buyers have always expected to have meaningful options when they make purchases. Why wouldn't that be the case in medical insurance and other benefits to ensure complete financial protection?

These concepts haven't changed from Liazon's earliest start-up days, when there were five of us and a whiteboard jammed into a 120-square-foot conference room, working through a lot of frigid Buffalo days. Liazon cofounder and former CEO Ashok Subramanian recalled in an interview,

> When you look at our first PowerPoint prototype, Version 0.0 of what we did, you see a high degree of similarity and consistency between our earliest vision and where we are now. We established our principles early on: transparency around the employer contribution and the full price of products; giving people the power to use the employer's contribution as a part of their compensation to spend those dollars as they do their salary; and offering smart guidance through what we call decision support. We were convinced that people would be able to choose the benefits that make the most sense for themselves and their family, not because they became actuaries overnight in health care, but rather because they would get quality advice delivered through the mass market by technology.[14]

We were convinced that people would be able to choose the benefits that make the most sense...because they would get quality advice delivered through the mass market by technology. –Liazon cofounder Ashok Subramanian

14. Personal interview with Ashok Subramanian, November 24, 2015.

Liazon cofounder Ashok Subramanian, pictured here with colleagues during Liazon's early days in Buffalo, sketching out company principles on a whiteboard.

Brokers Join the Bandwagon

As the ACA made exchanges a part of our daily vernacular, employers weren't the only ones interested in what new alternatives there might be to the benefits status quo. Insurance brokers saw the health care landscape experiencing early tremors of a major earthquake, and once the ACA was in motion, everyone in the benefits industry started seeking out information about the emerging benefits marketplaces.

> Insurance brokers saw the health care landscape experiencing early tremors of a major earthquake, and...started seeking out information about the emerging benefits marketplaces.

According to Ashok Subramanian, "Back in the early twenty-teens, every broker wanted to know what private exchanges were and how they might affect their business. Now the conversation is shifting. Brokers want to integrate exchanges into detailed account planning for their clients. Many brokers from large national outfits to smaller regional businesses have embraced private exchanges as a core part of their business strategy."[15]

Indeed, in 2012 Liazon reached a tipping point when it gained the support of 8 out of the 10 leading national brokerages. Liazon saw the value in brokerages such as Buffalo-based Lawley Insurance, Willis Group Holdings (now Willis Towers Watson), Arthur J. Gallagher & Co., and others, that have preexisting relationships with their clients as trusted advisors. Soon, these and many other firms joined the movement to develop their own white-labeled exchanges, powered by Liazon, to offer a marketplace system for choosing benefits as one tool in their arsenal to improve their clients' benefits strategies. These marketplaces are unique to each broker's specifications and branding, in an effort to serve their regional or national clients.

Summary

Understanding the development of employer-sponsored benefits as a response to post–World War II labor influxes helps us place benefits in its rightful context as a differentiator for companies looking to attract and retain the best employees. Knowing the original intention behind "exchanges" and the evolution to the modern-day usage of the term helps illuminate what we mean by a "free market" mechanism for buying and selling, rather than a commoditized one.

Just as the Dallas teachers dared to dream of a better way to get hospital coverage, innovation has always required that we do better by leaving our comfort zone for the next level. This is also true for the world of benefits. But before we can discuss what's required of all stakeholders to reach the next level in benefits, it's important to understand what's in the way of progress. In Chapter 3, we explore the biggest opposition faced by private exchange innovators and proponents.

---

15. Personal interview with Ashok Subramanian, November 24, 2015.

3

They Don't Know What They're Missing: Flipping the Status Quo on Its Head

For Liazon or any other private exchange operator, the greatest competition isn't other businesses providing benefits marketplaces, but the status quo itself. And this isn't surprising: There's tremendous comfort in the familiar, especially for employer teams trained on systems established decades earlier and still in use, despite how flawed they might be.

When it comes to health and other employee benefits, the status quo at midsized and large companies largely remains the employer-mandated plan, chosen and managed by human resources and offering little to no transparency into the true costs of the benefits. Employees pick from a prescribed list of benefit options—maybe a handful of different medical plans at most, depending on the size of the company.

As discussed in this book's Introduction, about half of private sector firms across all industries that offer health insurance still offer only one medical plan, and the number of firms offering two or more plan choices grew by only about 9 percentage points from 2010 to 2015, with nearly half of this growth occurring between 2014 and 2015.[1]

More firms are starting to offer consumer-driven health plans (CDHPs), plans with low premiums and high deductibles that qualify for health savings accounts (HSAs) or health reimbursement arrangements (HRAs); in fact, according to recent research from Willis Towers Watson, since the ACA was passed in 2010, 2016 enrollment in CDHPs has increased from 15% to 45%, largely because many employers replaced all their plans with CDHPs.[2] While consumer-driven plans are largely touted as the savior in the current cost crisis faced by many employers, there are some employees who might benefit from a different type of plan, such as those who anticipate a lot of medical expenses and are therefore likely to reach a lower deductible sooner and have more of their expenses paid for by their insurer. Therefore, each employee should be able to make a choice not only of the type of medical plan but from among different plan designs within a plan type as well.

To further complicate the issue of plan choice, plan designs often change annually, so even if an employee can find a suitable plan from among the options offered by his or her employer, chances are that plan won't be available the following year, or the consumer will have to switch carriers, perhaps losing a favored in-network provider in the process.

Despite the nominal growth rate in choice of plans offered, there still isn't much real choice, and little is being done to engage or educate employees about these choices. For as long as most of us remember, the "low" versus "high" plan benefits menu has also come with higher premiums across the board each year. As discussed in this book's Introduction, between 2006 and 2016, average annual worker contributions for family health coverage increased 78%, compared to 58% for employer contributions, according to 2016 Kaiser Family Foundation data.[3] Higher prices for less choice doesn't pass muster with consumers in other areas of life, and it and shouldn't for health insurance either.

1. U.S. Department of Health and Human Services, Agency for Healthcare Research and Quality, Center for Financing, "Access and Cost Trends. 2010–2015," Medical Expenditure Panel Survey Insurance Component, https://meps.ahrq.gov/mepsweb/.

2. Willis Towers Watson, "Full Report: 2016 21st Annual Best Practices in Health Care Employer Survey," www.willistowerswatson.com/en/insights/2017/01/full-report-2016-21st-annual-willis-towers-watson-best-practices-in-health-care-employer-survey.

3. Kaiser Family Foundation, "2016 Employer Health Benefits Survey," http://kff.org/report-section/ehbs-2016-summary-of-findings/.

Those of us who have worked in the insurance industry for years know that insurance has very little to do with providing health care. It's about providing financial protection against the *cost* of health care, which in turn provides peace of mind. Private exchanges exist to provide better performance for the benefit dollar and a shorter, surer path to the end result—the peace of mind that insurance provides.

> Private exchanges exist to provide better performance for the benefit dollar and a shorter, surer path to the end result—the peace of mind that insurance provides.

The Problem with the Status Quo

When your child gets sick and you take that child to the doctor, you're not thinking about what your insurance will cover, you're thinking about your child getting well. Or when your knee finally gives out, and it's time to repair the cartilage, you have enough to focus on in terms of your physical therapy, and you don't need to be sidetracked by a surprise bill from the anesthesiologist.

In many employer-managed programs, employees don't know what to expect from major health issues and are largely in the dark about how their health insurance will work should it be needed. If people took more of a role in their own health care decisions and understood how their coverage and benefits worked, these situations could be alleviated.

The problem is, when it comes to purchasing insurance, employers have for decades told their employees, "We'll tell you what's good for you." The implied message—*having meaningful choice is above your pay grade*—still exists, even as informed, quality shopping has revolutionized daily experiences in home entertainment (from cable to streaming on Hulu), food (from the local supermarket to FreshDirect), and even dating (from being "fixed up" to Match.com). So why is the benefits industry still locked in the pre-technology paradigm and so resistant to change?

The status quo can be quite comfortable from the employer's perspective. Employers know how they can cut costs in the traditional system: by switching carriers, reducing benefits, or passing on the costs. They don't know what they don't know in terms of the advantages of private exchanges when it comes to cost control.

The HR department is so busy navigating the pitfalls of traditional benefits enrollment that it has no time to imagine things can be any different. It's the devil, but it's the devil they know. And employees? Their expectations are pretty low, so they're not likely to complain too loudly. For them, enrolling in benefits is akin to filing taxes—something you just have to do, and then you can forget about it (hopefully). In fact, a recent survey from UnitedHealthcare found that

25% of respondents would rather do their taxes than complete their annual benefits enrollment.[4]

Fear of change and the unknown are powerful protectors of the status quo. Employers are hesitant to relinquish control over the benefits decision. They don't yet understand that they can trust the value of the offerings afforded by private exchanges, even if they are not the ones negotiating plans with the carriers.

> Fear of change and the unknown are powerful protectors of the status quo.

When we started our company, Liazon, we knew it would be challenging to disrupt the decades-old patriarchal benefits arrangement between employer and employee. As with other pioneers in the private exchange business, we understood the stakes were high. But we also knew that the potential for success for those employers and employees—and, yes, for Liazon—was much higher. Employer-sponsored insurance covers over 177 million people[5]—an amazing market opportunity for innovation in the benefits delivery system.

If disrupting the status quo means delivering a far superior alternative that wins on quality, price, selection, and service, how can this be a bad thing? Ultimately, if a product or service is good for business, the C-suite will respond. As T. J. Revelas, managing partner for employee benefits at Lawley Insurance (which offers its clients a Liazon-powered private exchange called the Lawley Marketplace) said, "Businesses don't want to be the first, but they don't want to be the fourth either when there are new strategies in the market."[6]

> "Businesses don't want to be the first, but they don't want to be the fourth either when there are new strategies in the market."
>
> —T.J. Revelas

When it comes to benefits, we're in the midst of a tipping point in many sectors and regions of the country, and employers are eager to explore innovative alternatives to traditional benefits distribution and management. With more and more "firsts" entering the market, the race for second will begin to reach critical mass.

---

4. UnitedHealthcare, "UnitedHealthcare Consumer Sentiment Survey," September 2016, www.uhc.com/content/dam/uhcdotcom/en/NewsRelease/PDF/UHC%20Consumer%20Sentiment%20Survey.pdf.

5. U.S. Census Bureau, Current Population Survey, 2014, 2015 and 2016 Annual Social and Economic Supplements.

6. Personal interview with T.J. Revelas, April 22, 2015.

For thousands of employers and millions of employees who have already moved to a private exchange, the insurance status quo is a quaint memory akin to watching TV with three channels. The economics of choice, and of who makes that choice, is happening; the word is out. Employers who have adopted private exchanges are talking about how doing so has improved the value of their benefits and given their employees more customized solutions.

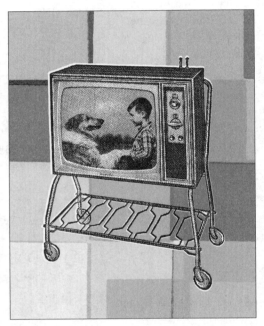

Credit: CSA Images/Printstock Collection/Getty Images

Disrupting the Status Quo

Each year, Liazon analyzes the experiences of the more than 1,000 employers that use our exchanges to understand the value they offer compared to traditional employer-managed benefits, and what employers like about them and what can be improved. Through these analyses, Liazon sees what has changed from the old to the new, what's evolving, and what is very likely to continue to change tomorrow.

The future of benefits is going to be based on four disruptors of traditional benefit arrangements: meaningful choice, price transparency, personalization, and consumerism.

> The future of benefits is going to be based on... meaningful choice, price transparency, personalization, and consumerism.

Meaningful Choice

As we discussed in Chapter 1, "Building a Better Benefits System," in most employer-sponsored plans, employees lack engagement with their benefits options due to lack of choice and control. People don't make meaningful choices; their HR department makes choices for them. Employees aren't offered many choices to begin with, nor are they given transparent, well-designed information to intelligently select from the few choices that are available to them. Employees are willing to accept less coverage for increasing cost because they don't actually know that's what is happening or that it could be different.

What Regina E. Herzlinger wrote in her landmark 2002 *Harvard Business Review* article "Let's Put Consumers in Charge of Health Care" is just as true today as it was then in terms of traditional employer-managed plans:

> And even when companies offer three or four options, precious little distinguishes them—most managed-care plans provide the same benefits, insure virtually identical levels of expenses, reimburse providers in similar ways for a limited array of traditional services, and last for only one year. In essence, managed care comes in just two flavors: plans that place constraints on access to physicians and hospitals for a lower price, and plans that offer readier access for a higher price.[7]

Fifteen years later, little has changed—as many employers have told us. Employees have a limited number of standardized choices in terms of benefits—even while the ability to customize is expected in just about every other consumer experience. Even if employees are given a choice of two or three plans, very often there is such a large spread between the plans, they are still shortchanged and can't find one that best meets their needs, as the "best plan" for a large number of individuals employed by that company might fall somewhere in the middle of the range of what's offered. It's like being able to buy a Sleep Number bed, but the bed has only two settings, soft and hard, and doesn't let you adjust that number for each person sharing the bed.

> Employees have a limited number of standardized choices in terms of benefits—even while the ability to customize is expected in just about every other consumer experience.

Taking this idea into the traditional benefits arrangement, a 58-year-old with a chronic health condition and three kids under 18 and a healthy 25-year-old recent college graduate will, most likely, be presented with the same health plan or plans from their

---

7. Regina Herzlinger, "Let's Put Consumers in Charge of Health Care," *Harvard Business Review*, July 2002, https://hbr.org/2002/07/lets-put-consumers-in-charge-of-health-care.

employer and won't be able to find a plan that truly meets their own preferences. In addition, they typically don't have transparency into the true cost of the plan and what percentage of that cost they are responsible for. It's a double slight: They don't know how much they're actually paying for a plan that's not even tailored for them.

What happens when people are empowered to shop for their own benefits and dial up or down among plans, based on their own wants and needs? They learn to choose a complete set of products that work together to provide the full protection they need. This might involve filling the gaps left by a medical plan by using money given to them by their employer to purchase additional products. So they can opt for the lower-cost medical option, but instead of leaving it at that and hoping for the best, they can mitigate their risks with hospital indemnity, critical illness, life, or disability insurance. (You'll see actual data on the range of products offered and purchased on Liazon exchanges in Chapters 4, "Making Sense of Benefits Solutions: Public Exchanges and Private Exchanges," and 8, "Brokers and Exchanges: Better Together.") They can configure their own alternatives, given the right support, based on their needs—and this represents a great stride forward from the traditional model. They learn how to make smarter decisions about their health care because they understand how their benefits work together and what questions to ask providers to make sure they put the products they've purchased to good use (see Figure 3.1).

Decision support helps employees make thoughtful choices for their benefits.

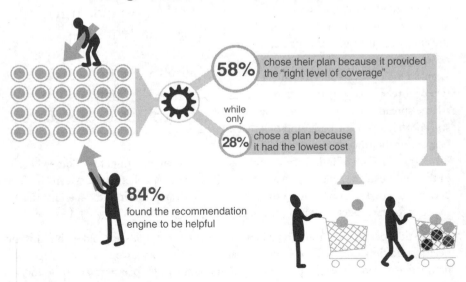

58% chose their plan because it provided the "right level of coverage"

while only

28% chose a plan because it had the lowest cost

84% found the recommendation engine to be helpful

Source: Liazon 2017 Employee Survey

Figure 3.1 *Employee Data on Recommendations Received Through Liazon Exchanges.*

In the most sophisticated exchanges, a *benefits portfolio*, composed of a unique combination of health, financial, protection, and lifestyle products, can make the experience more individualized. One of Liazon's longest-tenured account executives, Kevin Holler, said:

> Employees have diverse wants and needs when it comes to these products. They're personal. With exchanges, employees now have the right to educate themselves and say, "Gee, this is the right plan for me." If explained properly to an employer, it's very difficult for them to say "I don't believe in choice and I don't believe in consumerism." It's almost like saying I don't believe in America.[8]

Looked at this way, does it even make sense for benefits to be offered by an employer? If the company's goal is to attract and retain employees, it sure does. But the paradigm shift that needs to occur on the employer side is to go from deciding "What health plan do we select for our employees?" to "How much money do we want to allocate to our employees to spend on their health plan?" and to let the employees do the rest.

A company pays Employee X a salary, and then Employee X goes out and buys her own house, car, and TV and makes her own investments. So why does the company get to choose her health insurance?

> A company pays Employee X a salary, and then Employee X goes out and buys her own house, car, and TV...So why does the company get to choose her health insurance?

Price Transparency and Defined Contribution

Economists, CFOs, and CEOs would mostly agree that the traditional employer-sponsored benefits system has contributed to a serious distortion in employees' understanding of their total compensation. Health economist Uwe Reinhardt observed in a 2009 *New York Times* essay that this approach "keeps opaque who actually pays for the health care used by employees" and that "employees tend to view employer-paid health insurance as a gift, on top of their pay. Therefore they see little personal gain in attempts to control the cost of their care."[9] In the traditional system, employees perceive the value of their benefits to be 55% of their

---

8. Personal interview with Kevin Holler, April 21, 2015.

9. Uwe Reinhardt, "Is Employer-Based Health Insurance Worth Saving?" *New York Times,* May 22, 2009, https://economix.blogs.nytimes.com/2009/05/22/is-employer-based-health-insurance-worth-saving/?_r=0.

actual cost; in other words, according to a well-documented study done by MetLife, 45 cents of every benefits dollar spent is wasted.[10]

The lack of transparency into medical premium costs and who is paying for them explains why the value of total compensation is lost on employees. Private exchanges with defined contribution reveal the monetary value of benefits so that employees understand the nature and amount of the transaction—the total costs of benefits as well as the employer's and employee's contributions. When employees recognize the full value of their compensation package, including benefits, they come to value their employers more. (In a recent Liazon's survey of employees who chose their benefits through a private exchange, 87% said they are more aware of their employer's contribution and 83% said they value this contribution more.)[11]

This paradigm-shifting breakthrough started with the change from a financial model of "defined benefit" to one of "defined contribution"—the same shift that occurred when employers transitioned from paying guaranteed pension benefits to offering a choice of 401(k) retirement accounts, thereby putting control over how to save that money in the hands of employees. Rather than the employer defining the benefit by naming the health plan(s) (and maybe also a dental plan and one or two nonmedical options), the employer defines the amount of contribution and then gives employees the money and lets them shop. (Employees also have the option of adding their own money on top of their employer's contribution if they feel they need a more robust package of benefits.)

A 401(K) BACKLASH?

Often when describing defined contribution versus defined benefit, the conversation references 401(k) plans as being an example of an early shift to defined contribution, wherein, rather than the employer contributing funds to a long-term financial investment on behalf of an employee, the employee chooses how to invest funds provided by the employer.

---

10. MetLife, "4th Annual MetLife Employee Benefits Trend Study," 2006.

11. Liazon, "Liazon's 2017 Employee Survey Report: Health Care Consumerism in a Marketplace Environment," March 2017 http://liazon.hs-sites.com/liazon/employeesurvey-1.

A 401(k) backlash appears to be brewing because many employees have lost money in the Wall Street casino that is the investment market, and some of them associate their shortfall with the employer who gave them the money in the first place. But it's important to make a distinction between the company giving employees money and employees being able to bet on the future 10, 20, or 30 years out. It's not that companies aren't giving employees enough money to help them save for retirement, it's that employees in some cases are quite simply doing a bad job of predicting what certain funds will do over the long term. So the 401(k) backlash really shouldn't be against employers. Giving money to employees to put toward their long-term financial stability is a good thing. Making investments is a confusing matter.

With defined contribution for employee benefits, in the case of Liazon exchanges, employees are not expected to know what will happen any time beyond the next year in terms of their anticipated health usage, financial status, and personal preferences and lifestyle. And even within the Liazon system, these criteria are merely an indication of the best portfolio of benefits for them; no system can know for sure, as no one can know for sure what will happen to him or her in a year and what financial impact it might have.

When it comes to the value of defined contribution, employers are catching on. According to a 2017 report by PwC, 17% of employers are currently using a defined contribution approach, and the percentage is projected to grow to 35% by 2020.[12]

Employers can decide to allocate the same amount they are currently paying to the insurance carriers or the amount they would be paying if they stayed with the insurer after their rates were raised.

12. Private Exchange Evaluation Collaborative, "What Happened to Private Exchanges?" February 27, 2017, http://nebgh.org/wp-content/uploads/2017/03/FINAL-2016-PEEC-webinar-v8.pdf.pdf.

WHY PRICE TRANSPARENCY WITH DEFINED CONTRIBUTION MAKES SENSE

In order for an employer's contribution to be valued by employees, it has to be seen. Without transparency, employers run the risk of setting prices based on how many people they *think* should be in each plan at the time. Rather, the intent from an employer perspective should be to indicate true plan costs (which are visible in a private exchange) so that the choice makes sense from both the employee's and employer's perspective.

Consider an example. If the true plan costs aren't visible, and an employer opts to allocate the same percentage to each of three different plan costs and just show the cost that an employee is responsible for, the costs might look like the ones in Figure 3.2.

However, the cost differential between plans in this case is not nearly enough to offset the amount of risk the employee is taking on, for example, in the case of choosing a high-deductible plan and the likelihood of having to cover the costs incurred until the deductible is reached. A $50 difference in monthly premium, or $600 per year, is nothing compared to the thousands of dollars an employee may be on the hook for if anyone on his or her plan needs some form of medical care.

In a transparent approach with defined contribution, the cost scenario makes more sense because employees can truly gauge their own level of financial risk for the following reasons: (1) they see the true cost of the plan, (2) they see how much their employer is contributing and how much they are on the hook for, and (3) they see the differentials between plan deductibles versus premiums (among other costs, such as copays and coinsurance), so they can better gauge their own likelihood to need care (with the help of decision support tools).

Many employers that work with Liazon come to realize that they are, in effect, misleading their employees by not disclosing the true cost structure of their medical plans. A good number of them are very well intentioned in trying to provide an equal advantage across the board by covering the same percentage for each plan. But plan designs aren't that straightforward. The defined contribution approach works to level the playing field in terms of risk versus reward on the employee side, while helping employers who are making a valuable contribution get more from the benefits dollars they're offering.

From a financial perspective, plan cost should help employers control their exposure. The difference between the actual cost of a medical plan and the amount the company is contributing is the employee cost share. (For employees, their portion of cost matters substantially more in a self-funded arrangement because the employer is acting as the insurance company.) If the employer doesn't collect enough money from employees, they won't be able to pay future claims. This is why a company may be compelled to collect a disproportionate amount of money from employees who are in cheaper plans.

Plan Cost Comparison Without Defined Contribution: Employer contributes 75% to premiums across the board*

Plan	A	B	C
Type	Low Deductible	Small Network (HMO)	High Deductible
Deductible	$500	$500	$2,500
Monthly Premium (True)	$600	$500	$400
ER Contribution (75%)	$450	$375	$300
EE Cost	$150	$125	$100
Yearly EE Cost	$1,800	$1,500	$1,200
Yearly EE savings comparison	---	B to A: $300	C to A: $600 C to B: $300

Scenarios:

 If Employee chooses Plan B over Plan A: For a $300 yearly savings, EE is locking themselves into a smaller network and may have to pay more if they go out of network, or be restricted from using certain providers. Is it worth it?

 If Employee chooses Plan C over Plan A: For a $600 yearly savings, EE is betting they won't have to pay their deductible, which could quickly absorb the total cost of their yearly savings with just one unplanned doctor's visit and then some, should more needs arise. Is it worth it?

 If Employee choses Plan C over Plan B: For a $300 yearly savings, EE takes on the financial risk above, plus has a limited choice of providers. Definitely not worth it.

* For illustrative purposes only

Figure 3.2 *Hypothetical Illustration of Cost Scenarios Without Defined Contribution.*

However, the key in setting plan cost for an employer is to not let your employee migration assumptions (that is, thoughts about what plans employees are likely to select) affect your initial setting of rates. Trying to predict which plans employees will buy and manipulating plan cost based on that can cause adverse selection and may ultimately lead to a financial miss. Plan costs should be clear so that when employees are evaluating different plan choices, many times with the help of decision support, navigating the system is easy.

Employers can also decide to spend less, but this type of decision comes at the expense of providing value to employees. With employees scrutinizing their benefits packages more than ever—for example, 61% of employees surveyed by Aon Hewitt say "better than average benefits" is a differentiator among employers[13]—the competitive threat as measured by the benefits value being offered by another employer is not one to be taken lightly.

The value equation can largely be derived with a defined contribution that is on par with or slightly above the employer's current spending when their employees get more for their benefits dollars. As a case in point, one Liazon client, a 220-employee nonprofit based in Oklahoma City, set its defined contribution amount to slightly more than the renewal premium offered by its pre-exchange carrier. But the total medical premium after employee selections on the exchange was *1.6 percent less expensive* than the prior year. In other words, the company's contribution went further for employees, putting 7 percent of medical premium cost back in their pockets to put toward a much wider choice of nonmedical benefits than were previously offered (13 versus 7).

Defined contribution can lead to transparency when it comes to benefits costs (both the employer's and the employee's). Employees increasingly understand that an employer who is willing to turn money over to them to spend as they choose on benefits is a concerned, forward-thinking company. Putting the actual dollars out in the open shifts the conversation from being about how to get the most benefits *dollars* to being about how to get the most benefits *value*.

> Employees increasingly understand that an employer who is willing to turn money over to them to spend as they choose on benefits is a concerned, forward-thinking company.

Private exchanges make even more sense when premium rates rise higher than the rate of inflation and higher than the rate of employee wage increases, as happened

13. Aon Hewitt, "Aon Hewitt 2016 Workforce Mindset™ Study," 2016. www.aon.com/human-capital-consulting/thought-leadership/communication/2016-workforce-mindset.jsp?utm_source=vanity&utm_medium=aoncom&utm_campaign=2016-workforce-mindset.

in the late 1990s and early 2000s. This situation resulted in employers having to make really hard decisions about how to absorb the increases: Should they pass them on to employees? Cut benefits? Suck up the cost? All these are highly undesirable options. The determination of employers to control benefits costs will never be a thing of the past (see Figure 3.3).

Premiums Among Workers Covered by Employer-Sponsored Coverage, 1999 – 2016

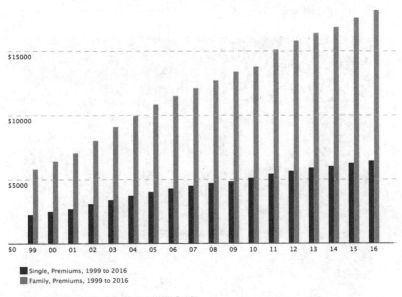

SOURCE: Kaiser/HRET Survey of Employer-Sponsored Health Benefits

Figure 3.3 *Premiums Among Workers Covered by Employer-Sponsored Coverage, 1999–2016.*

Here's where the status quo really is the enemy of common sense. These sanguine employers don't realize that by offering the same plans to everyone, they're squandering the value of their benefits by overinsuring some employees and underinsuring others. They're wasting money they could be putting in the hands of their employees, some of whom will require more insurance and others, less. Having too much insurance is lost on most employees, and not seen as generous. Having too little insurance leads to frustration and even anger when an employee has to face the music in the form of uncovered expenses. Blame the insurance company? Blame the boss? Blame everyone.

And here's where the common sense comes in: People do a better job of spending their own money than someone else's, as the economist Milton Friedman famously observed. So not only are employers inadequately insuring a large portion of their employees but these same employees have no idea this is the case or how much their employer is spending on them at all. They're in the dark—on both counts!

"It's amazing what happens when people see the employer contribution on their computer screen," Holler said. "They're actually shocked by how much their employer is giving them, especially when they discover that the annual cost of their family copay plan is often more than their mortgage (see Figure 3.4)."[14]

> "It's amazing what happens when people see the employer contribution on their computer screen..."
>
> —*Kevin Holler*

Source: Liazon 2017 Employee Survey

Figure 3.4 *Employee Satisfaction on Liazon Exchanges.*

Liazon research shows that most companies save money when they buy in to the exchange concept—but not because employees are seeking out and selecting plans based on price alone. Instead, Liazon findings confirm that employees are selecting the right insurance for their needs and avoiding paying for what they don't need. One survey we conducted found that 70% of employers who moved to a Liazon private exchange said their benefits costs decreased or remained the same as the previous year—which is a great story when you consider that insurers are steadily increasing their rates. As Liazon accumulates more data over time, we are seeing these

---

14. Personal interview with Kevin Holler, April 21, 2015.

employer cost savings improve as they continue to use an exchange; 86% of employers in their second year on Liazon exchanges said they either spent less than the year before or kept costs the same.[15] This only yields a positive outlook for the continued advantages of a defined contribution approach going forward.

86% of employers in their second year on Liazon exchanges said they either spent less than the year before or kept costs the same.[16]

Employers are not saving this money at their employees' expense. Of the employees Liazon surveyed, 94% who chose their benefits through Liazon exchanges said they were satisfied with their experience, and 92% said they were satisfied with their benefits one year later.[17]

Personalization

Before the emergence of private exchanges, employees were on their own in terms of understanding what's at stake in regard to their insurance choices. They weren't offered many options for effectively choosing the benefits that suit their lives and concerns. Liazon research shows that employees using exchanges are satisfied with how information tools, improved offerings, and deep expertise combine to empower them to personalize their benefits. In a recent Liazon survey, 96% of employees said they find expanded product choice important, 96% said they find extensive education and decision support tools important, and 97% said they find exposure to the true price of benefits important.[18] Employees can see their needs and concerns reflected back at them through their unique coverage portfolio in a Liazon exchange. When employees log in to their exchange's web portal and complete their personal profiles, they see the relative costs and details of plans in plain language, learn about benefits and benefits terms if needed, and then decide to accept the recommended portfolio and make adjustments or start fresh and go shopping in the store.

Employees can see their needs and concerns reflected back at them through their unique coverage portfolio in a Liazon exchange.

15. Liazon, "Liazon's 2017 Employee Survey Report: Health Care Consumerism in a Marketplace Environment," March 2017 http://liazon.hs-sites.com/liazon/employeesurvey-1.

16. Ibid.

17. Liazon, "Liazon 2017 Employer Survey Report: Employer Satisfaction with Private Exchanges," May 2017 http://liazon.hs-sites.com/liazon/employeesurvey-1-0.

18. Ibid.

Add/Edit These Recommended Plans	Start with an Empty Cart

The recommendation engine component of Liazon's decision support enables an individual to receive a personalized benefits package that is a smart fit for his or her particular situation. A recent college grad may only be concerned about making sure he's covered for his contact lenses, whereas a married woman with four children may be much more concerned about making sure she has adequate life insurance. Decision support is the big distinguisher that

> When shopping for benefits, people can and ought to be smart choosers *and* smart users.

empowers consumers to make informed, effective decisions about insurance products that they wouldn't otherwise understand. When shopping for benefits, people can and ought to be smart choosers *and* smart users.

The technology used by Liazon is based on a sophisticated algorithm that considers a user's health concerns, financial situation, and personal preferences, and creates a personalized recommendation of benefits that work together to meet their particular needs for financial protection. It takes into account the full spectrum of products and plans that will best match people's needs and wants, balances premiums with out-of-pocket expenses to find the most cost-effective option for a medical plan, and accounts for things like physician and network preferences. These recommendations are a big departure from the status quo, and this level of decision support distinguishes Liazon from other private exchanges. (See Appendix C, "Real-World Data and Applications," for a peek at the interface used on Liazon exchanges.) In addition, workers can access tutorials and videos to get further education about how to be a smart benefits consumer.

According to T. J. Revelas of Lawley Insurance, one of Liazon's broker partners:

> Decision support is one of the most innovative and most important aspects of the exchange model for employers to appreciate. When employers know they're removing themselves from the buying decision and allowing employees to become consumers, decision support builds confidence in the transition. It reflects the reality that employees have personal needs, and need to educate themselves about the mix of benefits that uniquely fit their situation. By knowing what

> Decision support is one of the most innovative and most important aspects of the exchange model for employers to appreciate.
>
> —T.J. Revelas

members of the workforce select for their benefits, and being able to understand how their employees utilize benefits, employers gain the perspective to better predict their budgets for three or four years ahead.[19]

When employees realize how exchanges help guide them to the products they need while eliminating coverage they don't, they're very likely to also choose plans that provide better value for them as individuals. This change alone can lead to a complete shift in mindset when the annual open enrollment season rolls around. What would it be like to have employees actually look forward to choosing their benefits? That's a *big* before and after difference, and one that Liazon is working toward. Before exchanges, the annual benefits meeting was invariably one of the most dreaded business experiences of the year. With private exchanges, that meeting may become one of the most rewarding as employees come to understand that they'll be given new freedom and flexibility—and that they like being in the driver's seat. Why do we think this can happen? Because now, it's about *their* money.

Using advanced decision support makes the process intelligent. The Liazon decision support system doesn't just spit back aggregated selections based on a few major inputs and filters, like a travel or real estate web site. Proper decision support actually learns about users' situations, lifestyles, and personalities—things that are key to determining coverage needs—in order to recommend the plans that are right for each person (see Figure 3.5).

Figure 3.5 *Examples of Benefits Portfolios in Liazon Exchanges.*

Decision support integrates advanced analysis on how best to combine benefits to cover particular situations and provide options that benefits consumers most likely have never considered. If employees aren't surprised when they use a private exchange, then we're doing

If employees aren't surprised when they use a private exchange, then we're doing something wrong.

19. Personal interview with T. J. Revelas, April 22, 2015.

something wrong. As a result of decision support guidance, employees understand that the choice of a less robust health care plan may be a wise decision if they can round out potential coverage gaps with other insurance products. Liazon data based on employee behavior on our private exchanges indicate that employees choose an average of five benefits offerings (including medical and nonmedical products) [20] which, together, create a personalized package that may cost the same or less than what they would have received in a traditional benefits arrangement.

According to T. J. Revelas of Lawley Insurance,

> "Employees have wanted things like this in the past but employers, by virtue of the market itself or their size, or a combination of both, have been precluded from making this kind of offering. With the decision support algorithm and other tools, the model clearly helps with retention and recruitment, and gives the small business CEO the opportunity to offer benefits that he never could have before, while still meeting his budget."[21]

Consumerism

What's the ultimate result of more choice, price transparency, and decision support?

At the most basic level, everything about private exchanges should be consumer driven—that is, designed with the consumer (in this case, the benefits consumer) in mind. An exchange succeeds when the focus is on consumers and giving them the information and access they need to shop, just as they shop in stores for so many other things. Liazon was founded on the rock-solid principle that people will do a better job choosing benefits for themselves and their families than their employers can do for them. But there's also a positive outgrowth of the exchange experience that is also focused on the consumer. *Health care consumerism* is a movement driving individuals to play a greater role in their health care decisions.

Ultimately, for health care consumerism to work, people need to be informed. They need to have their questions answered, they need quick access to information, and

---

20. Private Exchange Research Council (PERC) analysis, 2017, www.percinsights.com. Information here based on groups enrolling in benefits on Liazon exchanges with a benefits effective date of January 1, 2017. Based on employees who purchased at least one product.

21. Personal interview with T. J. Revelas, April 22, 2015.

they need to understand what they're buying and that they have responsibility for how they manage their purchase all year long. It's a responsibility we hope consumers will come to embrace; we can't just give them the keys to the car without teaching them how to drive. We need to give health care consumers the right tools so they can successfully manage their own benefits costs and reap the advantages of doing so (see Figure 3.6). Liazon exchanges cultivate informed benefits consumers through educational resources and videos; communication campaigns around open enrollment; access to health care expense management, price transparency, and provider lookup tools; health advocacy services; and more.

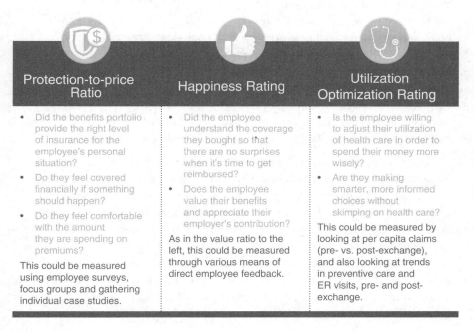

Protection-to-price Ratio	Happiness Rating	Utilization Optimization Rating
• Did the benefits portfolio provide the right level of insurance for the employee's personal situation? • Do they feel covered financially if something should happen? • Do they feel comfortable with the amount they are spending on premiums? This could be measured using employee surveys, focus groups and gathering individual case studies.	• Did the employee understand the coverage they bought so that there are no surprises when it's time to get reimbursed? • Does the employee value their benefits and appreciate their employer's contribution? As in the value ratio to the left, this could be measured through various means of direct employee feedback.	• Is the employee willing to adjust their utilization of health care in order to spend their money more wisely? • Are they making smarter, more informed choices without skimping on health care? This could be measured by looking at per capita claims (pre- vs. post-exchange), and also looking at trends in preventive care and ER visits, pre- and post-exchange.

Figure 3.6 *Does an Exchange Work for a Benefits Consumer? A Quick Checklist.*

When consumers are in charge, they create fertile ground for new markets to emerge, with innovative offerings. For example, with the increased responsibility to choose and manage benefits comes a parallel responsibility for employees to learn more about their costs and coverage. Smart benefits consumers know how to get more for their spending and how to avoid scary surprises in terms of unexpected bills. The term *price transparency tools* wasn't around just a few years ago, and it is one great example of new companies being created out of a need for better consumer information when it comes to choosing benefits.

Price transparency tools enable benefits consumers to shop around for a specific medical treatment or procedure in order to get the best price for it. Prices can vary greatly, and it can no longer be assumed that insurance will cover all costs; a benefits consumer becomes empowered by being able to save $200 on a procedure. With high-deductible health plans, in particular, a consumer has to spend a lot before something is actually paid for by the insurer. In addition to benefits consumers embracing online tools that provide objective third-party information on potential cost of care and insurance, they are also seeking out information on quality ratings and performance information on both physicians and hospitals, which bodes well for companies vying for market share in these disciplines.[22]

We've had lots of conversations over the years with insurers about designing plans and products they know people want to buy. For example, rising interest in alternative treatments has led to plans including coverage for acupuncture and chiropractic services. When employers

> When consumers take a more active role, products like pet insurance start to become mainstream.

were calling the shots, these types of services didn't matter. When consumers take a more active role, products like pet insurance start to become mainstream.

Typically, insurers have had virtually no outlet for "research and development" because their resources were largely spent dealing with plan design and marketing. On the employer side, HR managers have been so focused on getting employees to open enrollment and then handling their questions and problems afterwards that they have had too little time to devote to their core business function, which is attracting and retaining employees. Shifting to a new model that is more employee focused has the potential to benefit these other constituents as well; HR can get back to the job it was meant to do, and insurers can compete on innovation, thereby creating new products and services to improve costs, and potentially health care outcomes, for employees.

A 2001 *TIME* magazine feature titled "Click Till You Drop," about the early days of e-commerce, talked about Amazon.com, Yahoo!, and other blockbusters of the decade. The author carefully presented both sides of whether online shopping was a historic shift in consumer behavior. The innovators were facing heavy resistance that seems quaint now: A Wall Street analyst wondering if e-commerce would ever get big; Barnes & Noble defending its megastores and suing Amazon.com for its tagline "Earth's Biggest Bookstore"; Sears telling us it's "not rushing to build a

22. Sheryl Coughlin & Paul Keckley, "2012 Survey of U.S. Health Care Consumers," http://dupress.
deloitte.com/dup-us-en/industry/health-care/2012-survey-of-u-s-health-care-consumers-
five-year-look-back.html?id=us:2el:3lk:4dup_gl:5eng:6dup&highlight=type:textContent|
9503$9554$15$highlight$.

webstore." The article noted that Sears lost at least one customer based on staying locked in the status quo:

> It has already missed Lisa Fontes, a 36-year-old Massachusetts psychologist who went to sears.com last month hoping to buy a freezer. The Sears site, however, didn't have what she needed. "I assumed I couldn't find it because I was stupid or computer illiterate," she explains. But th e real illiteracy may have belonged to Sears. It doesn't yet sell freezers online.[23]

(I don't know where Lisa Fontes is right now, but maybe she's shopping for benefits on a private exchange.)

How much do employers who look away at the notion of private exchanges—the way Sears did in the early days of e-commerce—stand to lose?

"Some of the mature active exchanges that have been around for several years have recently released results indicating that their clients did experience cost reduction and better health care controls after implementing private exchanges," said Barbara Gniewek, noted industry analyst for PwC. "Savings resulted from employees right sizing their benefits to meet their individual needs, increased/enabled consumerism, and fixing/controlling the employer contribution through defined contribution,"[24] she said.

Summary

Fear of change can be a powerful protector of the status quo. But any good innovation requires disruption. Choice. Transparency. Personalization. Consumerism. These are private exchanges' answer to defenders of the status quo in benefits.

Chapter 4, "Making Sense of Benefits Solutions: Public Exchanges and Private Exchanges," takes a deep dive into the changing benefits landscape in which this disruption is taking place.

---

23. Michael Krantz, "Click Till You Drop," *Time Magazine*, June 24, 2001.

24. Personal interview with Barbara Gniewek, October 13, 2016.

4

Making Sense of Benefits Solutions: Public Exchanges and Private Exchanges

Seeing a market opportunity, dozens of companies from varied technological origins are creating their own takes on the private exchange concept to meet the demand of a hungry but often confused benefits market. When employers decide to radically change how they offer their employees benefits, they should take the time to carefully sift through their options. How can they sort through all the alternatives to find the right fit? What are the key attributes of different players in the benefits solutions space? What are various players known to do best?

The View from the Top: Public Versus Private Exchanges

As discussed throughout this book, the Affordable Care Act (ACA) brought the idea of insurance exchanges into the mainstream. *Public exchanges,* or *marketplaces,* are run by federal or state government agencies, or a combination of both, to offer health insurance to individuals who are uninsured or whom may or may not be eligible to receive benefits through their employers (see Figure 4.1). Those who are not able to access benefits through their employer may be eligible to receive a subsidy based on their income level to help cover the cost of their insurance premiums through the public exchanges.

At the time of this writing, there are 12 state-based marketplaces (including District of Columbia) which are responsible for all marketplace functions and accessed

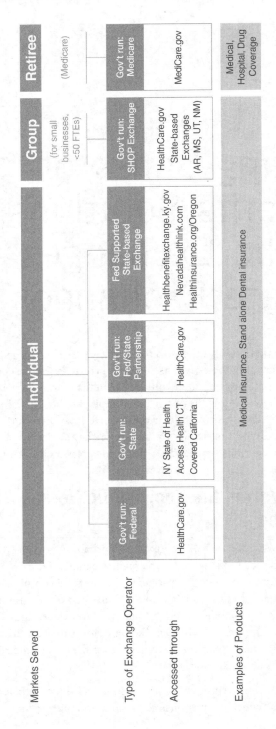

Figure 4.1 *The Public Exchange Landscape.*

online through their own websites—for example, Covered California (CoveredCA. org). The remaining states access the ACA exchange through HealthCare.gov; 28 of these use the federally facilitated marketplace, 6 are part of a state–federal partnership in which marketplace functions are split between the state and the Department of Health and Human Services (HHS), and 5 are run as a federally supported state-based exchange in partnership with HHS.[1]

The drafters of the ACA hoped that the public exchanges' online enrollment platform would make it easier for consumers to shop for health insurance, while also increasing transparency of costs and the benefits and services covered under a particular health plan. However, as of this writing, the public exchanges lack a robust decision support system, which is critical in helping consumers find a health plan that best fits their needs.

Private exchanges are not run by the government but rather by independent entities in the private sector. They are targeted to companies that offer benefits to their employees (see Figure 4.2). Under the ACA's employer mandate, as of 2016, this included all companies with 50 or more full time or full-time equivalent (FTE) employees, those individuals, or a combination of individuals, who work at least 30 hours per week on average.

The retiree market is actually trending ahead of the active employee market in the private exchange world. Willis Towers Watson estimates that 41% of companies have switched their Medicare-eligible retirees into a private exchange, and 60% expect to offer a retiree exchange in 2018.[2] This trend of the over-65 Medicare-eligible retiree market shifting to private exchanges faster than the active employee market is highlighted in a 2016 article in *HR Magazine* by Tamara Lytle:

> When Rockwell International, a Milwaukee-based industrial automation products and software business, decided to move its retirees from a company health plan to a private insurance exchange in 2015... so many people signed up to learn about the new coverage that Rockwell had to move the meeting to a ballroom twice as large as planned.
>
> Like Rockwell, a stream of companies are finding that moving Medicare-eligible retirees (ages 65 and older) out of their group health insurance plans and into private individual exchanges is a win-win for them and their former employees. Retirees often get more choices for less money, while HR departments are relieved of what can be a heavy administrative burden.[3]

1. Health Insurance.org, "What Types of Health Insurance Does My State Have?" December 7, 2016, www.healthinsurance.org/faqs/what-type-of-health-insurance-exchange-does-my-state-have/.

2. Willis Towers Watson, "Full Report: 2016 21st Annual Best Practices in Health Care Employer Survey," www.willistowerswatson.com/en/insights/2017/01/full-report-2016-21st-annual-willis-towers-watson-best-practices-in-health-care-employer-survey.

3. Tamara Lytle, "Strategic Moves: The Exchange Option for Retirees," March 1, 2016, www.shrm.org/hr-today/news/hr-magazine/0316/pages/strategic-moves-the-exchange-option-for-retirees.aspx.

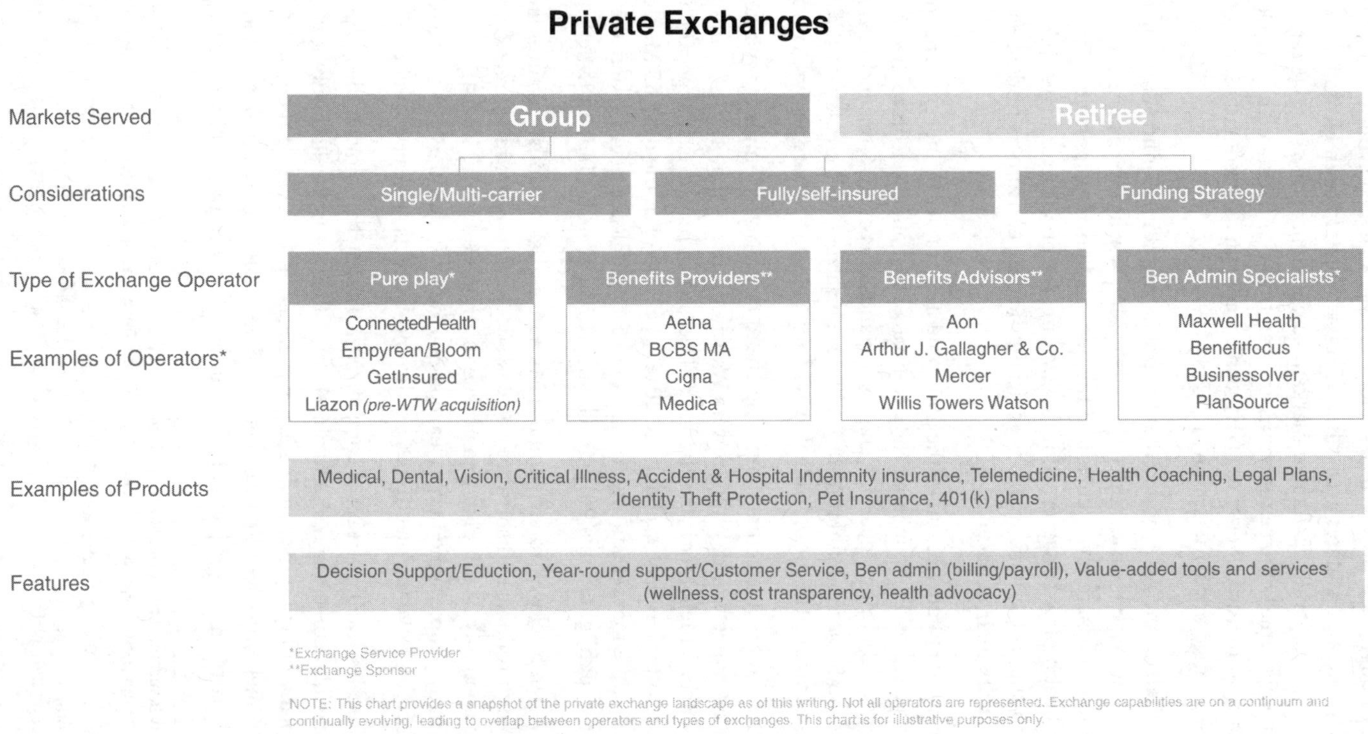

Private Exchanges

Markets Served	Group			Retiree	
Considerations	Single/Multi-carrier	Fully/self-insured		Funding Strategy	
Type of Exchange Operator	Pure play*	Benefits Providers**	Benefits Advisors**		Ben Admin Specialists*
Examples of Operators*	ConnectedHealth Empyrean/Bloom GetInsured Liazon (pre-WTW acquisition)	Aetna BCBS MA Cigna Medica	Aon Arthur J. Gallagher & Co. Mercer Willis Towers Watson		Maxwell Health Benefitfocus Businessolver PlanSource
Examples of Products	Medical, Dental, Vision, Critical Illness, Accident & Hospital Indemnity insurance, Telemedicine, Health Coaching, Legal Plans, Identity Theft Protection, Pet Insurance, 401(k) plans				
Features	Decision Support/Education, Year-round support/Customer Service, Ben admin (billing/payroll), Value-added tools and services (wellness, cost transparency, health advocacy)				

*Exchange Service Provider
**Exchange Sponsor

NOTE: This chart provides a snapshot of the private exchange landscape as of this writing. Not all operators are represented. Exchange capabilities are on a continuum and continually evolving, leading to overlap between operators and types of exchanges. This chart is for illustrative purposes only.

Figure 4.2 *The Private Exchange Landscape.*

The same article also quoted John Barkett, the senior director of health policy affairs for Willis Towers Watson, as saying that retiree exchanges are popular because they provide better customer service to retirees who typically have many questions for HR departments. Once retirees are shifted off company insurance, Barkett noted, "HR doesn't hear a peep from most of them, allowing staff to get back to the huge list of things the benefits team needs to accomplish."[4]

Who Runs These Things Anyway? Types of Private Exchange Operators

Many different types of companies are competing to design, operate, and market benefits exchanges to employers, and the lines are blurring between those that originated as traditional exchange service providers, also known as "pure play" operators, and those that lease the technology of another company to offer an exchange solution. Recent industry activity—including Connecture's acquisition of ConnectedHealth, and Willis Towers Watson's acquisition of Liazon—is rewriting the rules of what it means to be a private exchange operator. However, understanding the traditional differences will help illuminate the shifting landscape.

> Recent industry activity—including Connecture's acquisition of ConnectedHealth, and Willis Towers Watson's acquisition of Liazon—is rewriting the rules of what it means to be a private exchange operator.

Pure-Play Providers

Pure-play providers are companies built specifically for benefits shopping activity. These companies specialize in the development and installation of the system through which benefits are chosen, delivered, and managed. They aren't "verticals" that exist as part of a broader type of company; they're niche companies that specialize in technology and the building of "benefit stores," or marketplaces. They typically have strong decision support capabilities that help users choose benefits, with a focus on the experience; that's what their platforms were primarily designed to do. Liazon started out as a pure-play provider in 2007, and was acquired by Towers Watson, now Willis Towers Watson, a leading global advisory, broking, and solutions company, in 2013.

---

4. Ibid.

Benefits Providers

Many of America's leading insurance carriers now align with technology providers to offer their own benefits exchange options; among them are Cigna (Cigna Guided Solutions, powered by bswift) and Blue Cross Blue Shield of Michigan (GlidePath, powered by Empyrean Benefit Solutions, formerly Bloom Health). These companies are adept at ensuring client compliance and providing full back-office capabilities. These marketplaces are, by definition, "single-carrier" on the medical side, meaning all the plans offered are from one insurer. Other products besides medical may also be offered in these exchanges, usually provided by other insurers. What defines a system as a carrier exchange is being sponsored by an insurance carrier, but powered by a technology company, such as a pure-play provider.

> What defines a system as a carrier exchange is being sponsored by an insurance carrier, but powered by a technology company, such as a pure-play provider.

WHAT IS NEEDED FOR CARRIER EXCHANGES TO REALLY TAKE OFF?

For carrier-powered exchanges to really take off, the level of customer satisfaction with carrier experiences would need to be akin to that of customers of Apple products, for example. With customer satisfaction levels for insurance carriers ranking in the bottom 12 of all industries, carriers have a long way to go in adopting the "store" concept and making it successful.

Think about it: Apple can run its own store, where it carries nothing but Apple products. It may have competition, but no one is walking into an Apple store and complaining that there is nothing from Motorola in there. They're not even comparing their prospective purchase to Motorola before entering the store because they know chances are they will be happy with their purchase because it is made by Apple. Until we get to this "Apple-level" brand experience with an insurer, carrier-powered exchanges will just be a fledgling approach. As of now, though, carriers really have nothing to lose from it, as they are still offering their products alongside their competitors in competitive multi-carrier benefits exchanges, as well as through their trusted liaisons, the brokers.

Benefits Advisors

Global human resources management consultancies have long held a strong market share of the benefits exchange industry and include some of the pioneering organizations in the category. Key consultancies that act as benefits advisors include Aon,

Mercer, Arthur J. Gallagher & Co., and Willis Towers Watson. In addition, in early 2010 Xerox Corporation purchased the parent company of Buck Consultants, now Conduent, which offers the RightOpt private exchange solution and is now fully divested from Xerox.

Consultants, due to their history and sophistication, tend to offer a full-service "white glove" experience, which encompasses full consultative services such as day-to-day benefits administration, billing support, and client compliance management. But consultants also provide superior plan design knowledge and benefits administration capabilities.

A number of leading insurance brokerages have also entered the market with their own private exchanges. This is often accomplished through attaching their own branding to an established technology platform, as BB&T and Lawley do with Liazon's technology. Brokers are a natural fit for offering private exchanges due to their established customer relationships and trusted advisor status, along with knowledge of multiple carriers and their products, and an increasingly consultative role in the new benefits landscape.

> Brokers are a natural fit for offering private exchanges due to their established customer relationships and trusted advisor status...

Traditional Benefits Administration Companies

As mentioned earlier, benefits administration functionality is at the core of most companies that are calling themselves private exchanges; however, there are strong differentiators in the services offered among the numerous players in the space. Several benefits administration firms are entering the exchange industry already specializing in the technological systems and processes required to administer and manage benefits. These companies have typically been focused on automation, whereas pure-play exchanges entered the landscape more focused on the employee experience. Benefit administration companies have had no choice but to shift their focus to the employee experience, offering varying degrees of decision support and the ability to handle defined contribution, but they didn't start out that way.

One such player is the payroll services provider ADP, which launched its private exchange capabilities through the ADP Private Exchange in August 2015. ADP Private Exchange positions itself as "a benefits administration technology platform supported by human capital management systems"[5]; in other words, its offering

---

5. ADP Press Release, "ADP Launches Private Exchange," August 6, 2015 http://mediacenter.adp.com/releasedetail.cfm?releaseid=926345.

enables industry participants to launch a private exchange on ADP's robust human capital management (HCM) platform.

As Rhonda Marcucci, divisional vice president and HR and benefits technology consulting practice leader for the Benefits and Human Resources Consulting division of Arthur J. Gallagher & Co., has observed, "the benefits technology industry is relatively young—less than 20 years—compared with some workplace automation systems (for example, human resource information system [HRIS], payroll) that have been around for decades longer. This is only the beginning of the private exchange discussion."[6]

> "This is only the beginning of the private exchange discussion."
>
> —Rhonda Marcucci

THE CONVERGENCE OF HEALTH AND WEALTH

One of the latest entrants into the competitive field of private exchanges is Fidelity Investments, which launched Fidelity Health Marketplace as a fully integrated health and financial offering for small- and mid-sized businesses in early 2016. It's likely that the benefits industry will see increasingly more of this type of convergence between health care and retirement, with other financial services firms joining the fray.

6. Personal interview with Rhonda Marcucci, April 21, 2016.

As an example, Liazon has started a pilot program in which employees can take some of the dollars allocated for health care and put them into their retirement savings accounts. It's not surprising that a company like Fidelity would see an opportunity in this emerging space, and it validates the usefulness of private exchanges in the small- and mid-size employer markets as a vehicle for providing other types of benefits besides insurance.

Rhonda Marcucci agrees. "It makes sense from a 'total rewards' perspective," she said, "but it will take time for the market to warm up to this concept, just as it is still taking time to warm up to private exchanges overall. It's logical to integrate retirement savings with benefit spending through a defined contribution model, but as we've seen with the adoption curve for consumer-driven health plans (CDHPs), it will take time to really penetrate the market."[7]

---

7. Personal interview with Rhonda Marcucci, April 21, 2016.

What Should You Consider When Moving to a Private Exchange?

In addition to choosing the type of exchange operator that best suits their needs, an employer should consider how to configure their exchange in terms of the number of health insurers (carriers) offered as well as who will assume the risk of benefits utilization (a self-or fully-insured model). Employers should also consider their comfort level with price transparency, which will inform the extent to which a defined contribution model makes sense for them.

Single- Versus Multi-Carrier Exchanges

Most private exchanges are "single carrier," meaning one medical insurance carrier is offered; however, a virtually unlimited number of plans (including HMOs, PPOs, high-deductible health plans [HDHPs], and several different hybrid arrangements) may be provided by that carrier within the exchange. Multi-carrier exchanges, in which more than one medical carrier is offered (each offering a broad range of plans) may be appropriate for larger groups that have a significant number of employees in multiple markets. (For example, Liazon multi-carrier exchanges offer a choice of three national carriers and one regional carrier, where available.)

The difference between single- and multi-carrier exchanges comes down to who bears the risk (one carrier versus a shared responsibility across several carriers), and potentially lower costs resulting from competition among carriers participating in a multi-carrier model. (See the sidebar, "A Lesson in Fully Insured Multi-carrier Exchanges.")

Self- Versus Fully-Insured Models

Employers, when considering their benefits delivery, have the option of going with a fully-insured or self-insured model for funding health insurance. *Fully-insured* means the carriers assume the risk, and companies (and their employees) pay a fixed premium amount to the carriers. *The carrier then pays out the claims* based on the parameters of the coverage specified by the plan. The difference between the premiums collected and the claims payout represents the insurance company's gross margin.

Larger companies, however, also have the option of choosing a self-insured model, in which they are responsible for paying out claims to their employee population. A third-party administrator, or a carrier, charges self-insured employers a fixed amount per month for administrative expenses and other costs, *but the employer is responsible for payment of health care claims.* Most multi-carrier exchanges are self-insured, meaning the employer assumes the risk for the entire population, regardless of which carrier employees choose.

Many private exchanges are equipped to function in either a self- or fully-insured environment, even if they were originally designed with one model in mind.

A LESSON IN FULLY INSURED MULTI-CARRIER EXCHANGES

When moving to a private exchange model, employers need to consider whether they would rather avoid risk (that is, choose a fully-insured option) or bear the risk for the sake of possibly lower costs (that is, choose a self-insured option). The decision may depend in part on the size of the organization. For companies with a large number of employees (3,000+), the likelihood of a negative surprise is low because of the size of the risk pool. Also, there are tax advantages to being self-insured, as well as the ability to avoid state mandates for coverage (both typically resulting in total health cost savings of 3% to 8%). For example, California requires that every health plan and health insurer cover acupuncture; however, these rules don't apply to self-insured companies. For these reasons, some employers may opt for the self-insured model.

A single-carrier exchange in a fully-insured model means all risk falls to one carrier, so the results of one year can be used to project the expected risk the payer takes on during the following exchange year, and the rates established can be reflective of this anticipated risk level. However, a multi-carrier exchange in a fully-insured model is inherently challenged to predict likely usage levels due to the inability to forecast which carriers employees will gravitate toward. In the worst-case scenario, suppose that all the "sicker" employees in a company chose Carrier A. This would result in the carrier needing to pay out a disproportionate amount of costs, and without knowing this information in advance, it's virtually impossible to establish rates that reflect the actual risk in this type of model. For this reason, risk adjustment is a critical necessity for a fully-insured, multi-carrier exchange.

In a self-insured model, the employer may want to devote more toward disease management or wellness programs in order to reduce the risk of catastrophic claims down the road. In this sense, the employer has more control and flexibility. On the other hand, when carriers absorb the risk, they must compete for members each year, which could potentially lead to competitive pricing, new offerings, high-quality networks, integrated solutions, and other innovative developments. This is the concept on which the Aon fully insured exchanges were developed, but market realities eventually led to the company's decision to expand its offerings to include self-insured employer models as well.

Rick Strater is the divisional vice president and national exchange practice leader for the Benefits and Human Resources Consulting division of Arthur J. Gallagher & Co., which offers its own private exchange, the Gallagher Marketplace. One of the solutions available through the Gallagher Marketplace is powered by Liazon's technology. Rick said of the fully-insured model, "If you have bad claims experience as an employer, your rates are going up. A large part of medical plan pricing is claims exposure."[8]

> "A large part of medical plan pricing is claims exposure."
>
> —Rick Strater

With respect to funding, Strater believes that most large, complex employee populations should be self-insured, whether or not they implement a private exchange. "Many clients ask how they can manage their costs on a private exchange if they are self-insured," he said. "These costs can be controlled through an exchange's defined contribution budget, as well as specific and aggregate stop loss coverage."[9] Strater encourages self-insured clients to work with experienced underwriters or actuaries to complete in-depth migration analysis on plans in order to price them as closely as possible to what clients can reasonably expect to see during the actual claims year. He stresses that not doing so can result in unexpected outcomes.

8. Personal interview with Rick Strater, May 12, 2016.

9. Ibid.

Funding Strategies

Another factor that influences the type of private exchange that is right for an employer is the level of price transparency the company believes in and the capability of a private exchange to support it. For employers that believe in true price transparency (as discussed in Chapter 3, "They Don't Know What They're Missing: Flipping the Status Quo on Its Head"), a defined contribution model makes sense. With a defined contribution model, employers set a fixed amount of money that they will contribute to each employee toward benefits. This contribution, along with the full cost of premiums, is made apparent during the enrollment experience, thereby allowing each employee to see his or her share of premium costs as part of the total cost of benefits.

> With a defined contribution model, employers set a fixed amount of money that they will contribute to each employee toward benefits.

An employer must also consider whether the system enables multiple funding strategies to be implemented on the advice of a broker (such as varying defined contribution levels based on tier of coverage or type of product chosen, for example, medical versus nonmedical products; offering health saving account [HSA] seeds; and wellness incentives).

Another approach to funding involves setting a defined contribution but not displaying that amount to employees during the shopping experience. In a defined contribution model, the premium rate is displayed, along with the employer's fixed subsidy (defined contribution) as well as the employee's share of the cost, or "net cost." Alternatively, this approach just displays net cost to employees during the shopping experience.

Who Can Benefit from Private Exchanges? Markets Served

Public exchanges primarily serve the individual market (people not eligible for health insurance through their employer and who may be able to obtain a premium subsidy). Private exchanges largely serve the employer, or group market (people who are eligible for benefits through their employer or nonprofit association, trade association, or other member organization, such as Freelancers Union). Finally, a public or private exchange may offer medical coverage to those aged 65 and over (the retiree market).

HEALTH INSURANCE ENROLLMENT:
A LOOK AT THE NUMBERS

Public Exchanges

According to figures reported by the U.S. Department of Health and Human Services (HHS), approximately 12.2 million consumers selected or were automatically reenrolled in a public marketplace plan (both federal and state based) during the 2017 open enrollment period (see Figure 4.3).

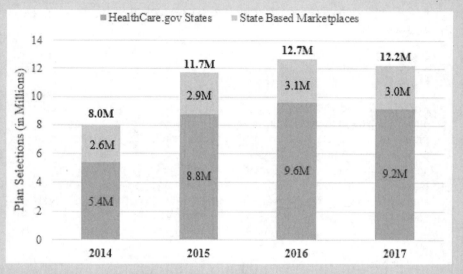

Source: "HEALTH INSURANCE MARKETPLACES 2017 OPEN ENROLLMENT PERIOD FINAL ENROLLMENT REPORT: NOVEMBER 1, 2016 – JANUARY 31, 2017," CMS.gov, March 15, 2017

The data for the 2014 OEP was from 10/1/2013 to 4/19/2014; the 2015 OEP was from 11/15/2014 to 2/22/2015; the 2016 OEP was from 11/1/2015 to 2/1/2016 (1/31/2016 for some states); the 2017 OEP was from 11/1/2016 to 1/31/2017. Plan selections by Marketplace model for each OEP reflects the status of the state's Marketplace model at the time of that OEP. Caution should be used when comparing plan selections across OEPs since some states have transitioned platforms between years. Additionally, state expansion of Medicaid may affect enrollment figures from year to year; Louisiana expanded Medicaid in July 2016, which may have affected Marketplace enrollments in 2017.

Figure 4.3 *ACA Marketplace Enrollment, 2014–2017.*

At the start of 2017, then Secretary of Health and Human Services Sylvia Matthews Burwell noted in an opinion piece for the *Boston Globe*:

> The reality of the Affordable Care Act is that 20 million people have gained coverage [since its inception]. Because of the law, nearly everyone's coverage is stronger today—whether they get covered through Medicaid, Medicare, private plans through the HealthCare.gov Marketplace, or their jobs. And the law has

helped hold down health care cost growth across the nation. It's made progress in the access, quality, and cost of coverage.[10]

Medicare

For enrollment through 2015, over 55 million Americans were enrolled in Medicare, according to the latest government data available.[11]

Retiree Exchanges

According to the "2016 Best Practices in Health Care Survey" from Willis Towers Watson, 41% of companies provide access to a private exchange for Medicare-eligible employees, and 60% are considering it for 2018.[12]

Private Exchanges

The latest research from Accenture indicates that 8 million people were enrolled in health insurance through a private exchange in 2016, up 35% from the previous year (see Figure 4.4).

Recent research from Frost & Sullivan indicates that "while the adoption of private HIX solutions among United States (U.S.) employers has lagged initial market expectations, the need to support a robust e-commerce experience for health plan beneficiaries among active and retired employees will accelerate uptake in coming years."[13] Frost & Sullivan projected that the total market for private health insurance exchange solutions among U.S. employers would grow at a compound annual rate of 41.9% between 2016 and 2020.

10. Sylvia Matthews Burwell, "The Reality of Repealing the Affordable Care Act," *Boston Globe*, January 9, 2017 www.bostonglobe.com/opinion/editorials/2017/01/09/the-reality-repealing-affordable-care-act/neZNjqiXjUSgO7unvEA57M/story.html.

11. Centers for Medicare & Medicaid Services, Press Release, "On its 50th anniversary, more than 55 million people Americans covered by Medicare," July 28, 2015, https://www.cms.gov/Newsroom/MediaReleaseDatabase/Press-releases/2015-Press-releases-items/2015-07-28.html.

12. Willis Towers Watson, "Full Report: 2016 21st Annual Best Practices in Health Care Employer Survey," www.willistowerswatson.com/en/insights/2017/01/full-report-2016-21st-annual-willis-towers-watson-best-practices-in-health-care-employer-survey.

13. Frost & Sullivan, "Private Health Insurance Exchanges Solutions Primed for Robust Growth Among U.S. Employers as Vendors Differentiate to Meet Evolving Consumer Expectations," April 11, 2017, ww2.frost.com/news/press-releases/private-health-insurance-exchanges-solutions-primed-robust-growth-among-us-employers-vendors-differentiate-meet-evolving-consume/.

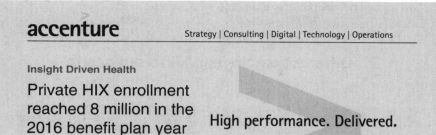

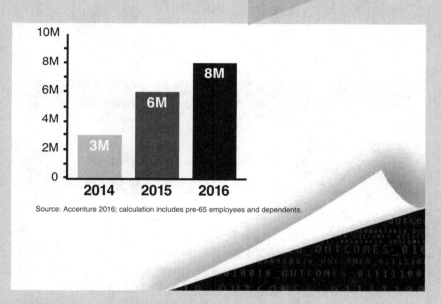

Figure 4.4 *Private Exchange Enrollment, 2014–2016.*

A Look at Products in Private Exchanges

A number of factors come together to form a shopping experience: the design (or navigation in an online store), customer support, merchandising (how the products are displayed on the shelves), and, most importantly, the inventory itself. Consumers have come to expect meaningful choices (not just one or two) with quality options at various price points, especially when shopping online. When we shop, we choose based on our needs and how the options are presented to align with those needs. For each person, these needs encompass complex personal desires that are addressed through the purchase. One individual may buy tickets to the opera at Lincoln Center to satisfy her intellectual interest, another might spend his hard-earned money on season tickets for his favorite football team. Different needs, different means, same measure of value.

Different employees, different needs

When it comes to private exchanges, "stores" are differentiated by the variety and quality of the merchandise being sold. Different benefit stores have different types of inventory. Some offer only medical insurance, or medical plus a few nonmedical options, such as life and disability; some exist to serve a company's active employee population, others their retiree population. What's important is the degree to which the offerings are curated to provide a meaningful selection in both the number and *types* of choices provided (see Figure 4.5).

> When it comes to private exchanges, "stores" are differentiated by the variety and quality of the merchandise being sold.

For example, offering a number of medical plans that are similar in design doesn't really make for meaningful choice. But if there are many plans, and they offer genuinely different options in terms of plan type (for example, HMO, PPO, HDHP), premium costs, networks, cost-sharing arrangements, and more, these choices are providing value in the shopping experience. A benefits consumer might choose one type of medical plan in absence of other nonmedical offerings to help fill any gaps in coverage, but with additional offerings such as hospital indemnity or critical illness insurance to help protect his or her income in the event of illness, a different medical plan type might become more attractive.

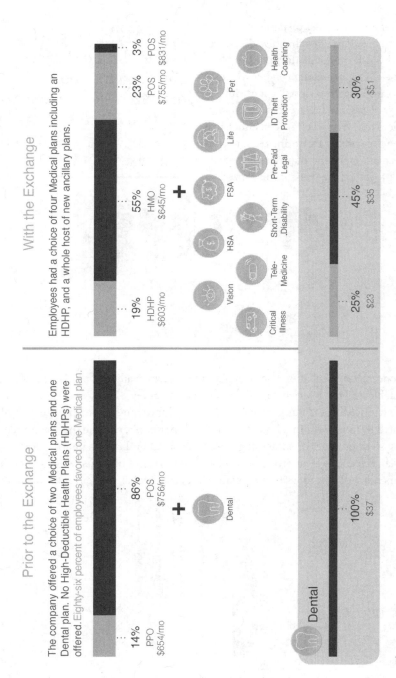

Figure 4.5 *Actual Employer Benefit Offerings Before and After Implementing a Liazon Private Exchange.*

Therefore, a benefits consumer needs to be able to see all the merchandise displayed side-by-side on the platform or be able to use a *recommendation engine* to select the plans that most closely align with his or her needs and preferences. Too many choices may overwhelm a consumer, but when the choices are optimized and presented as a portfolio of products that all work together, the stress is minimized.

> Too many choices may overwhelm a consumer, but when the choices are optimized and presented as a portfolio of products that all work together, the stress is minimized.

3 out of 4

selected a medical plan that was similar to what was recommended

Source: Liazon 2016 Employee Survey

A good recommendation engine makes the choices available on private exchanges palatable and not overwhelming. In one Liazon survey, 87% of employees said they were happy with the number of choices offered through Liazon's private exchanges or wanted even more.[15] In addition, a good number of people take the recommendation the system provides or something close to it; based on Liazon's internal 2015 analysis of plan selections by approximately 4,000 employees of one client, 48% chose the recommended plan, and 28% chose plans with costs similar to the recommendation.

On private exchanges, employees can "dial up" or "dial down" their plans based on their individual preferences.

15. Liazon, "Liazon's 2017 Employee Survey Report: Health Care Consumerism in a Marketplace Environment," March 2017 http://liazon.hs-sites.com/liazon/employeesurvey-1.

A PEEK AT THE DATA: WHAT DO EMPLOYEES CHOOSE?

PERC

Private Exchange Research Council

One of the clearest benefits of private exchanges is the ability to round out traditional health insurance with other types of coverage to tailor a unique portfolio to each person. On Liazon exchanges, there is a large uptake of nonmedical benefits to provide further financial protection. Consumers enrolled in high-deductible health plans (HDHPs), in particular, may find they have additional employer contribution dollars they are saving in medical premiums that they can put toward buying additional products tailored to their needs.

Employees choose an average of 5.1 products on Liazon exchanges,[16] including many of the ones shown in Figure 4.6.

---

16. Private Exchange Research Council (PERC) analysis, 2017, www.percinsights.com. Information here based on groups enrolling in benefits on Liazon exchanges with a benefits effective date of January 1, 2017. Based on employees who purchased at least one product.

Product Purchases on Liazon Exchanges, 2017

Percentage of employees who purchased a plan in each product category when offered

Product category	2017 (%)
Medical Insurance	76
Dental Insurance	74
Vision Insurance	60
Employee Life Insurance**	45
Short Term Disability**	45
Long Term Disability**	40
Health Savings Account	26
Critical Illness Insurance	21
Hospital Indemnity Insurance	21
Accident Insurance	20
Telemedicine	19
Spouse Life Insurance**	17
Child Life Insurance**	17
Identity Theft Protection	11
Pet Insurance	10
Legal Plans	6
Health Coaching	1

Source: Private Exchange Research Council (PERC) analysis, 2017. Based on groups enrolling in benefits on Liazon exchanges with a benefits effective date of January 1, 2017. www.percinsights.com
Sample: Employee study sample with at least one plan purchase.
*Based on employees who were offered the product and purchased at least one product in 2017.
**Net employer-paid products.

Figure 4.6 *What Do Employees Choose on a Private Exchange?*

What Else Can Private Exchanges Offer?

Exchanges can be largely distinguished by the degree and type of *decision support* they offer, and this is where pure-play operators tend to excel. (See more about decision support in Chapter 3.) "The best systems should include software capabilities that empower each user to not just understand their benefits but also empower them with the knowledge to avoid making ill-advised choices," Rhonda Marcucci said in an interview.[17] Examples of poor choices could be buying too much coverage, buying too little, or purchasing a high-deductible health plan (HDHP) but neglecting to set up the tax-advantaged health savings account (HSA) for which that plan is eligible.

Year-round customer support is another feature that sounds obvious but that can be a differentiator when it comes to selecting benefits on a private exchange. Marcucci encourages employers to ask, "Is the system largely set up for open enrollment, or does it serve employees year round, with options to review or change their benefits due to the occurrence of a life event?" A qualifying "life event," such as marriage or the birth of a child, is one of the most important determinants of the need to change benefits options during the enrollment year, and they invariably bring some degree of confusion on the part of employees. Marcucci also says it's important to ask, "Does the system provide access to a team dedicated to answering employee questions at the point of selection as well as while they're attempting to use their benefits throughout the year?"[18]

Employees should also consider to what extent *benefits administration features* are developed. In the case of systems that originated as benefits tech/automation platforms, discussed earlier in this chapter, this should be a no-brainer.

As the private exchange landscape continues to evolve, more and more opportunities for innovative companies to thrive are presenting themselves. The most recent examples of these provide added value to employees in the form of wellness programs and incentives, provider lookup and cost transparency tools, and health advocacy services. On

> As more..."value added" tools and services...appear... in the market, private exchanges should be well equipped to integrate their offerings into the exchange experience.

the employer side, the ACA has spurred new markets for dependent verification services, and companies specializing in nothing else but helping employers complete the forms required by the ACA have emerged! As more and more of

17. Personal interview with Rhonda Marcucci, April 21, 2016.
18. Ibid

these *"value added" tools and services* begin to appear and succeed in the market, private exchanges should be well equipped to integrate their offerings into the exchange experience.

Summary

This chapter has provided an overview of the public and private exchange ecosystem, with an in-depth look at the various players, offerings, and considerations for the private exchange space. There's no sugarcoating it: The current benefits landscape is complicated, and matters are not likely to improve anytime soon. The best we can do is work to understand the current system, keep abreast of the seemingly daily changes, and stay open to new ways to make it work better.

Now that we've examined the current landscape, along with what makes a true private exchange, how they came to be, and what's standing in their way, in Part II, "Stakeholders: Making the Move from 'One Size Fits All'", we turn our attention to some of the key constituents that are already benefitting from the paradigm shift, beginning with employers.

Part II

Stakeholders: Making the Move from "One Size Fits All"

5

Employers Find Skin in the Game

The following are some vignettes based on conversations with employers who have used Liazon exchanges:

- Housekeeping and maintenance workers gather around kiosks in the lobby of a resort on northwestern Florida's Gulf coast, excitedly talking to on-site advisors as they are introduced to a benefits marketplace for the first time. A young groundskeeper watches a short video and then picks out a medical insurance plan with a high deductible and a health savings account, comfortable that what the system recommended is the right choice for him.

- A 35-year-old store manager sits at her kitchen table in Savannah, Georgia, with her husband speaking Spanish to an employee services representative at 7:30 p.m. In a few minutes, they'll sign up for their first family medical insurance plan.

- An HR executive from a company with 5,000 retail stores in 18 states is reviewing enrollment figures during her company's open enrollment to see how many employees have yet to elect their plans when her phone rings. The caller ID shows it's her CIO on the line, and she is anxious; he could have some tough questions about the site's decision support, functionality, or reporting portal. Would she know what to say? Would her decision to try a new system prove out? The CIO tells her he just completed the online assessment profile questions. "Spot on," he says, "this is awesome," speaking of the recommendations the new marketplace enrollment platform has delivered to him.

Based on Liazon's annual employee and employer surveys, experiences like these are not uncommon. Legacy employer-provided benefits enrollments have typically resulted in much less active and engaged experiences.

While the old employer-knows-best model may have made sense in the past, industry players have long been unwittingly encouraging employees to be passive participants in the benefits process, rolling over their previous plan or choosing from two to three plans that aren't personalized to their needs. Through decades of the status quo in benefits, employees have become disengaged from some very important decisions regarding their physical and financial health. They've been spending more time figuring out what television to buy than on benefits decisions.

> [Employees] have been spending more time figuring out what television to buy than on benefits decisions.

Some companies, however, have decided things need to change, and they've done something about. This chapter tells the stories of two such companies.

A Big Bet Pays Off: TitleMax, Part of the TMX Finance Family of Companies[1]

TMX Finance Family of Companies ("TMX") is one of the nation's fastest-growing consumer finance companies. TMX employs more than 5,000 people in 15 states, and has its corporate offices in Dallas and Savannah. The company's most recognized brand, TitleMax, makes personal loans collateralized by a consumer's car title, thereby providing ready access to loans for clients who might not otherwise be able to secure them based on credit and cash flow alone. TitleMax maintains the bulk of its employees in the field at storefront locations. Their workforce's average age is 36, and 20% of them are native Spanish speakers.

During 2009, as national health care reform gathered momentum, TMX executives became concerned that the company would need to change its approach to providing medical insurance and other benefits. At that time, the company employed a stipend plan to partially support what employees could purchase on their own, outside the company. The company's rapid growth, concern for employees, and

---

1. The information in this section is based on a personal interview with Lauren Thomas, TMX's former senior vice president, human resources and administration, March 3, 2016.

commitment to attracting talent, along with the passage of the Affordable Care Act in 2010, made finding a quality corporate benefits plan an imperative.

"In 2011, we put into place our first employee benefits plan for medical and supplemental insurance, including dental and vision," explained Lauren Thomas, then human resources and administration senior vice president at TMX. TMX did not originally choose a private exchange and was immediately faced with the challenges of managing a large self-funded plan with a new population; the prospect of an RFP each year at renewal, ever-changing vendor relationships, and cost management were all concerns. While the new system was an important step forward, many employees had difficulty understanding the choices they were making.

"Our people didn't have enough guidance," Thomas recalled. "We had a number of employees taking lower deductible, higher premium plans who probably didn't need that much coverage. Some people took a high-deductible plan but didn't realize they also needed to pair that with a health savings account. Then we started getting clobbered on renewals for the next plan year. I jumped into researching more options."

Thomas reached out to peers in the industry and TMX's insurance broker for guidance. She had a few key requirements in mind. They wanted to remain with some type of "store" experience because the company's younger, decentralized workforce was used to technology-based HR services. A true benefits exchange could have a potentially superior approach to employee confidentiality and at-your-fingertips control over analytics and tracking, which would make life easier for her and her team. She also wanted a more intuitive, easy-to-use system, as well as consulting expertise to ensure that TMX was compliant with health care reform. By providing a competitive, quality enrollment platform, TMX could better attract and retain top management as well as frontline talent, an emerging concern for the growth-oriented, family-owned business.

When her broker introduced Lauren and her team to a Liazon-powered exchange, the groundwork was set.

For TMX, the exchange offered sought-after features missing from its previous system: a consumer-facing store with a rich array of choices, intuitive online navigation, Spanish translation and services, a new defined contribution funding strategy, and a commitment to educating employees so the company could empower its workforce to make the best choices for themselves and their families. (See Chapter 6, "Six Questions to Ask Before You Choose a Private Exchange," for a checklist you can use to evaluate different exchange offerings.)

See Chapter 6 ... for a checklist you can use to evaluate different exchange offerings.

Checklist of What TMX Wanted in a Private Exchange

The enrollment period started with an announcement to employees that an exciting change in the way they would be receiving benefits was on its way. The HR team members considered the consultants they were working with trusted advisors and assured employees that their enrollment choices and medical information would be treated with total confidentiality.

The education effort began with a series of online trainings, conference calls, and meetings. A guide to choosing their benefits was sent out via email, and employees were encouraged to open, read, and print it for later reference. The messaging was clear from the beginning that this change was a big shift that would positively impact the company's benefits offering. The team was not shy in communicating that employees, rather than the company, would now be making important benefits choices and that they would be educated on how to make smart, personalized decisions.

During open enrollment sessions, employees were introduced to the exchange's functionality and had core insurance concepts explained to them, such as the importance of balancing cost and coverage. Employees learned about the different types of products they'd find on the store shelves. Many learned for the first time how life insurance and health insurance work and why they might need both short- and long-term disability insurance. Advisors educated workers so they didn't buy too many benefits, a problem that had occurred in the past. They even held one-on-one sessions with employees to show them the site's navigation and talk about decision support and how the profile questionnaire helped clarify choices. It was critical for employees to understand how to purchase the right blend of coverage they needed—but no more or no less.

"People appreciated that no one tried to get them to sign up for coverage they didn't need, which had happened in the past," Lauren recalled. "For the first time, many employees understood the trade-offs between a high-deductible plan and health savings account versus a high-premium, low-deductible plan. Employees were able to ask questions about their coverage for one particular prescription or doctor choice that was particularly important to their families."

> "For the first time, many employees understood the trade-offs between a high-deductible plan and health savings account versus a high-premium, low-deductible plan."
>
> —*Lauren Thomas*

As people began spending time online and using the decision support features, they found many channels to use when they had questions or needed more information. Getting enrollment assistance had to be as easy as asking a sales associate questions at a Best Buy store or on the Zappos website. This support-rich environment included:

- An introductory video viewed when users first log in

- Online support through the exchange's educational hub as well as telephone support

- TMX's internal toll-free phone number, which offers an option to connect to Liazon's call center

- Bilingual assistance, which is particularly helpful for spouses who didn't speak English

- Extended hours for Liazon phone support staff to accommodate store closings in Mountain and Pacific time zones

- Rapid response assistance from TMX's HR office

- Additional onsite meetings in Savannah and Dallas for troubleshooting

Within a few weeks, TMX employees were making final decisions based on side-by-side comparisons of the plans offered and other educational tools available through the system. TMX continued to offer high-touch, one-on-one support. Lauren's team easily identified and double-checked on employees who hadn't purchased their benefits by a certain time. But for Thomas, the moment of truth arrived when the first paycheck deductions hit employee paychecks.

"We've had buyers' remorse before," she said. "Colleagues would have sticker shock when they opened their paychecks because they hadn't been given the educational opportunities to really know what they were buying. We'd have to show them what policy they picked and tell them unfortunately there wasn't much we could do about it until the next year. I was still dreading that a little bit. But as the implementation period passed, almost all of the emails and calls were positive; people here felt they understood what they'd bought. They got what they paid for and made the choices themselves, and that was a good thing."

> "They got what they paid for and made the choices themselves, and that was a good thing."
>
> —Lauren Thomas

Customer-Focused Luxury Resort Gives Back to Its Employees: Sandestin[2]

Sandestin Golf and Beach Resort is a 2,400-acre destination resort in Miramar Beach, Florida, on northwestern Florida's Gulf coast. It is a high-end family and vacation compound, offering golf, beaches, bays, spas, and racket sports.

Sandestin's customers expect flawless and courteous customer service, as they would with Ritz-Carlton or other elite luxury hotel chains. The resort employs approximately 350 people, a workforce with many faces of diversity. "Our workforce is as varied as they come," noted Sandestin's then benefits administrator and

---

2. The information in this section is based on personal correspondence with Amy Natalie, Sandestin's former benefits administrator and HR generalist, March, 2016.

HR generalist, Amy Natalie. "We have employment opportunities ranging from golf course and vehicle maintenance to housekeeping to finance to executive administration. Team Sandestin is made up of people of different genders, ages, ethnicities, and health concerns."

For Sandestin and similar resorts offering luxury experiences, a little-understood truth is that employees' interface with customers is one of the critical components of their brand experience. Therefore, the entire staff needs to be trained and supported in managing guests with seamless recognition, from the CEO to the parking valet. Sandestin's leaders consistently communicate to their workforce that they value employee feedback and meeting their employees' needs.

"Our number-one business challenge as a self-insured employer has been designing an offering for a diverse employee population that provides plan choices that both fit their health needs and that make sense for them and the company financially," Natalie said. "We needed to give employees choices that encourage them to be more proactive and less reactive with their health care needs so both parties benefit through happier, healthier employees and lower costs." And they also needed to give employees a reason to stay with the company.

> "We needed to give employees choices that encourage them to be more proactive and less reactive with their health care needs..."
>
> —Amy Natalie

By retaining more employees, reducing turnover, and offering choice and security in benefits offerings, Sandestin acts as the kind of employer it truly aspires to be. Sandestin's leaders know that their diverse workforce will always have diverse concerns about medical insurance and other benefits. Therefore, the annual selection of a benefits provider represents a big decision for Sandestin's executive benefits committee.

Sandestin received poor feedback from employees about its 2015 insurance options. The company offered one medical insurance plan with an HRA, a dental plan, and a vision plan, along with life insurance and short- and long-term disability. Employees wanted more choices and didn't like being forced into a high-deductible arrangement. Natalie and the benefits committee, which includes the general manager, VP of finance, VP of real estate, and VP of human resources, met with their benefits consultant Blake Hamby of Willis (now Willis Towers Watson).

Hamby recommended a private exchange powered by Liazon. Liazon's team, led by Tyler Davis, traveled to Sandestin to meet with the benefits committee and owner Tom Becnel to introduce Liazon's model and online portal. Sandestin greenlighted the exchange in August 2015, and Liazon worked on developing Sandestin's benefits store from September to November.

The store offered six medical plans instead of one, a choice of three dental plans and four vision plans, as well as a shelf of products consisting of short- and long-term disability insurance, an FSA and an HSA, telemedicine, accident insurance, life insurance, and critical illness insurance. Both sides agreed on a robust three-week communications launch, touting the exchange as a major new asset for employees with an array of educational opportunities and support.

It was open enrollment time in early November. Hamby and Davis made on-site presentations and recommendations from 10:00 a.m. to 3:00 p.m. for several days to reach as many employees as possible. Everyone received a "2016 Guide to Using Your Benefits" so they could follow along and have a handy resource outside the portal. More than 8 in 10 employees attended these meetings, and nearly all of those confirmed that the sessions were very helpful. During this time, Sandestin distributed pre-open enrollment communications materials to employees, including flyers, emails, and a video demonstration of how the portal worked.

Later in the month, one-on-one onsite meetings were held with employees. Because Sandestin has many employees who work outside the office and don't use computers, 15 computer kiosks were provided for employees to use for enrollment. The kiosks were extremely popular and the enrollment period was a huge success, according to Natalie:

> Our communication strategy worked well for a company of our size with such a diverse workforce. Approximately 95% of eligible employees completed the benefits process (signed on to the system and either elected or waived coverage).

> Of course employees saw this as a change, but change is what they wanted. We knew we had to provide more choices and most employees understood that this switch to an online portal was the best way to do that.

"Of course employees saw this as a change, but change is what they wanted."

—Amy Natalie

> There will always be individuals who are resistant to change and technology and because of our widespread demographic, I was somewhat afraid of the number of people who would not take to the online concept. I was pleasantly surprised by how accepting and engaged our employees turned out to be.

The biggest implication for employers, insurers, and perhaps to our economy as a whole is how important benefits are to employee satisfaction and retention. In a post-enrollment survey, nearly 7 in 10 workers told Sandestin that they are more likely to stay employed with the company because of its better benefits program. Benefits are another reason Sandestin's employee churn percentage is around 25% annually, a remarkable figure for the hospitality industry, where turnover can run as high as 75% per year. Natalie commented, "The effects of this change are so profound and much more than we could have initially imagined.

"Insurance and decisions related to insurance are far too important to our employees' well-being to not learn and grow from employee feedback and make changes," said Natalie. "Because we did this, employees feel ownership's commitment to their well-being and families and in turn our employees become more committed to the company. We also believe that a healthy employee is a happy employee and vice versa. Happy employees better serve our members and guests and directly lead to positive interactions and experiences."

> "The effects of this change are so profound and much more than we could have initially imagined."
>
> —Amy Natalie

Summary

This chapter provided firsthand employer accounts about what is actually needed for a successful enrollment experience. We know it takes some work and planning upfront to ensure positive results, but as demonstrated by the experiences of TMX and Sandestin, the payoff is indeed worth it.

Both of these HR professionals had the benefit of a trusted partner on their teams—their insurance broker—to help guide them through the process of deciding if a private exchange was right for them, and then, which private exchange to choose. We'll explore the broker/employer relationship later on in this section. But first, Chapter 6, "Six Questions to Ask Before you Choose a Private Exchange," offers a guide to what questions to ask to distinguish among various exchange operators to make sure your company's needs are met.

6

Six Questions to Ask Before You Choose a Private Exchange

In 2014, the Kaiser Family Foundation reported that private exchanges "have the potential to reshape employer-sponsored health insurance, which covers 149 million people, or nearly 56% of the U.S. non-elderly population."[1] Kaiser conducted interviews with several leading private exchanges, including Liazon, as well as many employers and health plans moving in this direction, to create a picture of this quickly growing landscape.

This chapter draws on Kaiser's research as well as that of leading benefits consultants Barbara Gniewek, a principal in PwC's Global Human Resource Services practice,[2] and Rhonda Marcucci, divisional vice president and national HR & benefits technology practice leader for the Benefits and Human Resources Consulting division of Arthur J. Gallagher & Co.[3] This chapter examines the factors organizations need to consider as they try to decide which private exchange option is the best fit. It also provides performance indicators for what qualifies as a true benefits "store"—in addition to the technology necessary to enable online enrollment, payroll and billing processes, benefits administration, and more.

---

1. Alex Alvarado et al., "Examining Private Exchanges in the Employer-Sponsored Market," Kaiser Family Foundation, September 23, 2014, http://kff.org/private-insurance/report/examining-private-exchanges-in-the-employer-sponsored-insurance-market/.

2. All of the quotes and ideas from Barbara Gniewek in this section are based on a personal interview conducted October 13, 2016.

3. All of the quotes and ideas from Rhonda Marcucci in this section are based on a personal interview conducted April 21, 2016.

In Kaiser's research, 20 of the platforms interviewed qualified as full private exchanges based on the following indicators:

- A set of health plans
- An Affordable Care Act (ACA)–compliant environment
- The ability to switch to defined contribution

Admittedly, Kaiser's three simple criteria are the minimum requirements. A true benefits store does much more. Best practices in exchanges have concentrated (appropriately) on customer experience, improved decision support, better education and guidance, and network design. As Barbara Gniewek explained:

> Exchanges are a modernization of employer-sponsored benefits. They provide a way to bring technology to enhance benefits offerings and/or accelerate strategies. They allow companies to help employees become meaningful consumers. Employers using exchanges are doing something different to provide choices and improve the employee experience.

"Employers using exchanges are doing something different to provide choices and improve the employee experience."

—*Barbara Gniewek*

The near future holds enormous promise for gains in wellness integration, portal enhancements, broader use of alternative networks, and innovative mobile apps and programs such as loyalty programs and rewards points. Some private exchanges are already including these features. (See Chapter 9, "Innovation in Benefits [Yes, Benefits]" and Chapter 11, "Who's Afraid of the American Consumer?" for a look at the future of private exchanges and benefits.)

What Makes for a True Private Exchange?

Earlier chapters in this book discuss choice and defined contribution as defining principles of a private exchange and as disruptors that will release the status quo from its stranglehold. (See Chapter 3, "They Don't Know What They're Missing: Flipping the Status Quo on Its Head," for a review of these essential principles.)

This chapter will take a deeper dive into some distinguishing characteristics among exchange providers and sponsors to help companies when evaluating different offerings. First, in Figure 6.1, we discuss some basics you should look for in a private exchange experience.

What should you look for in a private exchange?

A checklist:

Every benefits marketplace is different, and not every system can be expected to have every attribute. Use this checklist when considering the level of choice and guidance, or "decision support," provided by a benefits marketplace.

Does the benefits marketplace provide:	Yes	No	Need further info
• A wide variety of products, including medical, dental, supplemental health, vision, life, disability, money accounts, and more, to best protect the wellbeing of employees and their families?	☐	☐	☐
• A broad range of plans that provide meaningful choice along a range of dimensions such as price, provider network, and deductible?	☐	☐	☐
• Advanced decision support tools to help guide employees to a benefits decision that is right for them?	☐	☐	☐
• A sophisticated algorithm that matches employees' individual needs and preferences to the best combination of benefits?	☐	☐	☐
• A recommendation engine that considers an employee's health status, plan preferences, financial situation, comfort level with risk, concerns for the future, and more, when recommending plans and products?	☐	☐	☐
• Education about insurance via different learning formats?	☐	☐	☐
• Side-by-side plan comparisons of key coverages, plan features and costs?	☐	☐	☐
• Summarized plan information including deductibles, copays, prescription coverage, and out of pocket maximums?	☐	☐	☐
• Benefit summaries provided by the carriers of health and ancillary benefits offered through the private exchange, or a third-party administrator in the case of self-funded benefits?	☐	☐	☐

The more variety in products, and the better decision support a private exchange provides, the greater the likelihood that it will produce satisfying results for employees. If the information is not readily apparent from your early understanding of a proposed private exchange platform, it could be worth it to dig deeper to find out how the system fares on each of the measures above.

Figure 6.1 *What to look for in a private exchange.*

In order to realize the full advantages offered by private exchanges, it's important to consider the following six indicators when examining how robust the offering is.

1. Is Elasticity Built into Its Foundation?

A *health insurance exchange*, such as the public exchanges established under the ACA, is a marketplace stocked with various health insurance offerings, such as medical plans from leading national or regional insurers. A *benefits exchange* includes products beyond the standard health, dental, and vision offerings.

The shift to employee choice has motivated carriers and new entrants into the benefits landscape to innovate and experiment. The expansion and improvement of product lines by carriers is a positive outgrowth of the private exchange paradigm shift, one that encourages them to create products that people want to buy. Benefits exchanges often include varied products such as accident, critical illness, and hospital indemnity insurance; telemedicine; health coaching; identity theft protection; paid time-off buy-up options; pet insurance; legal plans; and more. (See a full explanation of each of these benefits and more in the Product Guide in Appendix B.)

Each of these lines of coverage can be thought of as an aisle in the store. Each shelf on the aisle has different plans from different carriers that you can compare, just as you would buy products in the supermarket. Conceptually, benefit stores were built on the concept of an aisle, medical insurance, which may be right next to the dental insurance and vision insurance aisles, and surrounding these are aisles that can expand to meet a broad range of products and needs, some of which may not even have been introduced yet. Who even heard of telemedicine 20 years ago? Within the store framework, innovation can be fueled such that aisles can be easily expanded to include new options, and that is the central concept of product merchandising within a benefits store. In private exchanges operated by Liazon, this can mean anywhere from 15 to 20 different lines, or aisles, of coverage, each with several options for plans on the "shelves"

> Innovation can be fueled such that aisles can be easily expanded to include new options, and that is the central concept of product merchandising within a benefits store.

(as many as 5 to more than 20 medical choices, along with options for each of the other lines of coverage).

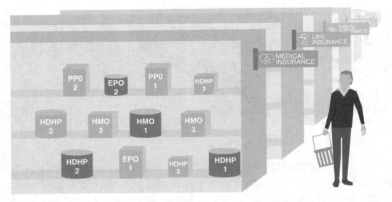

"Offering prepackaged benefits stores is one of the key differentiators of private exchanges from traditional benefits administration systems," said Rhonda Marcucci. "Employers should think of the products as inventory rather than think about each product on its own." She's right. If you as an employer don't like critical illness insurance, quite frankly, it doesn't matter. You don't get to pick for your employees anymore, and they will buy differently when they have more choices. "It's no longer a 'bring your own plan' type of system," said Marcucci. "It's a deeper, more integrated set of products that enables efficiency and brings meaningful choice to consumers."

> "Offering prepackaged benefits stores is one of the key differentiators of private exchanges from traditional benefits administration systems."
>
> —Rhonda Marcucci

2. Does It Include Decision Support and Educational Tools?

Without decision support, shopping in an online benefits store is like visiting a supermarket where the packaged goods offer no label information. Decision support tools are necessary to deliver a positive customer experience. Employees who face too many options can become confused and overwhelmed if they can't readily discern or understand the differences among products or make a value determination about how many products they need and at what cost. Numerous executives involved in adopting private exchanges have spoken about the importance of state-of-the-art user interface and decision support tools in increasing employee engagement. According to research compiled by Deutsche Bank Securities, when Walgreens shifted to a private exchange, employees increased their use of decision tools in the first year by 80%. Walgreens saw an additional 45% increase in the second year of adoption.[4]

"Giving employees choice and help in understanding the health care system is essential," said Barbara Gniewek. "They want the tools to identify the doctors they need and understand the costs. They want to make really good decisions like how much to put into their health savings accounts (HSAs) each year, how to pay for different benefits and how to determine if they need disability or dental coverage and, if so, how much." Gniewek pointed out that employees—especially Millennials—want to be able to minimize their out-of-pocket costs and payroll deductions. In a 2016 Liazon survey, 96% of employees consider extensive education and decision support tools an important aspect of the benefits marketplace, and 84% found the recommendation engine helpful.[5]

> "Giving employees choice and help in understanding the health care system is essential."
>
> —Barbara Gniewek

Rhonda Marcucci expanded on this point:

> Once you have the inventory, decision support becomes essential to help people choose the right plans. It should be something employers who are considering any private exchange pay special attention to when comparing offerings. And it's not just about guidance for choosing a medical plan; it's about the broader health and welfare risk portfolio in which differentiators, such as life stage, can lead to different recommendations of what's needed to protect each person's total risk.

---

4. "The Potential and Impact of Private Exchange Adoption," Deutsche Bank Markets Research, April 17, 2015.

5. Liazon, "Liazon's 2017 Employee Survey Report: Health Care Consumerism in a Marketplace Environment", March 2017 http://liazon.hs-sites.com/liazon/employeesurvey-1.

3. Are Prices Transparent?

As discussed in Chapter 1, "Building a Better Benefits System," and elsewhere in this book, defined contribution is best optimized in an exchange environment when employees are aware of the value of employer contributions. As employers consider the offerings of exchange providers, one thing that should be top of mind is the ability to make the cost information about those benefits transparent. Transparent pricing—about both the full cost of benefits as well as the employer's and employees' shares—is key to a good shopping experience. Barbara Gniewek explained the importance of price transparency:

> Understanding that the price for an MRI is not the same in a doctor's office, an outpatient clinic, and a free-standing MRI facility is very important to employees.
>
> Employees need to know the best places to go, the best providers, and all of the costs. There are also advocacy and second opinion programs interspersed in exchange programs. While some employers also offer similar programs, it is difficult to get employees to be aware that these tools are available. When someone needs to find a facility, he may not remember that he can use an employer resource to get help. However, with the exchange, if all the resources are available on one easy-to-use dashboard, the employee will have a very different—and favorable—experience.

Rhonda Marcucci also pointed out that transparency becomes even more important with all the confusion, controversy, and conflict over health care spending and insurance:

> If a private exchange doesn't offer a defined contribution model for benefits spending, it's clearly not one of the more robust platforms available today. Price transparency through defined contribution will become even more important as consumerism continues to take hold in light of the ACA, and you are really not doing all you

can for your employees if you don't let them know how much you, and they, are spending are on their benefits. The upside of this is that it changes the conversation you are having with your employees for the better.

Displaying how much employers are spending on their employees' benefits is a form of transparency. Some employers may prefer not to disclose this information but rather opt to display the "net cost" of plan prices in their exchanges. This is the cost of the plan minus the employer's contribution (which is not visible to employees) so that what is displayed is exactly how much the plan will cost employees.

> "The upside of [defined contribution with price transparency] is that it changes the conversation you are having with your employees for the better."
>
> —*Rhonda Marcucci*

Say that there is a choice of three different plans, priced at $500, $600, and $700 per month, and the employer has set a defined contribution of $500. In the defined contribution approach, the prices are presented to employees exactly as described above, and the employer's $500 contribution is also visible. In the second approach, the net costs to employees of $0, $100, and $200 are displayed.

In the net cost scenario, the employee does not see the value of the employer's benefit and, in effect, has to guess what role the contribution plays in his or her total compensation. Also, the concept of building a portfolio based on money the employer is providing is more difficult to grasp. Further, it can seem like little or nothing is left over for the employee to spend on other benefits that can enhance his or her portfolio and provide better protection.

On the flip side, with a defined contribution, behavioral economics are at work when the employee sees how generous the employer is being and that some of these plans end up costing the employee very little or nothing. In this scenario, employees might be more inclined to purchase certain plans because they seem more appealing in that a little more money can go a long way. That is to say, a small additional portion from the employee (relative to what the employer is investing) may be construed to yield even broader coverage that is well worth it for the peace of mind it brings.

With a net cost approach, the prices are transparent in that the employee sees his or her portion of the true cost of the plan, which looks desirable because the employer has effectively brought down the price of the plan. But the true value of the employer's contribution is lost on the employee. Benefits are and should always be viewed as a part of total compensation, and without knowing how much they are being compensated for their benefits, the overall value being provided by their employer is diminished.

4. Does It Integrate with Value-Added Services?

As the private exchange landscape grows, more companies are cropping up to help benefits consumers reap new forms of benefits and also make sense of it all. (See more about this in Chapter 8, "Insurers Find a New Way to Move Product.") The best exchanges provide integration with third-party providers to enhance the non-insurance offerings available through the system. With wellness offerings a key focus for employers over the past few years and various value-added programs such as cost transparency tools, health advocacy services, and provider lookup becoming more widespread, the best exchanges will allow for seamless integration of these types of services and more to round out their offerings.

"While health care has been the most important benefit in the employer–employee relationship, companies are now looking at benefits more broadly," Barbara Gniewek noted. "The ideal exchange, in my view, would not just offer health care and health and wellness programs but an overall rewards platform that could include education credits, credit and financial services, retirement planning, and an overall learning platform." Gniewek said that she has seen dashboards covering all aspects of financial planning. "Today's workforce is so diverse," she said, "that employers must give people what they want, and a 'one size fits all' approach is not giving them the right care. The exchanges give people access to the right information so they can make the right choices. It is about giving them tools and engaging people to help them."

"Private exchanges were set up as a technology solution," explained Rhonda Marcucci. "It only makes sense that they easily integrate with other technologies to improve the consumer experience; it's part of their DNA." (Chapter 9, "Innovation in Benefits [Yes, Benefits]" looks at some of the innovative companies that are integrating with Liazon and other exchanges to offer more of these value-added services to benefits consumers.)

5. Does It Provide Year-Round Support?

Enabling employees to choose benefits during open enrollment is the key function of an effective private exchange, but it's not the only function. A benefits exchange should be available all year so employees can review their benefits at any time, make changes to their benefits in the event of major life events (for example, marriage, birth of a child), make changes to their HSA contributions, and track and manage their health care spending.

Direct support for employees should be provided through an exchange in the form of customer service representatives who can be reached via phone or email to answer questions about benefits or using the system. Often a person signs up for dental insurance during open enrollment and has no idea who her insurer is when she goes to the dentist six months later. With an exchange, she can just log into her home page and see all her benefits information right there. And in certain platform configurations, she can easily contact someone if she has a question about what's covered—even while she's visiting the dentist!

According to Rhonda Marcucci, this type of support is another key distinguisher of private exchanges from traditional benefits administration systems. "Most standard enrollment platforms aren't flexible enough to handle things like life events throughout the year, dependent verification, and age-offs, she said. "These are services that can be found in a complete end-to-end solution. You're looking for more than just an enrollment platform with a private exchange."

> "You're looking for more than just an enrollment platform with a private exchange."
>
> —Rhonda Marcucci

6. To What Extent Does It Handle Benefits Administration?

A private exchange should be able to handle basic benefits administration functions when it comes to online benefits enrollment (such as eligibility requirements, processing new hires and terminations, life events, payroll deductions, carrier integration, billing, reporting requirements). However, a benefits administration system is not necessarily in and of itself considered a private exchange. Rhonda Marcucci spends every day of her working life understanding the differences, and this is how she explained them:

> A private exchange is built to cover various aspects of not only the benefits enrollment process but the benefits usage process. It should be able to handle basic benefits administration functions such as incorporating spending/health care accounts, billing and payment services, dependent verification services, and COBRA. But private exchanges go beyond these core capabilities of offering strong administrative functionality on the employer side, in that they are built with the employee user in mind.

"...private exchanges go beyond these core capabilities of offering strong administrative functionality on the employer side, in that they are built with the employee user in mind."

—*Rhonda Marcucci*

Summary

Marcucci advises her employer clients that private exchanges should have a simple user interface and high degree of decision support. In addition:

"They should help employees make the right benefits decisions. They should be able to accommodate defined contribution as a funding mechanism. Plus, the most advanced exchanges are flexible enough to integrate with other systems for anything they may not provide directly, such as price transparency tools and ACA compliance and tracking abilities. But the key distinguisher that makes a private exchange a true private exchange today is the inventory offered; in particular, pre-packaged medical plan inventory, and the efficiencies gained as a result of the curation of that inventory.

Armed with this information and these key questions to ask any exchange operator or provider, you can feel more comfortable about the prospect of identifying the system that can best meet the needs of your company. But employers never have to go it alone when deciding to make a change for the better for their employees. When it comes to benefits, having a broker on your team can be an asset. In Chapter 7, "Brokers and Exchanges: Better Together," we'll take a deeper look into why that is the case.

7

Brokers and Exchanges: Better Together

Moving to a private exchange represents change for employers and employees, and it also represents change for brokers. Not everyone is a fan of change. While some brokers remain concerned about private exchanges supplanting their business, these early fears are gradually dissipating—and with good reason. The opposite is actually occurring: In a private exchange environment, a broker or an advisor is more important than ever before.

> In a private exchange environment, a broker or an advisor is more important than ever before.

Insurance brokers have always provided great value to employers, but today they play a more complex, high-end consulting role, particularly if those benefits are sold through a private exchange. Brokers who embrace their enhanced role are well poised in this arena. Brokers are involved in helping employers choose a benefits strategy that is best for them, and if that strategy is a private exchange, it means making decisions regarding the cost and extent of coverage and helping to educate the workforce. In addition, the broker is involved in developing and selling new products through the exchange. Figure 7.1 provides a simplified overview of this evolving relationship.

The Role of the Broker: Then and Now

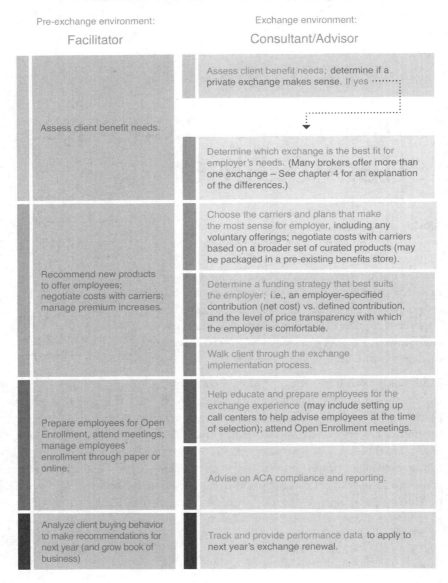

Pre-exchange environment:
Facilitator

Exchange environment:
Consultant/Advisor

Assess client benefit needs; determine if a private exchange makes sense. If yes ·········

Assess client benefit needs.

Determine which exchange is the best fit for employer's needs. (Many brokers offer more than one exchange – See chapter 4 for an explanation of the differences.)

Choose the carriers and plans that make the most sense for employer, including any voluntary offerings; negotiate costs with carriers based on a broader set of curated products (may be packaged in a pre-existing benefits store).

Recommend new products to offer employees; negotiate costs with carriers; manage premium increases.

Determine a funding strategy that best suits the employer; i.e., an employer-specified contribution (net cost) vs. defined contribution, and the level of price transparency with which the employer is comfortable.

Walk client through the exchange implementation process.

Help educate and prepare employees for the exchange experience (may include setting up call centers to help advise employees at the time of selection); attend Open Enrollment meetings.

Prepare employees for Open Enrollment, attend meetings; manage employees' enrollment through paper or online.

Advise on ACA compliance and reporting.

Analyze client buying behavior to make recommendations for next year (and grow book of business)

Track and provide performance data to apply to next year's exchange renewal.

Figure 7.1 *The Role of the Broker: Then and Now.*

In evaluating whether a private exchange strategy is right for a client, a broker should assess the client's current situation with regard to benefits, help the client understand their options, and recommend a strategy that best suits their needs. As discussed in Chapter 4, "Making Sense of Benefits Solutions: Public Exchanges and Private Exchanges," no one exchange platform fits every employer. Similarly, private exchanges aren't a panacea for all companies. Some companies may have employees who are perfectly happy with their benefits packages, and benefits are already a factor in helping attract and retain them. Companies with very homogenous workforces are well suited to having only a few plans. They may not be struggling with the issues of rising premiums, and benefits may not be a concern for them for a number of reasons.

HOW TO IDENTIFY AN EMPLOYER WHO IS READY FOR A PRIVATE EXCHANGE

A private exchange *may* be the best approach if the answer to most of the following questions is *yes*:

- Is the employer committed to attracting and retaining the best employees? Is turnover an issue? (Eight-seven percent of HR managers say that retention is a high or critical priority,[1] and 75% of employees surveyed who used a Liazon exchange said it made them more likely to stay with their employer.[2])

- Does the employer have a diverse staff in terms of age, location, life stage, and financial status? That is, do employees have different needs rather than being a fairly homogenous group of individuals?

- Is the company concerned about rising health care premiums and interested in hearing about ways to control them?

- Is the company committed to enhancing the corporate culture? That is, does it have a motivated HR staff that looks for new ways to engage employees? (Liazon found that, as a result of their benefits program, 85% of employees who use our exchanges become more engaged with their health care decisions and 79% are glad their employer made the switch.[3])

- Would the employer be willing to let their employees choose their own benefits? Do they believe their employees can make these decisions for themselves?

- Is the company forward thinking and willing to invest in its business, especially if changes yield positive results in the long run?

1. Kronos Inc. and Future Workplace, "The Employee Burnout Crisis: Study Reveals Big Workplace Challenge in 2017," January 9, 2017 https://www.kronos.com/about-us/newsroom/employee-burnout-crisis-study-reveals-big-workplace-challenge-2017

2. Liazon, "Liazon's 2017 Employee Survey Report: Health Care Consumerism in a Marketplace Environment," March 2017 http://liazon.hs-sites.com/liazon/employeesurvey-1.

3. Ibid.

One brokerage that saw the promise for its clients early on was Lawley Insurance, which was among the first companies to partner with Liazon to introduce its own branded exchange, the Lawley Marketplace. Brian Murphy, a partner in Lawley's Employee Benefits Group, told *Employee Benefit Adviser* in 2015, "We really thought it put us head and shoulders above our competitors.... Sure, it's an investment, but you have to constantly reinvest in your business."[4] He went on to say that his firm has seen significant new business through their private exchange and that many existing clients have expressed interest in moving to the exchange. Murphy explained that his company prides itself on innovation and investing in things that benefit customers; he noted that the cost to the company of starting its own exchange platform was merely the "cost of doing business."

> "We really thought [having our own exchange] put us head and shoulders above our competitors.... Sure, it's an investment, but you have to constantly reinvest in your business."
>
> —Brian Murphy

The timing of this kind of innovation for Lawley Insurance was apt: After the Affordable Care Act (ACA) was enacted, clients began to rely more on Lawley as a trusted advisor to help them navigate the new requirements and burdens on employers and insurance groups. Many employers needed to have questions answered about the contributions, which plans would best help to control costs, and how to make sure employees were comfortable with the change. These employers, curious about private exchanges but hesitant to commit, got reliable guidance in their decision-making process from their partners at Lawley.

For the employers and HR executives who take the plunge, the apparent novelty of exchanges has led to a remarkably effective benefits strategy, particularly for smaller companies. The technology helps smaller employers provide "as large an array of benefits as possible," according to T. J. Revelas, managing partner for employee benefits at Lawley, giving "more options and more choice" to employees. Lawley has been able to advocate the value of consumer-driven health care through its benefits offerings and has received immense positive feedback from employees. Still, Revelas recognizes that this strategy isn't immediately appropriate for every company, acknowledging that many are not yet ready to make the change. Many are still "sitting and waiting to see if exchanges really do

> The [exchange] technology helps smaller employers provide "as large an array of benefits as possible" giving "more options and more choice" to employees.
>
> — T.J. Revelas

---

4. Brian Kalish, "Private Exchanges: A Complex Process," *Employee Benefit Adviser*, January 15, 2015.

control costs" before making the shift, he said. In addition, many employers struggle with the concept of defined contribution and do not want to give up control of the products and offerings that employees choose.[5]

Developing partnerships with brokers like Lawley set the stage for more partnerships with other "white-labeled" exchanges, including those offered by Arthur J. Gallagher & Co., BB&T, Brown & Brown, HUB International, Lovitt & Touché, and Willis Group, now Willis Towers Watson. As Revelas indicated, many brokers remain skeptical about the ability of private exchanges to enhance their role with clients and prospects. We spoke with two of Liazon's early exchange partners to discover why this is still the case. The following sections relay their insights.

Rick Strater, Arthur J. Gallagher & Co.[6]

Rick Strater is the divisional vice president and national exchange practice leader for the Benefits and Human Resources Consulting division of Arthur J. Gallagher & Co., which offers its own private exchange, the Gallagher Marketplace. One of the solutions available through the Gallagher Marketplace is powered by Liazon's technology. Strater was also part of the initial team at Liazon earlier on in his career, so you might say he's been a part of private exchange solutions since the beginning. Strater views the concept of private exchanges as still being relatively new, despite all the noise in the industry about it. "There are still a lot of misconceptions about private exchanges," he said, and "this creates a lack of understanding on the part of employers."

"In the early days," Strater recalled, "we met with prospects to discuss the exchange concept. We said, here is the plan you have today, and here's what we can offer—which was a high-deductible plan—and provided a side-by-side comparison. We have a decision support tool that's built to help your employees decide which plan

---

5. Personal interview with T. J. Revelas, April 22, 2015.

6. The information in this section is based on a personal interview with Rick Strater, National Exchange Practice Leader at Arthur J. Gallagher & Co., May 12, 2016.

makes sense for them." The result? The lowest adoption rate for an HSA-qualified plan was 52%—an unbelievable turnaround from the trends at the time and a proof point of what can happen when employees are treated like consumers and understand the full cost of their benefits and how benefits work. "Suddenly, they got it," Strater said.

The Role of the Broker

The key role for the broker/consultant, Strater believes, is to provide advice. "Focus on the process. If you go into a client meeting selling an exchange as a product, that is a mistake," he said. "Rather, figure out whether or not the concept of defined contribution makes sense for the client. Explain that they'll need to be transparent with employees about costs. If an exchange isn't really right, then you shouldn't be trying to sell them on one."

> "If an exchange isn't really right, then you shouldn't be trying to sell [your client] on one."
>
> —*Rick Strater*

There is less emphasis on the individual products and choosing specific plans, and more consulting on an appropriate defined contribution strategy and then guiding the employer through the process once they see the benefit. "It's a shift from product to process," Strater said, "because moving to an exchange involves a culture change for companies; some company cultures are better suited to it than others." The role of the employee changes, too, from one of passive recipient to active buyer, and this is something the broker should help facilitate as well.

Overcoming Misconceptions

Strater recalled that when private exchanges were initially introduced, many employers were confused and unsettled at the prospect, for the reasons described in the following sections.

 ### Employees Don't Care About Choice

In Strater's words, "We said we wanted to offer multiple plans to a company so that the employees could select the plan that was right for them. Companies had a lot of questions and concerns around letting employees choose their own plans." Now, some employers on Liazon exchanges offer more than 20 medical plans and at least 10 dental plans.

Strater stressed that employees have different ways of using their coverage:

> Corporations traditionally tend to stress price and low deductibles when choosing plans to offer employees; yet about three-quarters of policy holders in traditional plans won't meet their lower deductible but will pay higher premiums for those deductibles nonetheless. Private exchanges work differently; they treat the end users—employees—as consumers who can make their own decisions when it comes to spending their own money.

According to a recent Liazon survey, 96% of employees on Liazon exchanges want to choose their own benefits, as opposed to having their employers choose for them.[7]

 ## Cost Is All That Matters

"We help employers understand that cost is not the only consideration and that the discussion around cost needs to change to one about the range of plan pricing that is appropriate based on the employee population," Strater said.

The reality is that exchanges with the right decision support guide employees to the best plans for them, considering their attitudes about costs as one, but not the only, factor. In fact, twice as many employees surveyed by Liazon in 2016 said that they chose their medical benefits because they provided the right level of coverage compared with those who chose them because they had the lowest cost.[8]

 ## Defined Contribution Is "Cost Shifting"

Strater is adamant that moving to defined contribution as a way to control costs doesn't mean companies are shifting the burden over to employees. "It may be the case that a client is in dire straits and needs to figure out ways to reduce costs, but a private exchange strategy with defined contribution in and of itself shouldn't necessarily be touted as the cure-all," said Strater. "Nor does the high cost of a plan automatically mean an employer will shift these costs to employees. Employers have the power over their budget and can still offer their employees more through a defined contribution approach. It needs to be considered on a case-by-case basis."

Strater sees promise in new data the industry is developing about exchange usage to address these misconceptions and increase exchange adoption rates.

---

7. Liazon, "Liazon's 2017 Employee Survey Report: Health Care Consumerism in a Marketplace Environment", March 2017 http://liazon.hs-sites.com/liazon/employeesurvey-1.

8. Ibid.

Rob Harkins, Willis Towers Watson[9]

Willis Towers Watson

Rob Harkins led the Exchange Practice for Willis Group Holdings until it merged with Towers Watson in 2016 to form Willis Towers Watson, for which he now serves as mid-market practice leader for private exchanges. The merger was a natural for these two complementary companies, leveraging Towers Watson's global consulting reach with Willis's broking and advisory services in the middle market.

The shift to private exchanges did not occur at that point, though, as Willis had already been selling its own private exchange, The Willis Advantage (powered by Liazon), since 2013, and eventually began using it for their own employees as well. Like Rick Strater, Rob Harkins recalled that those early days were largely about building out the model: "We were three years old—and still trying to explain what a private exchange was. It just didn't have the same acceptance across industries; many companies were unwilling to get involved."[10]

Even now, according to Harkins, there is a lot of resistance and "lots of misunderstanding and preconceived notions about what an exchange is." There's a fear of losing control on the part of the employer, when in reality, employers can get more control.

"The functionality that exchanges offer, which enables employees to choose their own benefits and create individualized portfolios of plans—can pose a real threat in terms of how employers perceive the transition, as well as their employees' autonomy," he said. "People are naturally resistant to change; they don't have the time and luxury of making large-scale transitions when it comes to the workforce. However, the reality we've seen with our clients is that an exchange platform gives employers the opportunity to configure an entirely different benefit program, with options and choices for their employees who are well equipped to make these decisions given the right guidance."

"The good brokers can work through all the objections and present the value," said Harkins. "The greatest ones who have delivered private exchanges successfully to their clients were able to alleviate those fears and create a new vision." But not all brokers are as forward thinking.

> "The greatest [brokers] who have delivered private exchanges successfully to their clients were able to alleviate [employers'] fears and create a new vision."
> —Rob Harkins

9. The information in this section is based on a personal interview with Rob Harkins, Mid-market Private Exchange Practice Leader for Willis Towers Watson, May 10, 2016.

10. Liazon, "Liazon's 2017 Employee Survey Report: Health Care Consumerism in a Marketplace Environment", March 2017 http://liazon.hs-sites.com/liazon/employeesurvey-1.

The industry knows about private exchanges, Harkins believes, but there is a huge resistance among many brokers due to the fear of the technology minimizing their role. In terms of a straight product focus, the broker's knowledge base and skills in product design may become minimized. This fear is causing some brokers to hesitate because they're focused on what it means for *them*. But they're missing the real opportunity. The most forward-thinking brokers recognize that they have a major role in the emerging benefits economy, provided that they are willing to change.

The Changing Role of Brokers

Willis's exchange proposition gradually shifted the company's focus. "Yesterday's role was focused on placing business with carriers, finding the best pricing and plan designs, helping employers figure out how to minimize cost," Harkins said. It was all about how to set up contribution strategies to support client concerns around cost, as inflation was a given. Today, price inflation is still a focus, but there are other concerns as well—most notably how to engage employees as their population changes.

Harkins pointed out that brokers need to understand that as the workforce changes, their role needs to change, too:

> Millennials created challenges for delivering benefits, as they are the most digitally savvy employees and are now the largest percentage of the workforce. This demographic expects sophisticated, digital access to their benefits, as well as the ability to choose them based on their unique needs. Give them anything less and they won't hesitate to move on to your competition. Providing a modern benefits platform that aligns with what they are seeing in just about every other aspect of their lives is crucial to attracting and retaining them.

How Can Brokers Win?

Varying plan designs and types of offerings becomes even more important because of the demographic realities. "Choice is the very framework of private exchanges," Harkins said, "and we have this tool that already recognizes that benefits are no longer a one-size-fits-all model. Individual desires need to be reflected in individual considerations, and private exchanges are the vehicle for delivering this to clients who are trying to address the realities of today's employee marketplace." Brokers now have to pitch employers on the

> "Individual desires need to be reflected in individual considerations, and private exchanges are the vehicle for delivering this to clients..."
>
> —Rob Harkins

benefits of the exchanges to their employees as *individuals*, Harkins said (see Figure 7.2). Among these benefits are the following:

- The ability to provide better health outcomes because employees are using the appropriate services for their needs.

- Tools to help guide employees based on their individual needs.

- Cost transparency of services. For example, price transparency tools such as Healthcare Bluebook allow employees to compare the costs of MRI and other services at different providers [see Chapter 8, "Innovation in Benefits (Yes, Benefits")]. This is very congruent with the way people are shopping online today.

What are the advantages of a private exchange?

Employers:

• Cost control and predictability

• Streamlined administration

• More value for benefits dollars

• End-to-end customer support

• Attract and retain talent

Employees:

• Empowerment to select the right
  benefits for their needs

• Expanded choice of plans and products

• Better understanding of how to
  choose and use benefits

• Comprehensive coverage for
  better protection

Figure 7.2 *The Advantages of a Private Exchange.*

The broker's role continues to evolve to meet these changing circumstances, said Harkins. "The broker can't set up a prepackaged model for private exchanges and walk away. The broker must navigate employer concerns using technology as a tool—just as employees use technology today." Brokers who come from a property and casualty background are seeing cross-selling opportunities. "We see the two coming together in the mid-market," said Harkins. "We are constantly thinking about how to engage that side of our business to see the value in private exchanges."

The Role of HR

HR personnel share many of the same fears and concerns as brokers. However, private exchanges can have a very positive impact on the primary goal of HR, which is hiring and retaining high-quality employees. HR staffers play a smaller role in benefits administration in an exchange environment. "With the exchange providing a high level of service, HR can wean itself from employees who expect HR staffers to have the answers. HR will not have to do all the administrative work and instead can focus on strategic human resources responsibilities, including developing corporate culture, communicating with employees, and being a value-added partner to the business," Harkins said. Findings from a survey conducted by Willis Towers Watson back up Harkins's assertions: The survey found that 56% of employers who use an exchange believe that exchanges improve their employee value proposition or total rewards strategy, compared to 18% who don't use an exchange. In addition, 56% of employers who use an exchange believe that exchanges ease their administrative burden, compared to 44% who don't use an exchange.[11]

> "[With a private exchange] HR will not have to do all the administrative work and instead can focus on strategic human resources responsibilities..."
>
> —Rob Harkins

It is likely that HR staffers involved in the transition will ultimately end up with useful benefits data leading to a new role for HR in analyzing and using this data. The benefits team can understand what employees are doing with the money that has been allocated to them and whether they are getting value from it. Ultimately, this can substantiate the value of the exchanges to employers in serving their employees.

"The exchanges' offerings don't automatically mean a loss of HR positions," Harkins stated. "Instead, this department should embrace the change management opportunity and refocus its work on activities that can help grow their companies."

Technology Is the Future of Benefits

Harkins is optimistic about the future of brokers working with private exchanges because of the opportunities afforded by technology. "The future is integrating benefits with the smartphone," he said. "It is not just about enrollment; the technology will evolve to a mobile environment—a single-source highway system to deliver all components—things like 401(k) and other wellness components could be prebuilt into this platform." Offering other types of insurance with one-stop pricing/group

---

11. Willis Towers Watson, "2017 Emerging Trends in Health Care Survey," May 19, 2017 https://www.willistowerswatson.com/en/insights/2017/05/insights-from-the-2017-emerging-trends-in-health-care-survey.data, URL.

discounts will provide greater value and help employees feel more connected to their employers. And they'll be easier to deliver at a much lower cost, Harkins believes, "because it's built into the structure—it's just not there yet, but it's coming. It's the next logical thing for the industry."

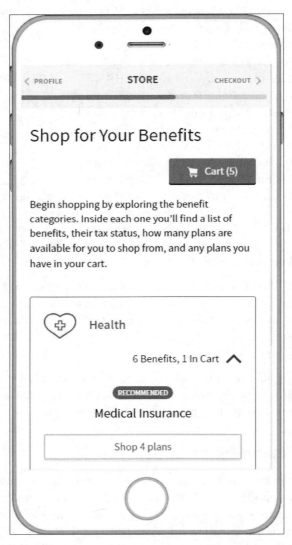

Shopping for Benefits on a Liazon Exchange via a Mobile Device

According to Harkins, the exchange model fosters engagement and involvement among employees so they are active participants. Now people might go to a physician or a hospital without really being engaged in the process. However, the first step of a private exchange is involving the individual in an electronic conversation around what is the best benefits package. Previously, when the employer chose the plans, employees selected either a middle-of-the-road plan or a high-end plan. With exchanges, engagement lets the individual think about nuances such as accident benefits or hospital coverage to fill in the gaps in many of today's medical plans.

"We make our decisions based on research. That's the way we engage today. That model has transitioned into the private exchange and benefits world. It is a vehicle of simplicity of communication so people can become more intelligent consumers," Harkins said. "Technology has changed how we engage; now part of what had been a cumbersome process is much simpler. We need a true set of standards around a new industry that is embracing the future, not the past," he added.

Harkins concedes that insurance is a very slow-moving industry:

> We need to move away from an industry that has been driven by "broker-consultant" to one where there is energy created around the private exchange concept. We need to move into the recognition that we're talking about a better way of doing benefits as an industry. The reality is that technology has changed around us, and the industry has to catch up. We shouldn't compete on plan design but on capabilities and service. This is generally true around any new industry. We need to embrace the future, not get stuck in the past.

> "We need to move into the recognition that we're talking about a better way of doing benefits as an industry."
>
> —Rob Harkins

There's a large portion of the insurance industry that's saying technology isn't here; not only is it here, but it's a better way of doing things and we need to move forward.

Summary

The role of the broker is indeed changing, thanks in part to a shift toward more employee-centered benefits and technology. The most successful brokers see the changes as a step forward for their clients, themselves, and the industry overall.

Brokers aren't the only ones who need to see the changes that are occurring and figure out ways to adapt. Insurers also have to brush up their game if they want to stay competitive in today's changing benefits landscape. Chapter 8, "Insurers Find a Way to Move Product" explains why some insurers are seeing the current landscape as one ripe for innovation.

8

Insurers Find a New Way to Move Product

The passage of the Affordable Care Act (ACA) in 2010 along with the resulting transformation in the health care industry created many challenges for health insurers in the United States. Already confronting rising costs, insurers needed to find innovative ways to retain existing clients and also grow their business portfolios because the public exchanges would dramatically change how people purchased their health coverage. For carriers of medical plans, in particular, pricing and merchandising policies in the public exchanges weren't anything like what they'd experienced in the past. In fact, as every insurer knew all too well, their companies were usually the first consumers would blame for the costs and inaccessibility of their coverage.

U.S. News

Aetna's Exit From Obamacare Constricts Insurance Choices

Rural counties are i   threat of only one
– or no – health in

health insurance .org

About **Blog** Exchanges FAQs Glossary Medicaid Obamacare Repeal & Replace States

Your carrier's leaving the exchange. What now?
Some health carriers have announced plans to exit the marketplaces.
Where will policyholders will be affected? and what are their options?

CNN Money

If three of the nation's largest insurers can't make it on the
Obamacare exchanges, can anyone?

That's the question hanging over President Obama's signature health reform law less than three
months before enrollment begins for 2017.

Some in the industry felt maligned or misunderstood. They were targets of many politicians, but that was unfair because carriers primarily sold to HR and finance executives and brokers; they were mostly focused on the business-to-business sector in a highly regulated industry with enormous price pressures. Outside government programs like Medicare and Medicaid, health insurers had not answered to individual consumers since the days of vertical managed care. The ACA effectively created a market of tens of millions of individual consumers that challenged insurers to design plans that would be attractive to them.

Exacerbating the problem was that health insurers generally had a poor reputation among consumers, and the rollout of the ACA didn't help. A 2016 poll by Kaiser found that health care was among the top issues, along with the economy and immigration, Americans would like to see addressed by the incoming president and his administration in 2017. Sixty-seven percent of those surveyed said lowering the amount individuals pay for health care should be a "top priority."[1] Furthermore, in terms of satisfaction, health insurers placed at the bottom of the list, below the U.S. Postal Service and airlines, according to the American Customer Satisfaction Index for 2016, which interviews about 70,000 consumers annually to get their views on a wide range of consumer goods and services (see Figure 8.1).[2]

ACSI: Lower 12 Industries

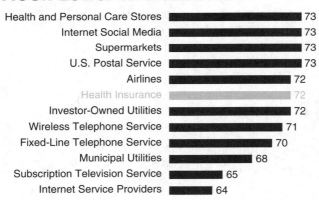

Figure 8.1 *American Customer Satisfaction Index: Lower 12 Industries.*

1. Ashley Kirzinger et al., "Kaiser Health Tracking Poll: Health Care Priorities for 2017," Kaiser Family Foundation, January 6, 2017, http://kff.org/health-costs/poll-finding/kaiser-health-tracking-poll-health-care-priorities-for-2017/.

2. American Customer Satisfaction Index, "National Sector and Industry Results," November 2016 as appeared in the blog post, "Health Insurers Doing a Better Job at Basics," December 21, 2016 https://acsimatters.com/2016/12/21/health-insurers-doing-a-better-job-at-basics.

In the health care industry in 2016, several proposed mergers of large corporations included the union of Aetna and Humana and the combination of Cigna and Anthem. Proponents said that consumers would benefit from these mergers because they would lead to more choices in health insurance at lower costs. The companies involved said the positive impact of the mergers would include sharing of best practices, research, and technology; stronger bargaining power with hospitals, doctors, and drug manufacturers; and greater company diversification. In February 2017, however, the Aetna/Humana merger was shot down due to the likelihood that it would substantially lessen competition, primarily around the market for Medicare, and the Anthem/Cigna deal was blocked due to its likelihood to decrease competition and lead to higher prices. Antitrust advocates agreed that the public would be better served if these large entities competed independently to provide services.

Furthermore, innovation is typically the first casualty of cost-cutting and restructuring moves, a concern for direct-to-consumer initiatives. Before any final approval is granted, regulators will conduct a careful review of coverage from each company in specific regions to see whether the merger would actually reduce competition rather than expand it. If the regulators feel there would be less competition after a merger, then adjustments to the merger proposals would have to be made. In addition, with a projected national health spending increase of 5.8% per year between 2015 and 2025, according to the Centers for Medicare & Medicaid Services,[3] higher costs could offset any marginal benefits gained through these mergers.

The Private Exchange: A Bridge to the Future?

Credit: INDECraft/DigitalVision Vectors/Getty Images

---

3. U.S. Centers for Medicare & Medicaid Services, "National Health Expenditure Data," 2016. www.cms.gov/research-statistics-data-and-systems/statistics-trends-and-reports/nationalhealthexpenddata/nhe-fact-sheet.html.

Private exchanges mixed new incentives, new threats, and new opportunities into this challenging environment for insurers. By partnering with various exchanges, carriers could offer a range of insurance options to meet employee needs and wants. However, aligning with an exchange required inventive and even alien approaches for insurers.

> By partnering with various exchanges, carriers could offer a range of insurance options to meet employee needs and wants.

Before the establishment of both public and private exchanges, most employers provided a limited number of options for medical coverage, and employees chose the plans with little guidance. Human resources staff would occasionally receive complaints from employees, but there was little direct contact between the insurers and the employees during the selection and enrollment process. The development of private exchanges altered this dynamic. Suddenly, insurers could provide coverage options to benefits consumers who had a much wider range of choices, sometimes from more than one insurer.

The challenge for the insurance companies is to design products that appeal to multiple consumers. Before exchanges, insurance companies rarely had to create products to offer directly to consumers who had varying needs. At most, the insurers had to worry about satisfying their employee customers to the extent that the workers wouldn't complain to their HR departments. As a result, most insurance companies shifted their focus to pricing in order to make plans seem more attractive, potentially at the expense of network size, and tilting the cost-sharing burden more toward the consumer. Now some insurers are realizing that wasn't a smart strategy. If you have a choice, do you want to be the cheapest or the best? Over the long run, you want to be the best.

Exchanges offer insurers a paradigm shift: They can sell their products to the people who use them. Consider this analogy: If the dominant economic model for decades was to have employers make mass purchasing decisions about the clothes their employees wore, the types of clothes people would purchase would be vastly different than if people were making those decisions themselves. Today, instead of designing products that companies agree to offer, more and more insurers can design products that people actually *want to buy*. The innovators who adapt to a consumer-focused business strategy will be rewarded. But as in any other struggle to adapt during profound upheaval, not every dinosaur will survive.

> Today, instead of designing products that companies agree to offer, more and more insurers can design products that people actually *want to buy*.

OSCAR'S APPROACH TO FIXING HEALTH CARE

As consumerism and e-commerce become increasingly dominant, the economic environment over the next decade may be a great opportunity for new entrants, like Oscar, that can win market share. Oscar was founded in 2012 by venture capitalist Josh Kushner, entrepreneur Mario Schlosser, and former Microsoft employee Kevin Nazemi. It caught the eye of venture capitalists. Oscar "is a rare example of a health insurance company with the valuation of a hot Internet startup," *Fast Company* noted in 2016. "It has 125,000 members in four states, and is valued at a massive $1.75 billion (a report from *Fortune* in January 2016 speculates that the valuation is closer to $3 billion). By contrast, much larger rival insurer Health Net, with 6 million members, was valued at its sale at $6.8 billion."[4]

Banner ad from Oscar when it began offering insurance to individuals in 2014. Copyright 2017,
Oscar. Banner image reprinted with permission from Oscar. All rights reserved.

Oscar's core customer base originated in New York City and nine counties in New Jersey, and the company now sells individual plans in New York, Texas, and California. The industry is very interested in the success of Oscar's consumer experience and its ability to simplify health care decision making. At Liazon, we know a thing or two about decision support technology, and we love what Oscar is doing with its user experience in this area. Consumer-friendly graphics compare provider costs, experience, and qualifications. Accessing customer medical history is as easy as accessing Amazon.com

4. Christina Farr, "Warning: Trying to Disrupt Health Insurance May Cause Headaches," January 26, 2016. www.fastcompany.com/3055700/warning-trying-to-disrupt-health-insurance-may-cause-headaches.

order history. Oscar makes board-certified doctors available by phone any-time, to give medical advice and even send common prescriptions to local pharmacies.

Some of Oscar's appeal is attributable to its marketing approach. From catchy, casual, and hip advertisements to an easy-to-navigate website, the company is clearly positioned as a consumer-friendly approach to health care. A short animated video on the company website emphasizes the ease of signing up for the plan and the access to medical professionals 24/7.

The video essentially walks visitors through the steps to finding help from the company. On the website, users can type in a symptom or problem, search for a doctor (either a specialist or primary care physician), and then speak to a physician on the phone via a free telemedicine call known as "Doctor on Call." Consumers can also use the site to make appointments to see a doctor in their network or send photographs of symptoms (such as an arm with a rash) to a doctor. Members can search for a physician by location, experience, and price and can make an appointment request on the website; Oscar sends a follow-up email within 30 minutes.

Oscar's new "concierge teams" include registered nurses who can help members find a doctor, understand their benefits, and save money. Members can also earn points toward Amazon gift cards by reaching certain goals, such as walking a particular number of steps in a day. All health-related activity—from doctors' visits to prescriptions to follow-up calls—are tracked for easy access.

Oscar's long-term future depends greatly on the company's ability to manage costs while keeping its premiums competitive with those of other plans sold on and off the public exchanges. Larger insurers scaled for millions of customers of different types are better able to absorb the costs of chronic disease that account for more than three-quarters of hospitalization and other costs among insureds.

Oscar has now broken into the group market by selling plans for small businesses in New York, with plans to expand to other markets in the works. As of November 2017, Oscar expects to offer health plans co-branded with the Cleveland Clinic, a world-renowned, patient-centered integrated health system, to residents of northeastern Ohio. Mario Schlosser posted on the company blog in June 2017:

> "The new Cleveland Clinic | Oscar health plans will bring us both closer to our vision of what better healthcare looks like. We believe that strengthening the quality of care and access to it requires a relentless focus on the member/patient. By linking a member engagement platform to a first-rate health system, we can deliver a seamless, unified health care experience—one that can improve health outcomes, lower costs, and make it easier than ever for the member to navigate the system..."

Shortly after announcing the deal with Cleveland Clinic, Oscar lined up a similar agreement with the Kentucky-based insurer, Humana. The new partnership will focus on providing commercial health insurance to small businesses, with a focus on personalized care, beginning with a test market in Nashville.

When it comes to innovation in health insurance, Oscar is one to watch.

Insurers that can adapt and offer a range of products will benefit from participating in private exchanges. A number of companies, including UnitedHealthcare, MetLife, Oxford, Horizon, and Blue Cross Blue Shield in Florida, Michigan, and Texas, have been redesigning their offerings. These insurers have the advantage of market share and name recognition, but in the past, adapting to change in the insurance industry for medical providers has been challenging and slow. Companies offering nonmedical benefits such as life and disability insurance, or complementary services such as identity theft protection, already have a strong direct-to-consumer orientation and are flourishing in the exchange environment.

> Insurers that can adapt and offer a range of products will benefit from participating in private exchanges.

Some insurers have been putting their names on their own exchanges, but I tend to advise against this practice. All the signs point to the future being dominated by multi-carrier exchanges, not a large constellation of smaller branded insurer exchanges where choice is limited. Insurers should be devoting resources to making products better rather than spending money on distribution, which is a drain on resources. The product needs to be better and available wherever people shop. That's a lesson the book publishing industry took too long to understand when it came to Amazon.com, for example. (See the sidebar "What Is Needed for Carrier Exchanges to Really Take Off?" in Chapter 4, "Making Sense of Benefits Solutions: Public Exchanges and Private Exchanges.")

What Insurers Can Gain from Private Exchanges

Yes, the enactment of the ACA had a significant impact on consumers, human resources administrators, and insurance brokers. Equally important was the impact on insurance companies, though that has not been as widely discussed as rate hikes and announcements of pullouts from the public exchanges due to uncertainty in the legislative environment.

Private exchanges give insurers far more freedom to innovate and expand into new markets, while gaining a deeper understanding of their end customers' concerns, choices, and cost sensitivities. Over the long term, the advantages to insurers can be substantial, provided that the companies embrace the opportunities offered to them through the store concept.

In order for insurers to get the most from the marketplace concept, they need to manage their businesses in new ways. As Liazon cofounder and former CEO Ashok Subramanian has said, these companies must modify aspects of their day-to-day operations. "They need to interact with brokers differently and change how they develop products. How they think about plan design and underwriting will be changed," explained Subramanian. "It's a bit of a hybrid. You have to cater to individuals who are buying your products, but you also have to cater to employers because they are involved in the servicing and keep much of the responsibility in terms of sponsorship."[5]

> "[Insurers] have to cater to individuals who are buying your products, but you also have to cater to employers...
>
> —*Ashok Subramanian*

> ...insurers entering the private exchange arena have to offer the products people want, or they're going to quickly lose market share.

Based on results of surveys of people who signed up for the public exchanges, according to Subramanian, consumers are willing to trade off the dollars they have to spend on insurance for some of those modifications in provider access. Some 40% of people are opting for a narrow network option, when given the choice of one.[6] As a result, insurers entering the private exchange arena have to offer the products people want, or they're going to quickly lose market share. (Figure 8.2 provides a breakdown of products that are offered on Liazon exchanges.)

Traditional health insurers have dealt primarily with employers and have had no direct interaction with individual consumers. On the other hand, nonmedical, or ancillary, providers such as MetLife have had experience selling to individuals because of their nonmedical products, such as auto, home, and life policies. Their experience in the direct-to-consumer market explains in part why these companies have been more involved with private exchanges than other insurers that only offer health coverage.

---

5. Personal interview with Ashok Subramanian, November 24, 2015.

6. The Commonwealth Fund, "Americans' Experience with ACA Marketplace Coverage: Affordability and Provider Network Satisfaction," February–April 2016 http://www.commonwealthfund.org/publications/issue-briefs/2016/jul/affordability-and-network-satisfaction.

Product Offerings on Liazon Exchanges, 2017

Percentage of companies offering a product category

Product category	% of companies offering product
Medical Insurance	100.0
Vision Insurance	97.7
Dental Insurance	96.4
Health Savings Account	95.6
Employee Life Insurance*	87.0
Child Life Insurance*	86.3
Spouse Life Insurance*	86.3
Legal Plans	70.5
Identity Theft Protection	67.9
Short Term Disability*	66.8
Accident Insurance	66.6
Critical Illness Insurance	62.4
Long Term Disability*	61.4
Pet Insurance	54.4
Medical Flexible Spending Account	48.7
Telemedicine	44.3
Dependent Care Flexible Spending Account	44.0
Health Coaching	36.0
Hospital Indemnity Insurance	24.9
Auto/Home Insurance	21.0
Spouse Critical Illness Insurance	13.5
Child Critical Illness Insurance	9.1
Transit Flexible Spending Account	6.5
Parking Flexible Spending Account	4.9

Source: Private Exchange Research Council (PERC) analysis, 2017. Based on groups enrolling in benefits on Liazon
exchanges with a benefits effective date of January 1, 2017. www.percinsights.com
Sample: Data representative of all firms in the study sample.
*Excludes employer-paid products.

Figure 8.2 *Product Offerings on Liazon Private Exchanges, 2017.*

Forward-thinking insurers operating in the exchange arena should view their involvement as a growth strategy that allows them to expand their business, increase their branding, and heighten consumer satisfaction of their services. Participating in a private exchange can benefit an insurer in several ways:

- **Improved enrollment technologies**—Employers and insurers are looking for administrative relief in the wake of the ACA's requirements. Private exchanges can simplify plan enrollment, with the development of user-friendly signup programs along with clear communication among employers, insurers, and employees. Rob Harkins, the mid-market practice leader for private exchanges at Willis Towers Watson, remarked, "Private exchanges can give employers a sense of control and stability. Their employees also want easier-to-use enrollment and tracking interfaces, including mobile apps. Private exchanges are modernizing technology to meet the changing workforce and benefits needs of people."[7]

> "Private exchanges are modernizing technology to meet the changing workforce and benefits needs of people."
> —*Rob Harkins*

- **Increased support for employees**—From getting their questions answered during open enrollment to better education on products and access to online educational resources or one-to-one support, employees better understand their benefits and are more engaged in the process of using them. (Eighty-three percent of employees who use Liazon exchanges better understand what their insurance and other benefits cover and 85% are more engaged in their health care decisions, according to Liazon's 2017 survey of employees.[8]) This, in turn, can lead to employees forming longer-term relationships with insurers, even after they transition to new employers.

- **Broader-based offerings focused on overall protection**—This coverage would go beyond health and dental to include financial, legal, auto, and other types of nonmedical policies. Recent data from the Private Exchange Research Council (PERC) shows that consumers are spending more on these types of products. For example, purchases of legal plans, hospital indemnity, and critical illness insurance each more than doubled from 2013 to 2017 on Liazon exchanges.[9]

---

7. Personal interview with Rob Harkins, May 10, 2016.

8. Liazon, "Liazon's 2017 Employee Survey Report: Health Care Consumerism in a Marketplace Environment," March 2017 http://liazon.hs-sites.com/liazon/employeesurvey-1.

9. Private Exchange Research Council (PERC) analysis, 2017, www.percinsights.com. Information here based on groups enrolling in benefits on Liazon exchanges with a benefits effective date of January 1, 2017. Based on employees who purchased at least one product in 2014–2017.

- **Expansion into other valuable services**—Given the uncertainty about health care costs in the future, the proposed taxes on employers, and increasing administrative burdens, insurers and their exchange partners can share data easily and use it to expand into other valuable services. For example, numerous studies point to telemedicine and other mobile uses being of particular interest to the Millennial demographic, which will continue to be a powerful and important consumer market. Additionally, MetLife began offering pre-paid legal services for the first time to their small business employers in 2017, in recognition of the expanded wants of their employees. Increased access to secure data for both insurers and employers will ensure more of these needs are identified so they can be met by developing and offering new products and services. Not only will the data show whether employees are making smarter choices on physician visits, drug purchases, and reduced spending, they will empower insurers to provide them more effective support.

For insurers, selling through private exchanges provides an opportunity to experiment. Somewhat analogous to the experience in an app store, insurers can offer a range of options, from traditional medical insurance to pet insurance and telemedicine, and they can evaluate which products are most valued by employees. According to Ashok Subramanian, "We're trying to array as broad a set of merchandise as possible to help people make good decisions and maximize their dollars; it may make more sense for someone to buy a high-deductible or narrow network plan and pair that with telemedicine; that small buy-up is probably a lot more cost-effective for them than buying a richer plan."[10]

Insurers have found that two-thirds or more of second-year users on a private exchange stay in the same plan or choose one that's very similar in the second year, indicating that they're satisfied with the plan's coverage. Research from Liazon's own data pool backs this up, as do industry sources such as the Kaiser Family Foundation, which found that 77% of employees in their first year on an exchange chose a health plan that was different than what they had previously; however, in their second year, this percentage decreased to 30%.[11] Similarly, Aon reported that 68% of employees change plans in their first year on an exchange but only 19% do so in the second year.[12]

10. Personal interview with Ashok Subramanian, November 24, 2015.

11. Alex Alvarado et al., "Examining Private Exchanges in the Employer-Sponsored Market," Kaiser Family Foundation, September 23, 2014, http://kff.org/private-insurance/report/examining-private-exchanges-in-the-employer-sponsored-insurance-market/.

12. Aon 2013 and 2014 press releases, as reported in Alex Alvarado et al., "Examining Private Exchanges in the Employer-Sponsored Market," Kaiser Family Foundation, September 23, 2014, http://kff.org/private-insurance/report/examining-private-exchanges-in-the-employer-sponsored-insurance-market/.

Dr. Vidya Raman-Tangella wrote a *MedCity* column on consumerism and health care insurers. In it she mentioned the importance of "various mobile applications, including Health4Me for iPhone and Android devices, which put crucial health and plan information, and decision support, at consumers' fingertips, including the ability to comparison shop for health care services based on both quality and cost." [13] Raman-Tangella cited a UnitedHealthcare study which showed that price transparency services, which can include quality information in addition to cost estimates, "enabled people to more frequently select quality health care providers across all specialties, including primary care physicians (7% more likely) and orthopedists (9% more likely)." [14]

Innovators Embrace Private Exchanges Early On

Throughout my career, I've learned a lot from a number of insurance executives in the vanguard of the industry's mega-shift to consumerism. The following sections provide two examples of innovators who "got" the exchange concept early on.

Jessica Moser, MetLife [15]

MetLife started focusing on private exchanges about three years ago but began collaborating with Liazon nearly a decade ago. "We decided that the Liazon exchange was ahead of its time in terms of innovation as well as delivering products and services. We recognized that this channel was expanding, and our leadership team believed it was worthwhile to have a dedicated group focused on it," said Jessica Moser, vice president, Regional & Small Market Business Strategy at MetLife.

---

13. Vidya Raman-Tangella, "The Three Pillars of Engaging Healthcare Consumers for Health Insurance Companies," *MedCity News*, January 15, 2016.

14. UnitedHealthcare, "Study: People Using myHealthcare Cost Estimator Are More Likely to Select High-Quality Physicians," September 16, 2014, www.stage-app.uhc.com/news-room/2014-news-release-archive/cost-estimator-leads-to-quality-physicians.

15. The information in this section is based on a personal interview with Jessical Moser, vice president, Regional & Small Market Business Strategy at MetLife, June 21, 2016 and citations from "MetLife's 15th Annual Employee Benefits Trend Study," April 3, 2017, https://benefittrends.metlife.com/media/1382/2017-ebts-report_0320_exp0518_v2.pdf.

Customer feedback about buying insurance influenced MetLife's strategy regarding private exchanges. Moser explained, "Private exchanges are a channel through which we can easily offer a broad portfolio." According to Moser, the exchanges offer organizational efficiency, particularly in regional markets serving smaller to midsize employers. MetLife's alliance with Liazon is especially effective, she believes, because of the Liazon salesforce's dedicated knowledge of the insurer's offerings.

"At MetLife, we believe offering employee benefits solutions through third parties enhances our portfolio. Our partnerships are another way to meet employer needs, including choice, true decision support, simplification of benefits administration, and easy access to enrollment technology," Moser said. The more guidance employees receive, the better benefits selections they make. Furthermore, through an exchange, employers provide employees access to a range of benefits they might otherwise not receive, including critical illness, accident, hospital indemnity, and group legal benefits. According to MetLife's 15th Annual U.S. Employee Benefit Trends Study, more than half of employees want an employer to provide a wider array of nonmedical benefits. Private exchanges are a perfect way to get there."

As to the role of employers in today's benefits environment, Moser said, "Now more than ever, employers need to know their employees and consider their benefit needs as individuals, rather than one homogenous group. For example, there are more single women in the workforce than ever. There is a variety of lifestyles among the general working population that needs to be accounted for." This variety is creating a new reality for employers—one that goes beyond typical demographic breakdowns. MetLife's 15th Annual U.S. Employee Benefits Trends Study found that employees identify their needs across a broad spectrum of interests; for example, 58% of employees want customized benefit options based on their personal information, 47% want their company to adjust benefits communications to incorporate same-sex partners, and 43% of employees expect to postpone their retirement due to their financial situation. As a result, Moser said, "Employees want their benefits to reflect their changing lives, and respond to the diversity of their needs. Addressing this range of needs will be a big responsibility for employers."

> Now more than ever, employers need to know their employees and consider them as individuals, rather than one homogenous group.
>
> —*Jessica Moser*

Moser sees the future benefits landscape as one ripe with opportunity for new products. "I think we'll be seeing more attention being paid to helping alleviate employee concerns—everything from gym memberships to paternity leave," she said. "Forty-nine percent of employees are concerned, anxious, or fearful about their current financial wellbeing, and they are increasingly looking to their employers for financial guidance and planning support. As employees will generally be in the workforce longer, more emphasis will be placed on financial planning by different life stages." Additionally, adding more offerings and giving employees the ability to customize their own benefits has been shown to drive employee loyalty and satisfaction, helping employers to meet their top benefit objectives.

"As the volume on private exchanges grows, we will continue to improve the experience. It's all about the consumerization of ancillary benefits and different ways to talk to customers," Moser said.

Kevin Hill, Oxford Health Plans/UnitedHealthcare[16]

From 1999 through 2004, Kevin Hill was the Executive VP of Sales, Products and Pricing, for Oxford Health Plans' $5.5 billion business, reporting to the company CEO. Upon Oxford's sale in 2004 to United Healthcare (UHC), Kevin was named CEO of United's Northeast Division and was with UHC until 2006. Now an advisor to several VC-backed companies, including pre-acquisition Liazon, Hill has been involved in start-ups and innovations in the health care landscape for many years.

At Oxford, Hill was involved in creating IDEA (Interactive Design and Electronic Administration), an automated renewal system aimed at simplifying and reducing the cost of renewals. Hill explained the thinking behind the program: "What can we do to take stress and hassle out of renewing? We wanted to increase our retention rate. We sent out a letter with the current plan and pricing and options. With a simple check of a box, the renewal was done. It made a tough decision easier and simpler." Hill said the broker and the employer were given a simple tool to toggle price and benefits designs. "The goal was for employers to say 'the rate goes to X, and I get it. No need to shop around.' We wanted to minimize the comparison shopping process."

"Liazon has been a pioneer in setting a course for the future when the brokers will be saying 'here is your exchange platform, and we can put any product we want on this exchange.' The issue will be what is the best technological platform with the best price and range of choice," said Hill. The underlying platform may be more important than the actual insurance company.

> "The underlying platform may be more important than the actual insurance company."
>
> —*Kevin Hill*

---

16. The information in this section is based on a personal interview with Kevin Hill, former EVP, Oxford Health Plans, June 8, 2016.

According to Hill, many insurance companies haven't examined the consumer experience or focused on the small business employers. The evolution of the health care business has revolved around dealing with brokers or large employers, so insurers have never before had to put themselves in the mindset of individual consumers. "If you focus too much attention on brokers, then your engagement with consumers is hindered," said Hill. In his view, the sales and marketing staff at Oxford engaged with individuals far more than the staff at other companies did.

Hill contends that health insurance needs more transparency. (See Figure 8.3 for an example of a price transparency tool for consumers.) While there is dynamic pricing in other businesses, such as sporting events, the same doesn't exist in health care. "Why can't someone do a Google search for the cost of a particular surgery in Oklahoma City? Technology allows for the communication of this information. Why would transparency work for every consumer decision except health care?"

> "Why can't someone do a Google search for the cost of a particular surgery in Oklahoma City? Technology allows for the communication of this information."
>
> —Kevin Hill

Much of the innovation around private exchanges came from financing and choices about the purchasing decision, but these changes don't address underlying health care costs, noted Hill. The providers and insurers need to unleash more innovation around major medical costs: "Small businesses can do cool things around virtual, telemedicine, and price transparency, but they need to be embedded in health insurance, or they won't make a big difference."

There are other opportunities with technology, Hill believes. Insurers could send text notifications to patients if their records have been accessed or text about other programs and offerings that would be useful to members. "The engagement has to be mobile. Marriott, Hertz, and every other company sends you alerts via phone," he said.

Hill believes the trend of consumers buying a higher-deductible plan and making smarter decisions when given a range of choices will continue. "Employers have to rally around the concept, but not everyone will get their arms around it if it is viewed as being a pain in the neck. Obstructionists are often the brokers because they want higher health care costs, so their commissions go up. They don't want to have to explain things," said Hill. "The employer has to believe in choice for the consumer," he added.

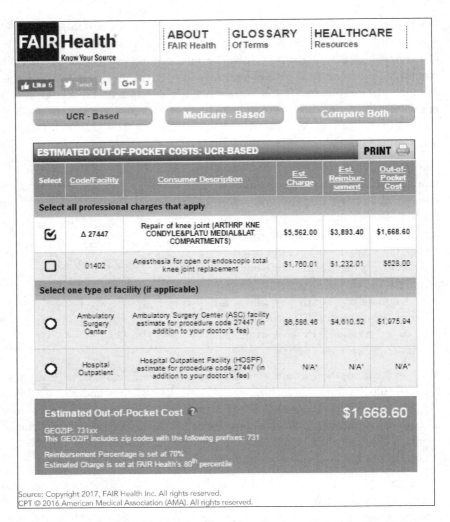

Figure 8.3 *Example of a Price Transparency Tool for Consumers (for illustrative purposes only).*

Insurers Aren't the Only Ones Innovating

Private exchanges broaden the definition of what it means to have full protection, and that means insurers aren't the only ones that can stock their merchandise in benefit stores. By enabling a mechanism for new types of products that protect your wallet, in addition to traditional insurance products that protect your house, your car, and even your life, new entrants are finding that exchanges help them move products, too.

For example, one new benefit employees have been clamoring for recently is identity theft protection. According to a 2016 article in *Employee Benefit News*, "concerned employees are seeking protection as an employer perk more than ever"[17] due to the alarming rise in data breaches pervading the headlines in recent years. The good news is that the government is taking notice, and the IRS now allows employer-provided identity theft protection benefits on a pre-tax basis, despite the absence of a data breach, whereas previously the tax code allowed these benefits only in the event of a demonstrated breach and only for individuals for whom personal information may have been compromised. This action has alleviated concern among many employers that were interested in offering the benefit but hesitant due to the impact on employee income taxes. Thus, the popularity of identity theft protection has grown and is expected to grow further in coming years, underscoring the idea that insurance and benefits exist to provide peace of mind to employees more than anything else.

> ...the popularity of identity theft protection has grown... underscoring the idea that...benefits exist to provide peace of mind to employees more than anything else.

Identity Theft Protection

The numbers back up this assertion: On Liazon exchanges, employee purchases of identity theft protection rose by 60% from 2014 to 2017, a classic example of "if you build it, they will come" in terms of benefit offerings. Another welcome addition? Protection for Fido. Pet insurance has been a perennial favorite on Liazon exchanges, seeing a comparable rise in employee purchases over this same four-year period. [18]

---

17. Melissa A. Winn, "Regulatory Clarity Makes ID Protection a More Attractive Employee Benefit," January 20, 2016, www.employeebenefitadviser.com/news/regulatory-clarity-makes-id-protection-a-more-attractive-employee-benefit.

18. Private Exchange Research Council (PERC) analysis, 2017, www.percinsights.com. Information here based on groups enrolling in benefits on Liazon exchanges with a benefits effective date of January 1, 2017.

Photo: akindo/DigitalVision Vectors/Getty Images

Summary

The continued expansion of private exchanges offers opportunities for insurance carriers to increase their customer pools by marketing their wares directly to employees who are choosing the types of insurance they need and want. It also opens the doors for a host of providers of nontraditional coverage options, such as identity theft protection, along with legal plans, pet insurance, telemedicine, and more. As traditional carriers and these other innovative manufacturers establish ongoing relationships with a rising crop of savvy benefits consumers, they'll become more adept at delivering the customer experiences that build loyalty. And we'll be looking to incorporate more diverse products on Liazon exchanges, some of which may not have even been thought of yet. That's the beauty of the exchange model.

Part III, "Future Vision," takes a look at some other innovations that can be enabled when technology meets consumerism in the benefits space.

Part III

Future Vision

9

Innovation in Benefits (Yes, Benefits)

Innovation has come at the health care industry in many forms during the past decade. Start-ups and major health providers partnered around innovations in data analysis of patient risk and behavior, wellness monitoring, and consumer satisfaction. Hospital and health care institutions sought out venture funds, developed new products, and formed partnerships in health and wellness. For example, Seattle's mega not-for-profit chain Providence Health & Services, through its investment arm Providence Ventures, invested in Sqord, a children's wearables company committed to increasing childhood exercise. Providence worked with community partners in five states to roll out Sqord's technology in health and wellness programs.[1] It also partnered with Binary Fountain, a social intelligence start-up that provides near-real-time monitoring of online patient experience reviews, ratings, and social media content.[2] The University of Pittsburgh Medical Center partnered with a Silicon Valley start-up to create technology that helped health systems measure and manage risk for populations of patients.[3] And, in a major partnership with Regeneron Pharmaceuticals Inc., Geisinger Health System began collecting genetics data from its patients (who had given consent) to develop new ways to prevent, diagnose and treat medical conditions before they cause harm.[4]

1. St. John's Health Center, Providence Health & Services, "ProvidenceHealth & Services Provides Kids with Fitness Technology; Challenges Them to Increase Activity, Improve Health," January 7, 2016, http://california.providence.org/saint-johns/news/2016/01/providence-ventures-in-fitness-technology-startup/.

2. Binary Fountain, "Providence Health & Services Partners with Binary Fountain," December 9, 2014. www.binaryfountain.com/providence-health-services-partners-with-binary-fountain/.

3. Lola Butcher, "Investing in Innovation to Disrupt Health Care's Status Quo," *Hospitals & Health Networks*, September 15, 2015, www.hhnmag.com/articles/3214-investing-in-innovation-to-disrupt-health-cares-status-quo.

4. Regeneron, "Regeneron and Geisinger Health System Announce Major Human Genetics Research Collaboration," January 13, 2014, http://investor.regeneron.com/releasedetail.cfm?ReleaseID=818844.

The venture firm Bessemer sees "a massive market opportunity for entrepreneurs and venture capitalists to pursue"[5] in health care and has identified nearly 200 companies that are leading the way based on the following groupings: technology infrastructure, payment models, disease management, and care models

The venture firm Bessemer sees "a massive market opportunity for entrepreneurs and venture capitalists to pursue"...

(see Figure 9.1). It seems like there is a new language sprouting up just to deal with this burgeoning field, as exemplified by new companies with one-word names such as ZeOmega, Fibrolast, joyable, livongo, and Avizia.

The growing interest of venture capitalists in investing in health care stems from the rapidly changing industry and its enormous economic footprint. "Health care is at a historic inflection point. No size institution is unaffected. As the paradigms shift, we believe innovation is going to be the margin of interest," said Thomas J. Graham, chief innovation officer at The Cleveland Clinic, at a 2014 *U.S. News & World Report* conference on the growing role of venture capital in the health care market.[6]

Graham's growth forecast is holding up. With consumers wanting more information and choices about their health care as well as control over their benefits, start-ups as well as expanded offerings from current companies are cropping up. In fact, entrepreneurs have created nearly 100 companies focused on consumer-driven innovations in the fields of telemedicine, education, model innovation, process improvement, and wellness. They're entering a wearables

"We are incredibly excited to use iPhone, iPad, and Apple Watch to create ... personalized technology solutions that will transform the health and wellness experience for our members."

—*Mark Bertolini*

space already known to Apple with its Apple Watch. In September 2016, for example, Aetna announced a major initiative to integrate Apple Watches into its analytics-based wellness and care management programs. It not only made the data-collecting watch available to some of its large employers and individual members during open enrollment season, it also gave the watch free to its own nearly 50,000 employees, who participated in the company's wellness reimbursement program. "We are incredibly excited to use iPhone, iPad, and Apple Watch to create simple, intuitive,

5. Stephen Kraus et al., "Fee-for-Value Drives Trillion-Dollar Healthcare Opportunity," May 9, 2016, www.bvp.com/blog/fee-value-drives-trillion-dollar-healthcare-opportunity.

6. U.S. News and World Report, "Venture Capitalists Make Inroads Into Health System," October 8, 2014, https://www.usnews.com/news/articles/2014/10/08/venture-capitalists-make-inroads-into-health-system?int=news-rec.

and personalized technology solutions that will transform the health and wellness experience for our members,"[7] Aetna chairman and CEO Mark Bertolini said in a statement at the time. The Apple Watch gives consumers tools such as medication reminders; integration with Apple Wallet to allow consumers to check their

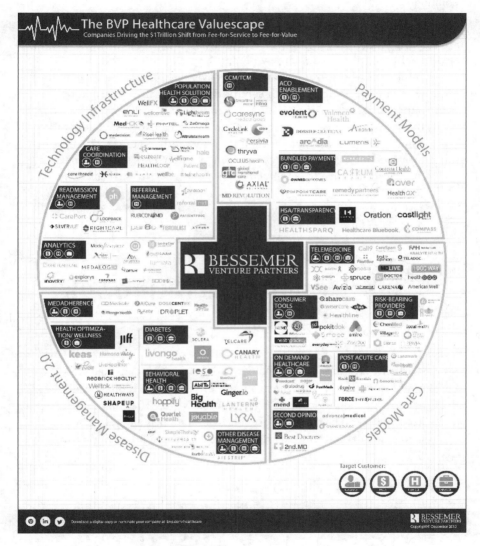

Figure 9.1 *Companies Leading the Health Care Sector.*

---

7. Aetna, "Aetna to Transform Members' Consumer Health Experience Using iPhone, iPad, and Apple Watch, September 26, 2016, https://news.aetna.com/news-releases/aetna-to-transform-members-consumer-health-experience-using-iphone-ipad-and-apple-watch/.

deductible and pay a bill; personalized health plans; messaging and decision support; and information on medical events such as a new diagnosis.

Apple is one of the most widely touted companies to make inroads into the health tech race. The following are among the throng of companies also offering inventive solutions:

- **Healthcare Bluebook**—With more financial responsibility steadily being placed on consumers for health care services, price, and quality of care remain largely hidden from patients, as well as the employers who sponsor their health coverage. Healthcare Bluebook was founded to bring health care pricing and quality information out of the shadows for patients and employers. Healthcare Bluebook's purpose is to protect patients by exposing the truth and empowering choice, two tenets Liazon fervently embraces. Healthcare Bluebook's transparency solution gives patients the information they need to move from *purchasers* of health care to real *consumers*. This solution makes it easy to compare providers, see how the prices and quality of procedures vary, and choose the providers that offer the best value.

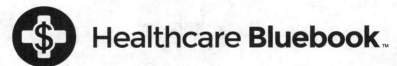

- **RedBrick Health**—The technology and services company RedBrick Health, founded in 2006, offers a range of services, including health assessment, biometric screening, phone and virtual coaching, and a health tracker. The company uses behavioral models along with technology to help consumers easily and efficiently monitor and improve their health.

- **HealthPatch and Fitbit**—HealthPatch, Fitbit, and other wearable technologies are part of a $14 billion market that is expected to reach

$34 billion by 2020.[8] These devices help individuals monitor their physical activity as well as specific health conditions such as diabetes.

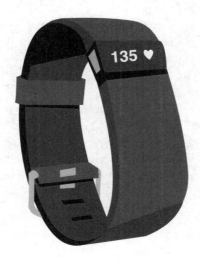

- **Castlight**—Debuting in 2008, the health benefits platform Castlight enables users to compare doctors and medical facilities based on quality of care and cost. In addition, users can easily access and track their annual medical spending, including deductibles, from all their physicians and medical providers. Employers using the platform are better able to evaluate their benefits plans and communicate with their employees about benefits. In April 2017, Castlight completed its acquisition of Jiff, a platform that organizes and curates vendors and incentivizes employees to use the solutions to create more value through a comprehensive experience that drives employee engagement and reduces administrative burden for employers.

8. Paul Lamkin, "Wearable Tech Market to Be Worth $34 Billion by 2020," *Forbes*, February 17, 2016, www.forbes.com/sites/paullamkin/2016/02/17/wearable-tech-market-to-be-worth-34-billion-by-2020/#2f3b16b03fe3.

These companies and many others are leading the way in improving many outdated health care systems and processes, while also uncovering long-term solutions to the failures of legacy benefit approaches for consumers. They're making significant inroads into what matters to the most powerful change makers in our society.

> [These companies are] making significant inroads into what matters to the most powerful change makers in our society.

People want more than efficient ways for institutions to monitor and measure their behavior, however. They want a health care experience to match their involvement with Amazon, where they can find a product, see the reviews, and easily place an order. "Anything that helps health care follow that same model will surely prosper," said venture capital investor and health care industry consultant Lisa Suennen.[9]

We're still only at the beginning of the sea change. The future of health care and benefits can be much more dynamic for consumers, employers, insurers, and practitioners. Private exchanges are one way employees can get the support they need to make informed decisions regarding new entrants. They increase engagement with benefits products, so what better way to introduce new platforms and services? They lead to improvements in health insurance costs and transparency. Exchange technology can harness the Internet's resources, smart navigation, decision support, and advanced e-commerce tools to become a daily dashboard for personal and financial well-being. (This might be a good time to review the seven principles for creating an optimal benefits store in Chapter 1, "Building a Better Benefits System," to see how this all works.)

Private exchanges are designed to integrate with game-changing innovations that will improve people's lives now and in the future. The following dramatic advances in benefits and health care are on the next frontier for private exchanges:

- Expanding the concept of a benefits store to give consumers the freedom to view and manage more of their entire health and wealth portfolio

- Letting individuals research and make a range of health service and benefits purchases, including the design of their own health networks, directly and without intermediaries

- Merging group and individual marketplaces for insurance to create a free market so consumers can purchase their own coverage

The following sections explain these three potential mega-trends in consumer-driven innovation enabled by private exchanges.

---

9. Lisa Suennen, "Ante Up! Where I'd Place My Healthcare Bets," November 17, 2014, http://venture-valkyrie.com/ante-up-where-id-place-my-healthcare-bets/.

Expanding the Aisles in the Benefits Store

Consider purchasing insurance as being analogous to shopping in a grocery store. A single aisle includes medical insurance, and other aisles have vision and dental coverage. However, employee benefits such as health, disability, and life insurance should not be viewed narrowly under the lens of "health coverage." They should be considered financial well-being tools. Health insurance helps preserve financial stability when doctor bills roll in. (Health insurance doesn't cure you, health care does; insurance lets you pay for your medical costs without negatively impacting your finances.) Disability coverage helps pay the bills if work income is not available due to illness or injury. Life insurance makes sure loved ones are provided for financially in the event of tragic circumstances.

Consequently, you should think of health insurance in the context of your overall financial decision making, which includes your investment goals, planning for retirement, estate planning, and more. Sound financial planning requires that you consider all relevant factors, based on your specific goals, family situation, investment targets, and other considerations. You may consult an advisor about investing in the stock market, but any reputable investment advisor will need to know your retirement strategy and your debt, as well as your other savings and investments. You can't make decisions about where to put your money in a vacuum; you need to consider the complete financial picture and how one decision may affect other areas.

The same principle applies to your health coverage: The amount of money you put into your health savings account should be part of your overall financial decision making, including how much to contribute to your 401(k), your child's 529 plan, and other investments. When you're shopping in one aisle, you need to consider what you're buying in the other aisles and how all your purchases fit together for your

> When you're shopping in one aisle, you need to consider what you're buying in the other aisles and how all your purchases fit together for your financial well-being.

financial well-being. You should get financial analysis or advice—perhaps one day using artificial intelligence—on how one move integrates with your other money decisions. Liazon's decision support systems are among those that are already sophisticated enough to perform these types of functions.

Following this approach allows portfolios to expand, practically without limits. Money that would otherwise be used to purchase a critical illness policy might be better off split between an investment account and long-term disability coverage. For example, an employee may not want to put $300 toward a critical illness policy if he or she hasn't maxed out contributions to their 401(k) account. Each individual needs to consider—based on their particular circumstances—whether it is better to buy a certain type of coverage or put the money into a retirement account. The answer may depend on tax implications, as well as their risk tolerance, retirement goals, and health concerns. These decisions need to be considered together; one cannot choose health or any coverage without first understanding his or her goals and what impact a medical crisis would have on their financial stability. One person may want to put more money into their investments instead of paying for any nonmedical insurance, while their more risk-averse colleague in the next office may want to do the opposite.

A viable benefits marketplace needs to be able to expand to accommodate these overarching decisions. Employees need to manage their global financial well-being in one place. Imagine having one financial management dashboard that includes health, dental, life, identity theft protec-

> Exchanges can help people manage asset allocation in ways they've never before considered...

tion, legal plans, and other products. Unfortunately, today people still think about coverage in silos, which is a mistake. Exchanges break down these silos so people can manage all of their financial life. Benefits stores are not simply about health care. They are about managing your financial life. For example, dental insurance may only cost an individual $350 a year, but there are typically caps on the maximum amounts that will be paid for treatments; therefore, someone might prefer to pay for a discounted dental service when it's needed and put the rest of the funds he or she would have spent on dental insurance toward repaying a student loan. Exchanges can help people manage asset allocation in ways they've never before considered, especially as aisles continue to expand with new offerings.

Letting Individuals Create Their Own Preferred Networks

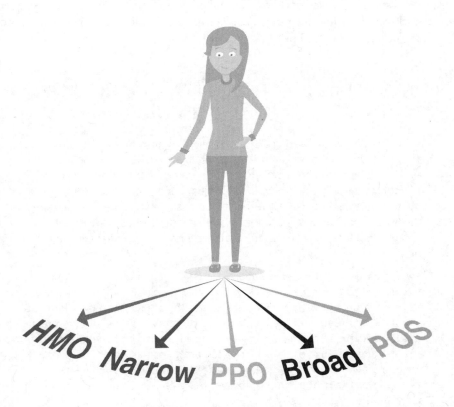

Create Your Own Network

Another area of consumer-driven innovation lies in individuals creating their own networks of providers and facilities. Until recently, the health care industry focused on creating larger networks to serve vast numbers of consumers.

However, given that many people see only one or two doctors a year, why not create a preferred network that includes the local doctors and specialists you want to see, based in the community where you live? The trend of coordinating health care systems between hospitals and group practices is evident in CareMount Medical Practice in Upstate New York, which has 500 doctors in 40 locations, as well as Accountable Care Organizations (ACO), which unite a group of doctors, hospitals and other systems in administering value-based care with financial incentives based on patient outcomes, as opposed to fee-for-service systems. Using only one medical group or ACO has the potential to reduce costs and improves health outcomes. These early inroads bode well for an individual one day specifying the 20 or so doctors and facilities that he or she would like to have access to—a DIY health plan network, if you will.

Essentially, a person would be able to build a customized network, including a location, specific physicians, a hospital, and other preferences. Having such smaller networks would reduce the problem of lack of coordination in sharing data records among providers and facilities.

THE TORINUS EFFECT: PROVING THE VALUE OF COMPETITION[10]

A number of change-making CEOs and analysts have blazed an impressive track record in the move toward "value pricing," which is all about making health service providers compete on price and, yes, the value of service offered at a given price. Their accomplishments demonstrate how close we are to implementing point-of-service purchasing through benefits stores. They show that competition works in the benefits market, as with all other markets, and that individuals can be trusted with the power to make purchasing decisions.

I was pleased to interview a national pioneer in this effort: John Torinus, author of *The Company That Solved Health Care*, CEO of the Wisconsin based Serigraph, Inc., and consultant on health care reform. When Torinus's company was faced with bankruptcy because of soaring health care premiums in the early 2000s, he became a self-taught expert on benefits financing and instituted a range of consumer-driven practices that saved his company. Value pricing is a voluntary part of the health coverage this company offers its employees, and the option provides Serigraph and its employees with substantial savings annually.

---

10. This information in this section is based on a personal interview with John Torinus, CEO, Serigraph, September 12, 2016.

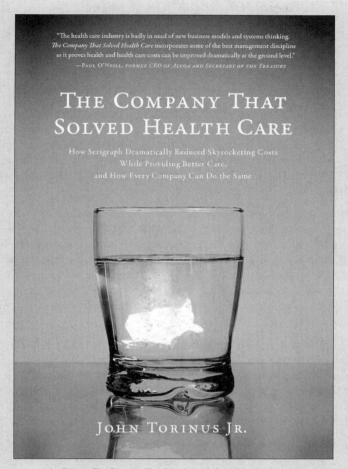

John Torinus, The Company That Solved Health Care: How Serigraph Dramatically Reduced
Sky-Rocketing Costs While Providing Better Care, and How Every Company Can Do the Same
(Dallas: BenBella Books, 2010). Cover reprinted with permission. All rights reserved.

Torinus and his team found that employees could pay 10 different prices
for the same procedure in the Milwaukee area alone, with fees for a procedure being as much as 300% to 400% higher at one provider compared to
another. Torinus knew that finding independent providers to perform procedures at a fixed price made sense. Thanks in part to this move, Serigraph has
saved some $7 million over the past few years in health care costs. Medicare
and CALpers, the state employee union of California, use a similar approach,
adopting flat rates for procedures.

Here's how the approach worked for a Serigraph engineer who needed a double knee replacement, as Torinus recounted it:

> Our employee waived his deductible and out-of-pocket expense, which is $6,500. He used a facility participating in the flat rate network where the company had negotiated a rate of $26,000 per knee.
>
> The patient had both knees replaced at the same time. So the cost was $52,000, compared to about $95,000 at other facilities. Serigraph ended up negotiating a lower price because the patient was under anesthesia only once so that brought the cost down to $39,000. The employee essentially paid nothing for the surgery and the company saved $49,500!

Setting up this type of coverage isn't too difficult. Benefits staffers look to providers that are rated well in a particular region. Serigraph uses infection rates of facilities as a way to gauge quality. In addition, some 21 states have a database of health care ratings that can also help select facilities for flat-rate pricing. Ideally, there should be two or three facilities available to give employees choice. These days, providers are actually approaching companies, saying they have a certain number of procedures that they will offer for a flat price.

"Our employees are pretty well educated. The best way to communicate is people talking. With the engineer talking about how much money he saved and how quickly he recovered from surgery, everyone in the company knew how happy he was with the surgery," said Torinus. "We're not shy about spreading the word; we have signs in the office; we tell stories in our newsletters," he added.

"I use my training as a Marine. You need to get people across the board engaged within your organization. You have to co-manage from the top down and the bottom up," stressed Torinus. He lets his employees know that if everyone works together and uses this arrangement, there won't be any increases in the medical coverage for the next year.

At Serigraph, this consumer-driven approach is embedded in the company culture. At monthly meetings with employees, health care coverage is discussed, and there are also free generic drug samples available. In addition, there is a nurse practitioner on site. This "primary care clinic" is a strategy that is increasingly being used throughout the country by school districts and companies. This type of clinic provides cost savings to both companies and individuals because the employee is able to see a nurse practitioner or a physician's assistant, who can order tests, recommend specialists when necessary, and write prescriptions.

"Although some employees were initially resistant about leaving their primary care physicians, they have gotten very comfortable using the primary care clinic. We do health assessments of every employee and his or her spouse so they get comfortable with the nurses and nurses' assistants. Two-thirds of our staff use this clinic. It is absolutely voluntary," said Torinus. More than 90% of employees who have diabetes now have their condition under control, largely because of the educative approach at the clinic, which includes monitoring, support, monthly check-ups and free insulin.

Creating a National Individual Insurance Market

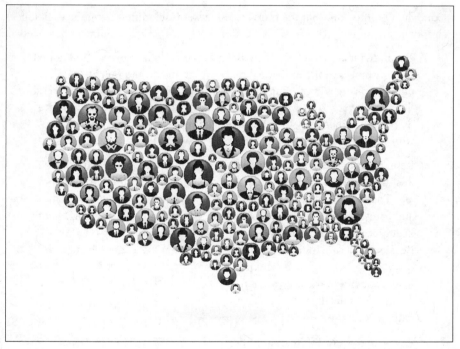

Credit: bubaone/DigitalVision Vectors/Getty Images

If we want to create a truly competitive, high-quality free market health insurance economy, then all individuals need to buy insurance for themselves. That's the third mega-trend—and it's a lot closer than many people think. As of this writing, many insurers have dropped out of the government exchanges, and other companies are eliminating coverage in certain states. Despite the best of intentions of the Affordable Care Act (ACA), the individual marketplace for insurance has sustained damage that must be repaired—or replaced with a bolder design. Chris Condeluci, who served as Tax Counsel to the U.S. Senate Finance Committee, where he participated in the development of portions of the ACA, explained in an interview:

> The drafters of the ACA recognized that the individual market was a dysfunctional market, and in an attempt to make that market functional, applied many of the rules and regulations applicable to group health plans to individual policies. For example, insurance companies are no longer permitted to underwrite individual insurance based on the health status of the policyholder. In addition, similar pre-existing condition protections are now imposed in *both* the individual and group markets. Again, these efforts were undertaken to essentially make the individual market look much like the group market.[11]

Condeluci pointed out that the individual market (including the public exchanges) simply hasn't moved in a positive direction, and the market remains unbalanced:

> The individual market is not evolving as the drafters expected and hoped. All consumers in the individual market both inside and outside of the public exchanges are feeling pain. Why would any employer want to send their employees to a dysfunctional market that generates daily headlines on premium increases, the pitfalls of narrow network plans, and plans with very high deductibles? The employer would take a huge PR hit.
>
> Remember that this individual insurance market as of 2016 comprised less than ten percent of the number of insurance policyholders nationally. That doesn't offer much incentive for carriers to live with the bumps and bruises of the long-game transition to a larger individual market with healthier risks. People ask: Why are major insurers dropping out? Answer: Because they can. In tandem with this trend, employers are reluctant to drop group coverage and send people with a stipend to the individual market. It's not a death spiral, but it's not a path to recovery either.[12]

The benefits store can become a superstore when more individuals have access to more options offering quality and choice.

However, if there were 150 to 175 million individuals purchasing their own coverage, these carriers would not be dropping out. Insurers need access to many more people who need coverage in order to survive and compete in the public exchange marketplace. As of 2016, insurers could access only a tiny corner of the overall benefits market, which is why so many companies have failed in their efforts on the public exchanges. A super-innovative company may be trying to attract enrollees in Cleveland, but with a potential market of only

---

11. Personal interview (and ongoing correspondence) with Chris Condeluci, November 15, 2016.

12. Ibid.

100,000 people, the company simply can't survive in that market. The benefits store can become a superstore when more individuals have access to more options offering quality and choice. Employers should be giving their employees money and letting them shop for their own coverage, without limiting the insurance options.

A MATTER OF POLICY

Private exchanges have already established a wealth of consumer and business field research on choice needed by policymakers in order to embrace the individual insurance market scenario. For example, employees who use private exchanges are very satisfied, according to a recent Liazon survey. Of those employees surveyed, 96% preferred to select their own benefits rather than have their employer choose them. In addition, 94% of the respondents said they are satisfied with their experience, and this number tends to increase with more time on the exchange. A year later, 92% said they were satisfied with the choices they had made one year earlier. In addition, 83% of employees said that they value their employer's contribution more than they did prior to the exchange experience.[13] Among employers, 70% said the exchange had helped them control costs, and 81% said they were glad they had made the move to an exchange.[14]

Further, from a policy perspective, the same regulations that are designed to protect consumers now can be transferred to the national individual market.

Chris Condeluci offered his perspective:

> Policymakers will run around asking themselves how are they going to regulate this national consumer-driven market. I suggest the answer they'll soon arrive at is this: they will be very similar to the insurance regulations we have today. No underwriting based on health status, rules relating to how premiums can be varied, the whole shebang of regulations that protect people in the group market such as HIPAA and COBRA.[15]

Congress took a major first step toward a national individual benefits market by passing a law that has found bipartisan support. The Small Business Healthcare Relief Act of 2015 (H.R. 2911 and S.1697), which later became part of the 21st Century Cures Act passed in December 2016, was

---

13. Liazon, "Health Care Consumerism in a Marketplace Environment," March 2017, http://liazon.hs-sites.com/liazon/employeesurvey-1.

14. Liazon, "Liazon's Employer and Employee Survey Results," October 2015, http://liazon.com/wp-content/uploads.php?link=Liazon-2015-Employer-Employee-Survey-Report1.pdf.

15. Personal interview (and ongoing correspondence) with Chris Condeluci, November 15, 2016.

enacted to roll back Treasury Department guidelines issued in conjunction with the Affordable Care Act (ACA) that prohibited the use of health reimbursement arrangements (HRAs) to purchase an individual market plan on a tax-free basis. Introduced by U.S. Senators Chuck Grassley (R-IA) and Heidi Heitkamp (D-ND), and Congressmen Charles W. Boustany, Jr., MD (R-LA) and Mike Thompson (D-CA), the law is aimed at allowing employers with fewer than 50 employees to give their employees a tax-free contribution through an HRA, which can be used to purchase an individual market plan on or off a public exchange. Importantly, the legislation does not allow an employee to "double-dip," meaning an employee cannot get both the tax-free employer contribution and a premium subsidy that is now offered under the ACA.

Calling for passage of this bill, R. Bruce Josten, executive vice president of the U.S. Chamber of Commerce, said in a letter supporting the legislation,

> This bill would give small employers the ability to provide money to their employees to pay for coverage or qualified medical expenses, while at the same time allowing employees the flexibility to choose the health care coverage that works best for them....This bill is an important first step in restoring flexibility to all businesses and their employees.[16]

Condeluci wrote in a 2016 newsletter:

> I support making the individual market one big marketplace. In other words, I believe that the on-exchange/off-exchange markets should go. A governmental entity—headed up by a Board which simply adds more red-tape—should not be in the business of operating an electronic enrollment platform. Private companies—with their innovative technology, decision support, and education tools—are better positioned to help consumers shop for a health plan. And, these private companies can simply be regulated by a State's Insurance Department (through the same office that currently regulates agents/brokers). As a result, we should modify the Exchange rules to allow private companies that meet specific requirements (and become certified) to serve as the distribution channel for all individual market plans. Insurance carriers can also continue to directly enroll consumers. Here, the premium subsidy would be available no matter where a consumer purchased a health plan.[17]

---

16. R. Bruce Joston, in a letter to The Honorable Charles Boustany and The Honorable Mike Thompson of the U.S. House of Representatives, July 7, 2015, https://www.uschamber.com/sites/default/files/150707_hr2911_smallbusinesshealthcarerelieftact_boustany_thompson.pdf.

17. Christopher Condeluci, "Policy & Regulatory Update," Week of August 29, 2016.

What a game-changing innovation this could be for Americans throughout the country! By eliminating group insurance and putting everyone into a national individual insurance pool where consumers could shop individually as they do for car insurance (and just about everything else), the incentives would encourage carriers to improve their products, lower deductibles, and give people better choices.

In the recent years of partisan warfare, it seems quaint to consider that such a disruptive shift as a national individual benefits market could come together with major elements that please both parties as well as industry and consumer groups. Add up the features:

- Access for all with subsidies intact
- Free market choice that trusts the consumer
- No watering down of regulations
- A new frontier of competition for insurance carriers to win customers
- Retention of tax preference
- Lifting of the benefits administration burden for corporations

Disruptive, indeed.

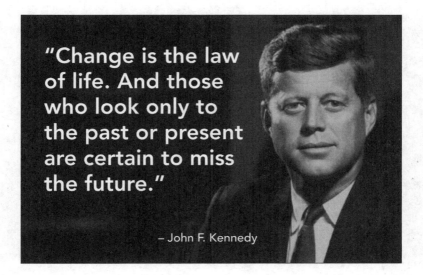

"Change is the law of life. And those who look only to the past or present are certain to miss the future."

– John F. Kennedy

Summary

From expanding the benefits store concept to include a virtually limitless product set, to influencing policymakers in Washington, innovation in benefits can take many forms. Sometimes it can take the U.S. democracy far too long to figure out the best way forward. But, in most cases, we do find that way when the people have a strong enough voice. As John Kennedy famously said, "Change is the law of life. And those who look only to the past or present are certain to miss the future."

The next two chapters dive more deeply into the current legislative environment, which is changing as these very words are being printed, as well as a future vision for benefits in this country.

10

The "Law of the Land," Insurance Tax Reform, and the November Surprise

The end of 2016 left hordes of pundits and political scientists to explain why thousands of polls turned out to be wrong on November 8, as President Donald J. Trump emerged victorious in the Electoral College while losing the popular vote to Hillary Clinton. The November elections and ensuing efforts to "repeal and replace" the Affordable Care Act (ACA) are not likely to dramatically affect group health plans and private exchanges "for the foreseeable future." Still, the success or failure of the ACA repeal-replace efforts deserves our interest, attention and focus.

The battle over the ACA and the role of government in working toward universal, quality health insurance took a dramatic turn in the early days of 2017, as President Trump vowed to dismantle President Obama's signature health care law as one of his first orders of business in the White House. Americans and their elected officials were grievously divided over the best course of action moving forward. The political emotions involved are not likely to subside before the ultimate fate of the ACA is decided, despite all attempts at its dismantling capped by the Senate's answer to the House-passed American Health Care Act (AHCA)—the Better Care Reconciliation Act (BCRA). As of this writing, Congress and the country are reeling from a prolonged process of partisan bickering a la "my bill is better than your bill." Depending on who you ask, the ACA, with all its flaws, looks pretty good in comparison to alternatives offered up by Speaker of the House Paul Ryan and Senate Majority Leader Mitch McConnell. This sentiment is underscored by this rare statement from former President Obama, who posted on Facebook on June 26, 2017, the day the BCRA was released:

The Senate bill, unveiled today, is not a health care bill. It's a massive transfer of wealth from middle-class and poor families to the richest people in America.[1]

Unfortunately, due to the politicization of health care, we may have lost sight of the point that every household needs financial protection against the extraordinary costs of getting the health care we and our families need. Every American wants affordable, quality health care. And these expectations affect anyone working in the benefits industry. The debates over health care spurred people to worry about the security of their benefits, thereby keeping public interest keen in the quality and viability of their own plans.

> The debates over health care spurred people to worry about the security of their benefits, thereby keeping public interest keen in the quality and viability of their own plans.

The continued focus on the future of "good" health insurance and other benefits will contribute to the ongoing success of private exchanges that has already been demonstrated in the thousand-plus workplaces that have implemented Liazon's marketplace technology. Exchanges have become a strong platform to deliver this financial protection to employees through their group health plan, through a variety of vehicles all working together.

---

1. Facebook post by former President Barack Obama, June 22, 2017, https://www.facebook.com/barackobama/posts/10154996557026749.

No matter how the Republican-led Congress and White House seek to improve, repeal, or replace the ACA, AHCA, BCRA, or any other "A" going forward, their actions will likely have little effect on private exchanges, which serve the employer-sponsored group market. Yes, the market for individual insurance could still change, with more power turned over to the individual states, as one likely possibility. But the ACA has always been primarily about providing protection for the uninsured and offering more comprehensive health coverage for those who don't have health insurance through an employer—through the individual market. None of the employers we have talked to expect a dramatic impact on their group health plans as a result of the policy wars in Washington that largely characterized the first six months of the Trump presidency.

> None of the employers we have talked to expect a dramatic impact on their group health plans as a result of the policy wars in Washington...

For example, some have suggested that the AHCA would have had a negative impact on employees because employers would add annual and lifetime limits to certain medical services that would no longer be considered one of the ACA's "essential health benefits" by a particular state. However, health care policy expert Chris Condeluci[2], who participated in the drafting of the Patient Protection and Affordable Care Act (PPACA), observed in his May 17, 2017 e-newsletter, "Employers offer health care coverage to employees to attract and retain talent. And based on this, there is a strong desire to offer more comprehensive benefits than what may be covered by

2. The thoughts and opinions of Chris Condeluci in this chapter are as a result of ongoing personal interviews and email correspondence obtained between November, 2016 and August, 2017.

an 'individual market' plan." As a result, Condeluci believes that it is highly unlikely that employers will shop around for a state that requires coverage for only a limited set of "essential health benefits," and in the end, employees will not be adversely affected. The Congressional Budget Office agreed in its May 24 cost estimate of the AHCA.[3]

How will we talk and think about affordability and access to health care in the years ahead? What are the potential contours of the policies, opportunities, and threats to innovation that will unfold? In this chapter, we turn to the views of Chris Condeluci and other trusted health care and legislative experts on what to watch for in the near term and the long term. Naturally, you should use these insights as useful filters through which to evaluate events as they happen. As the nation rediscovered on November 9, 2016 most political predictions are fools' gold.

> As the nation rediscovered on November 9, 2016 most political predictions are fools' gold.

"The Law of the Land...for the Foreseeable Future"

House Speaker Ryan brought a hiatus to the partisan bickering surrounding "repeal and replace" of the ACA when he withdrew his party's efforts to create a new health care bill on March 24, 2017. Just six weeks later, on May 4, 2017, the American Health Care Act (AHCA) resurfaced with some "revisions" (to the tune

---

3. Congressional Budget Office, H.R. 1628, American Health Care Act of 2017, May 24, 2017
   https://www.cbo.gov/publication/52752.

of $100 to $200 billion in savings) to pass in the House of Representatives by three votes. Most notably, the revised bill called for turning more power to individual states, as opposed to the federal government, in defining a minimum package of benefits that individual market health plans—including individual plans sold through the ACA exchanges—must cover. The states would receive more money ($130 billion over a decade), according to the proposed legislation, to help stabilize their insurance markets, including paying for "high risk" pools—a way to categorize individuals with preexisting conditions such that costs are lowered for healthier people.

CONGRESSIONAL BUDGET OFFICE
COST ESTIMATE

May 24, 2017

H.R. 1628
American Health Care Act of 2017

As passed by the House of Representatives on May 4, 2017

SUMMARY

The Congressional Budget Office and the staff of the Joint Committee on Taxation (JCT) have completed an estimate of the direct spending and revenue effects of H.R. 1628, the American Health Care Act of 2017, as passed by the House of Representatives. CBO and JCT estimate that enacting that version of H.R. 1628 would reduce the cumulative federal deficit over the 2017-2026 period by $119 billion. That amount is $32 billion less than the estimated net savings for the version of H.R. 1628 that was posted on the website of the House Committee on Rules on March 22, 2017, incorporating manager's amendments 4, 5, 24, and 25. (CBO issued a cost estimate for that earlier version of the legislation on March 23, 2017.)[1]

In comparison with the estimates for the previous version of the act, under the House-passed act, the number of people with health insurance would, by CBO and JCT's estimates, be slightly higher and average premiums for insurance purchased individually—that is, nongroup insurance—would be lower, in part because the insurance, on average, would pay for a smaller proportion of health care costs. In addition, the agencies expect that some people would use the tax credits authorized by the act to purchase policies that would not cover major medical risks and that are not counted as insurance in this cost estimate.

---

1.   Congressional Budget Office, cost estimate for H.R. 1628, the American Health Care Act, incorporating manager's amendments 4, 5, 24, and 25 (March 23, 2017), www.cbo.gov/publication/52516.

CBO cost estimate of House-passed bill to replace the ACA, "The American Health Care Act of 2017." The bill was later voted down by the Senate.

**CONGRESSIONAL BUDGET OFFICE
COST ESTIMATE**

June 26, 2017

H.R. 1628
Better Care Reconciliation Act of 2017

*An Amendment in the Nature of a Substitute [LYN17343]
as Posted on the Website of the Senate Committee on the Budget on June 26, 2017*

The Congressional Budget Office and the staff of the Joint Committee on Taxation (JCT) have completed an estimate of the direct spending and revenue effects of the Better Care Reconciliation Act of 2017, a Senate amendment in the nature of a substitute to H.R. 1628. CBO and JCT estimate that enacting this legislation would reduce the cumulative federal deficit over the 2017-2026 period by $321 billion. That amount is $202 billion more than the estimated net savings for the version of H.R. 1628 that was passed by the House of Representatives.

The Senate bill would increase the number of people who are uninsured by 22 million in 2026 relative to the number under current law, slightly fewer than the increase in the number of uninsured estimated for the House-passed legislation. By 2026, an estimated 49 million people would be uninsured, compared with 28 million who would lack insurance that year under current law.

Following the overview, this document provides details about the major provisions of this legislation, the estimated costs to the federal government, the basis for the estimate, and other related information, including a comparison with CBO's estimate for the House-passed act.

CBO cost estimate of Failed Senate bill to replace the ACA, "The Better Care Reconciliation Act of 2017."

When the bill made its way to the Senate for a vote, a group of 13 senators led by Senate Majority Leader Mitch McConnell met behind closed doors to draft a revised version of the so-called "reconciliation bill", called the Better Care Reconciliation Act (BCRA), which it released on June 22, 2017. In its Cost Estimate of June 26, 1017, the Congressional Budget Office said of the revised bill:

> The Senate bill would increase the number of people who are unin-
> sured by 22 million in 2026 relative to the number under current
> law [that is, the ACA], slightly fewer than the increase in the number
> of uninsured estimated for the House-passed legislation. By 2026,
> an estimated 49 million people would be uninsured, compared with
> 28 million who would lack insurance that year under current law.[4]

---

4. Congressional Budget Office Cost Estimate, H.R. 1628, Better Care Reconciliation Act of 2017, June 26, 2017, https://www.cbo.gov/system/files/115th-congress-2017-2018/costestimate/52849-hr1628senate.pdf.

In late 2016, I was pleased to interview John Barkett[5], the senior director of policy affairs for Willis Towers Watson about the aftereffects of the election. At that time, John discussed the election as a crossroads, one not necessarily offering safe passage for Republicans in the Congress and the White House. He rightfully observed that they must go down a path fraught with repercussions if they seek to undo the ACA:

> The only thing we know [as of December, 2016] is how much the Republicans don't know about what they'll do. Making health policy is filled with pitfalls. Whenever new laws are considered, they involve trade-offs. Some folks will be better off, and others will be worse off. In Washington, the ones who are worse off tend to be more vocal, and that gets politicians' attention. That's key to evaluating where this goes.

Fast-forward seven months, and still another revised bill was introduced by the Majority Leader on July 13, 2017. This 172-page piece of legislation was withdrawn four days later when four Republican Senators expressed their opposition to it, ensuring certain failure. In a last-ditch effort, the Republicans sought "a repeal of Obamacare with a two-year delay to provide for a stable transition period," otherwise known as repeal now, replace later, or "repeal and delay." The Majority Leader also acknowledged in the same statement, "Regretfully, it is now apparent that the effort to repeal and immediately replace the failure of Obamacare will not be successful."[6]

> "Regretfully, it is now apparent that the effort to repeal and immediately replace the failure of Obamacare will not be successful."
>
> —*Senate Majority Leader Mitch McConnell*

But McConnell and company were determined. In the early morning hours of July 28, yet another attempted bill, the so-called "skinny repeal bill," also lesser known as the Health Care Freedom Act, was voted down by a 49-51 tally, with the deciding "no" vote being attributed to Senator John McCain of Arizona. The bill would have repealed both the individual mandate (a penalty tax imposed on individuals who fail to obtain health insurance coverage) and the employer mandate (a penalty tax on employers with 50 or more full-time equivalent employees that fail to offer an affordable/minimum value plan).

---

5. The thoughts and opinions of John Barkett in this chapter are as a result of ongoing personal interviews and email correspondence obtained between November, 2016 and August, 2017.

6. The Honorable Mitch McConnell, Majority Leader United States Senate "McConnell Statement on Upcoming Vote to Repeal Obamacare," July 17, 2017, https://www.mcconnell.senate.gov/public/index.cfm/2017/7/mcconnell-statement-on-upcoming-vote-to-repeal-obamacare.

IN THE SENATE OF THE UNITED STATES—115th Cong., 1st Sess.

H. R. 1628

To provide for reconciliation pursuant to title II of the concurrent resolution on the budget for fiscal year 2017.

Referred to the Committee on _____ and ordered to be printed

Ordered to lie on the table and to be printed

AMENDMENT IN THE NATURE OF A SUBSTITUTE intended to be proposed by _____

Viz:

1   Strike all after the enacting clause and insert the fol-

2   lowing:

3   **SECTION 1. SHORT TITLE.**

4   This Act may be cited as the "Health Care Freedom

5   Act".

Failed Senate bill to replace the ACA, "The Health Care Freedom Act," aka the "skinny" bill. After the bill's rejection, the ACA remains the law of the land.

Majority Leader McConnell conceded on the Senate floor shortly after the vote:

> "I regret that our efforts were not enough at this time…We didn't achieve what we hoped to accomplish…We look forward to our colleagues on the other side suggesting what they have in mind. So now Mr. President, it is time to move on…"[7]

Chris Condeluci said of the week leading up to skinny bill repeal, "The past week has been the most unpredictable time period in the Senate that I have ever experienced. I checked in with many of my former Senate colleagues to see if they agreed. They agreed."

---

7. PBS News Hour footage as reported by The Hill, "McConnell: 'Time to Move On' After Health Care Defeat," July 28, 2017.

What can we expect next in the rousing debate over access to affordable health care? It's possible that Republicans and Democrats will come together in a rare show of unity, as Mr. McConnell suggested, and as Chris Condeluci said in his e-newsletter of July 10, 2017, "to 'save' the ACA's newly reformed individual markets." In that same e-newsletter, he also said "a strong argument can be made that there is a 'crisis' in the individual markets. And, Congress typically responds in a bipartisan way when there is a crisis."

Condeluci's words proved prescient, as it turned out a group of 40 Republicans and Democrats, collectively known as the "Problem Solvers Caucus," were working on a plan to "repair" the ACA, rather than repeal or replace it. This occurred throughout the last few weeks in July while McConnell and company were trying to get their (supposed) last ditch effort through. The latest approach, announced on July 31, 2017, focused on stabilizing the individual market and lowering premiums. Condeluci said that while enacting this type of bipartisan proposal may be hard-pressed to gain enough support, it is refreshing to see Republicans and Democrats attempting to come together to provide relief for individual market policyholders. A lot rests on whether the Trump Administration or Congress will fund the cost-sharing reduction subsidies for low-income ACA exchange policyholders, and to what extent. As of this writing, a resolution remains unclear.

But what does seem clear, according to Condeluci: "Because Republicans have failed to come to any sort of consensus up to this point, I do not believe there will be any repeal-replace legislation considered in the near future. That means that the ACA will remain the law of the land. That also means that it is back to business as usual from an operational and compliance perspective."

> "...the ACA will remain the law of the land...it is back to business as usual from an operational and compliance perspective."
>
> —Chris Condeluci

The Viability of the Individual Market

Why is the stability of the individual markets so important? According to John Barkett,

> The defined contribution model could be the future of health care. It relies on the individual health insurance market being a stable and viable marketplace—one that offers plans that employers would be happy to offer to their employees. And, for that to be the case, you need consumer protections in that marketplace that guarantee that all of your employees will get decent and affordable coverage.

> The Affordable Care Act took a major step in that direction by changing the rules of the individual market to ensure that anyone who applied for a health plan would be accepted, even if they had previously existing conditions. It includes other rules to ensure affordability of those products. If lawmakers degrade or turn back these standards, it makes the individual market much less appealing to employers.

Federal health law and policy expert Chris Condeluci agrees on the insurmountable task the Republicans took on:

> Republicans had the challenge of repealing enough of the ACA to pass muster with their base voters without at the same time blowing up people's benefits coverage or adding to the cost spiral. Whatever policies they ultimately would have passed (or still might) to replace the ACA would have fallen under the Pottery Barn Rule: if the GOP breaks health care, they'll have to own health care. And some may argue they already own it by virtue of winning the election. But just as many would argue that the Democrats own health care as well, as the original sponsors of the ACA.

> There is still going to be a lot of activity on this in the months and years ahead. Will it be comprehensive "repeal and replace"? Probably not. That is contingent, however, on whether congressional Republicans and Democrats can come together to improve the individual markets. It is also contingent on actions—or inaction—taken by HHS and the IRS. The big turning point will be whether the president and congressional Republicans will continue to fund the cost-sharing subsidies (money provided by the federal government to low-income individuals who obtain health insurance through the public exchanges), and to what extent. And one way to mitigate all of the damage that may flow from Washington, DC, is states taking the bull-by-the-horns and coming up with their own health reforms through what is known as a Section 1332 Waiver, which allows states to waive portions of the ACA, provided certain requirements are met.

Condeluci believes that in the near term, the new administration and Congress will have their hands full with other priorities and will avoid meddling with employer group insurance. "The private exchange industry's growth targets are in the group market, and not among individu-

> "Employers want to retain high-quality benefit packages because employees want and value this aspect of their compensation."
>
> —*Chris Condeluci*

als who are candidates for the public exchanges," he said. "Employers want to retain high-quality benefit packages because employees want and value this aspect of their compensation."

Despite claims made during the initial ACA debate, almost all employers who offer employees health benefits want to continue doing so well into the foreseeable future. The latest research from Willis Towers Watson points to more employers being "very confident" that they will be offering benefits 10 years from now (65% in 2017 compared to 54% in 2016, and nearly triple the lowest confidence level of 23% in 2012).[8] More employers are also considering health care benefits within a total reward context (43%) in order to attract and retain employees, and this number is expected to nearly double within two years. Few employers ever considered abandoning their benefits offerings and sending people to the public exchanges. The same research from 2016 found that only 6% of employers are considering offering a "skinny" or "minimal value" plan for 2018.[9]

What Else to Note on the Legislative Front

The following sections present some pending legislation that could have an impact on the employer-sponsored market.

8. Willis Towers Watson, "2017 22nd Annual Best Practices in Health Care Employer Survey," https://www.willistowerswatson.com/en/press/2017/08/us-employers-expect-health-care-costs-to-rise-in-2018.

9. Willis Towers Watson, "Full Report: 2016 21st Annual Best Practices in Health Care Employer Survey," www.willistowerswatson.com/en/insights/2017/01/full-report-2016-21st-annual-willis-towers-watson-best-practices-in-health-care-employer-survey.

The "Cadillac" of Taxes—And Other Pending Legislation

The "Cadillac tax" (the excise tax on high-cost group plans set to go into effect in 2020, despite all attempts by both the House and Senate-proposed bills to delay it) may no longer be an immediate topic of concern for employers as this book goes to print. However, experts agree there's a chance that another a similar policy—a cap on the tax exclusion that individual employees can take—could take its place. The point is to reduce the deficit by going "where the money is," whether it be via something like the Cadillac tax, a cap on the tax exclusion, or something else. Experts agree that this type of legislation will likely continue to be in play in future tax and health care reforms—not so much for deficit-reduction reasons but because policymakers in Washington believe that limiting the tax exclusion in some fashion will reduce health care spending. According to Chris Condeluci, "Many lawmakers believe that the open-ended tax preference for employer-sponsored insurance contributes to over-utilization of medical services, which raises health care costs for everyone. Limiting this tax preference—it is believed—will bend the proverbial cost curve downward."

While the ACA includes tax penalties for failure to comply with its individual and employer mandates (which require all individuals to have some form of health care coverage and all employers with more than 50 employees to provide it), proposed tax legislation tried with all its might to eliminate the tax penalties on one or both of these for noncompliance. As of this writing, it appears that the penalties are still in place with the Trump administration, just as they were under the Obama administration, despite all attempts of all versions the AHCA and BCRA, to, in effect, repeal the individual and employer mandate penalty taxes.

Another piece of legislation to watch in the saga of the ACA and its attempted replacements involves health savings accounts (HSAs). The original intent of the AHCA was to expand HSAs by increasing the maximum contribution limits for these accounts to match the level of out-of-pocket maximums (OOP max) defined for high-deductible health plans (HDHPs). "Attempted replacement legislation would have allowed consumers to rely on HSAs to help them pay for their out-of-pocket costs, like buying out the deductible of an HDHP," Condeluci said. The Senate's failed version of the bill as of July 13, included the ability for HSAs to also be applied to the payment of health insurance premiums, but this change was limited to individual market plans, *not* employer-sponsored plans.

The Medicare Marketplace as a Model

For many of us who would like to see a national infrastructure for an individual benefits market with tens of millions of participants, the success of federally approved private exchanges for Medicare recipients is encouraging.

John Barkett said:

> I think the interesting thing about Medicare as an individual marketplace is that it's had bipartisan support. Over the years whether Democrats or Republicans held the White House, the Senate or the House, we have passed laws that strengthened the Medicare individual marketplace. Because both parties worked together on improving that marketplace over time it became a viable place to get coverage that supplemented or replaced Medicare. Because the marketplace is fundamentally sound, thousands of employers have essentially said, "Let's allow our retirees to choose their own plan. Let's give our retirees access to health plans that are more competitively priced and offer benefits that are just as good as we are offering them." I don't think that's going to change. Future Congresses and future presidents don't want to disrupt that marketplace.

> "...thousands of employers have essentially said, "Let's allow our retirees to choose their own plan...I don't think that's going to change."
>
> —*John Barkett*

Chris Condeluci agrees:

> Both sides are proud of the reforms in Medicare and the moves toward value-based insurance designs and pricing. And, both sides want to keep Medicare solvent. For example, House Republicans have already pushed back the effective date of repeal of the Medicare payroll tax on high-income earners to 2023 (instead of 2017), which is a tax that is paid into the Medicare Trust Fund. Senate Republicans actually proposed to maintain this tax for the foreseeable future by dropping the Medicare payroll tax from the list of proposed ACA repeal items.

Small Businesses and Individual Benefits Marketplaces

The Small Business Healthcare Relief Act of 2015 (the so-called "HRA bill") passed as part of the 21st Century Cures Act, gives employers with fewer than 50 employees the ability to use health reimbursement arrangements (HRAs) to provide their employees with tax-free contributions to purchase individual market plans, either directly from insurers or through the public marketplaces. This is great news for the future of health care for all Americans as it means millions more employees can shop in individual benefits marketplaces with money provided to them by their employer. *Forbes* said the bill, tucked away in the 21st Century Cures Act, "past the billions spent on medical research, past the streamlined regulations for new drugs and medical devices, past the hoped-for improvements to mental health and substance abuse care, and past the changes in Medicare and Medicaid payments—is a gift to small business."[10]

"The politics of 2017 just about guarantee that we'll have the ability for small businesses to finance their employees' purchase of individual market plans on a tax-free basis," Condeluci said . The bipartisan bill introduced in 2015 by Reps. Boustany (R-LA) and Thompson (D-CA), and Sens. Grassley (R-IA) and Heitkamp (D-ND) had the votes to pass both chambers already in 2016. Now, Republicans may include even more employers in the bill's proposed tax-exemption by raising the lid on the size of the employers covered under the law.

> "The politics of 2017 just about guarantee that we'll have the ability for small businesses to finance their employees' purchase of individual market plans on a tax-free basis."
>
> —*Chris Condeluci*

---

10. Robb Mandelbaum, "New Law Eases Small Business Health Care Burden (but May Make Repealing ObamaCare Harder)," *Forbes*, December 14, 2016, www.forbes.com/sites/robbmandelbaum/2016/12/14/repealing-obamacare-just-got-harder-thanks-to-small-business-relief-in-21st-century-cures-act/#6a0111692e85.

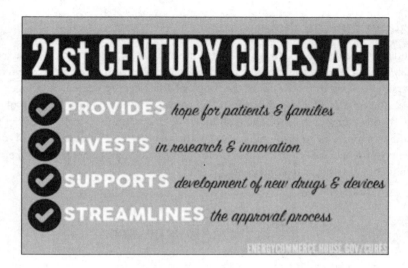

No one in Washington, DC, explains the bill's importance as well as Condeluci. Here's what he advised in late November 2016:

> Why is the HRA bill significant? First, it gives small employers the ability to act as the "financier" of their employees' health care coverage. As most know, a small employer will serve as the "financier" of health coverage by sponsoring a "group health plan." But, with the onset of the ACA's small group market insurance reforms, "small group" health plans experienced large premium increases.

> For many small employers, the premium increases are too great to bear, yet these employers still want to point to their "employer contribution" as an employee benefit to attract and retain talent. The HRA bill gives small employers the flexibility to essentially stay in the game as a "financier," while not being weighed down by the ever-increasing cost of sponsoring a group health plan.

> Second, the HRA bill may actually help out the individual market risk pool. How? In some industries, employees of small employers are on the younger, healthier side. Allowing these healthier risks to purchase an individual market plan with a tax-free employer contribution will likely improve the risk pool. In my opinion, such a change in the law would not have an adverse impact on the employer-based system.

Tweaking the Tax Code

I hope Congress seeks to study pro-consumer, market-oriented ideas that have circulated in the industry and media but not reached the legislative arena. I'd encourage policymakers to follow up on the proposal advanced by Regina Herzlinger, Barak Richman, and Richard Boxer in their *New York Times* opinion piece published on November 2, 2016. The authors wrote that a "minor tweak to our tax code could go a long way to bring more choice, affordability, and personal control to how workers purchase health insurance."[11] How? By having employers transfer their tax-favored benefits status to consumers.

The New York Times

The Opinion Pages | OP-ED CONTRIBUTORS

How Health Care Hurts Your Paycheck

By REGINA E. HERZLINGER, BARAK D. RICHMAN and
RICHARD J. BOXER   NOV. 2, 2016

If there is a coherent theme to this year's election, it is the growing economic frustration of working Americans. While trade has been the chief scapegoat, a major culprit has received much less attention: the rising cost of health insurance.

Recent news of large price increases for plans on the Affordable Care Act's insurance exchanges was the latest example of an unsustainable trend. But those exchanges sell insurance to only about 12 million individuals. Most people with private health insurance, about 150 million individuals, receive coverage through employers. And for those people, prices have been rising for years.

Under their plan, employers would give each employee a budget to purchase insurance but make part of that grant eligible as wages. Therefore, if an employee purchases insurance for a price under the agreed-upon budget ceiling, they keep the difference remaining (or some share of it) as tax-free wages. The authors wrote, "This slight change would turn the economic tables for the millions of Americans who get

---

11. Regina Herzlinger et al., "How Health Care Hurts Your Paycheck," *New York Times*, November 2, 2016. www.nytimes.com/2016/11/02/opinion/how-health-care-hurts-your-paycheck.html?_r=0.

health insurance through their employers. Abundant research has shown that low- and middle-income workers have a strong preference for low-cost plans, much more than what their employers currently offer." What's more, the authors go on to say, "If workers know they can increase take-home wages by purchasing less expensive insurance, they will demand more insurance options, and insurers are likely to respond."[12]

> "If workers know they can increase take-home wages by purchasing less expensive insurance, they will demand more insurance options, and insurers are likely to respond."
>
> —*Regina Herzlinger et al.*

Summary

As the country watches and awaits the ultimate fate of the ACA, and well into the future, we encourage progress on bipartisan efforts, including the House's 21st Century Cures Act, which will accelerate biomedical research in the development and approval of safe and effective drugs. We also support increasing funding to improve oversight of federal mental health programs and tackle the nation's opioid addiction crisis begun by the Comprehensive Addiction and Recovery Act, enacted with huge bipartisan support in 2016. Congress should continue to hear ideas about reducing prescription drug prices, finding more sensitive and sensible approaches for providing long-term care to the chronically ill, and advancing the use of remote technology so clinicians can deliver care to patients virtually, via telemedicine. Remote patient monitoring services can be cost-effective and can reduce stress for patients with chronic conditions. (Research from Willis Towers Watson indicates that 78% of companies of all sizes offer telemedicine services today, compared with only 11% in 2012, and this number could increase to as high as 94% by 2019.)[13]

As these and other legislative sessions continue to unfold throughout 2017 and beyond, the question of where the future will take us and the benefits industry will only become more pertinent to the work we do every day. But our role as industry innovators doesn't stop there. Next, we take a look at several components of one possible "future vision" for benefits and health care in this country.

---

12. Regina Herzlinger et al., "How Health Care Hurts Your Paycheck," *New York Times*, November 2, 2016. www.nytimes.com/2016/11/02/opinion/how-health-care-hurts-your-paycheck.html?_r=0.

13. Willis Towers Watson, "2017 22nd Annual Best Practices in Health Care Employer Survey," https://www.willistowerswatson.com/en/press/2017/08/us-employers-expect-health-care-costs-to-rise-in-2018.

11

Who's Afraid of the American Consumer?

In consideration of the "new health care landscape"—which may be more aptly called the "evolving health care landscape"—there has been a critical ingredient missing from the current debate in Washington: Why do we find it so hard to trust the consumer when it comes to health care decisions? Consumer involvement has impacted food and drug safety; led to fuel-efficient vehicles; ended product hazards such as flammable pajamas; stopped dolphin bycatch in the commercial tuna fishing industry; and called out entities from cable companies to the U.S. government on everything from rate hikes to travel bans. Anyone remember New Coke? Consumer behavior is powerful enough to impact how the world's favorite soft drink is made. Similarly, the consumer is driving innovation and change and will be an indispensable force in the future of health care and benefits.

> ...the consumer is driving innovation and change and will be an indispensable force in the future of health care and benefits.

John Barkett, the senior director of policy affairs for Willis Towers Watson, who worked on the drafting, passage, and implementation of the Patient Protection and Affordable Care Act (PPACA) as a staffer in Congress and in the Department of Health and Human Services, put it well:

> In the years to come—and we are well on the way there—I see exchanges driving insurers to become more consumer friendly. As exchange adoption grows, insurers will compete over how they treat their customer, not just their customer's employer. My belief is this will lead to some new thinking on the old frustrations that plague our health care system.

I also see the other groups that have been involved in health insurance purchasing, such as employers, becoming more consumer oriented themselves—for example, making more health consumerism tools available to employees and retirees. A key consideration for this consumerism sea change is the question: *If we all got to choose our own health insurance plan, would we all pick the same one? The answer is "Of course not!"*[1]

> *"If we all got to choose our own health insurance plan, would we all pick the same one? The answer is 'Of course not!'"*
>
> —*John Barkett*

Credit: Elina Viele-Pritzker

Consumer involvement in action: The Women's March on Chicago, January 21, 2017

I also applaud the leadership of global pioneers such as Dr. Don Berwick, the former head of the Centers for Medicare & Medicaid Services, who advocates tirelessly for consumer-driven practices and shifting power to the patient. Empowering people in benefits and health care must include the approaches detailed in this book for how we purchase benefits but must also extend through the entire cycle of experience in the health care system. In the United Kingdom, Denmark, India, some U.S. health care systems, and many other facilities worldwide,

---

1. Personal interview with John Barkett, November 18, 2016.

patients are being given more information, more tools, and more encouragement to become active partners in their own care. We were raised to be passive recipients of a doctor's care, but it doesn't have to be this way. Berwick said this to the December 2016 28th Annual Institute for Healthcare Improvement annual forum:

> I can fill out my tax returns. I can fly my craft. I can make terrific Italian meatballs. I can counsel my adult daughter on how to handle her son's new fears at school. I can finish the Saturday *New York Times* crossword puzzle. I can binge on three episodes of *Game of Thrones* while answering 50 emails at the same time. And then I show up at health care's dinner party and health care strips me. It silences me; it dresses me in a sheet; it takes away my work; it takes away my pleasures, my family; it tells me exactly what to do. "Take a breath, hold your breath." What if, instead, health care asked me what I can do, and thanked me for doing it? What if, instead, health care asked me if I would like to sit or stand? If I would like to speak or remain quiet? What if health care asked me for instructions, not doctor's orders, but people's orders?[2]

"...I show up at health care's dinner party and health care strips me...It silences me; ...it tells me exactly what to do."

—*Don Berwick*

We need to apply Berwick's perspective to the ways people manage the cost and utility of premiums and deductibles. Health plans must empower people to feel like they're spending their own money and help them figure out what matters to them so they don't buy any more insurance than they need—but no less than that either.

2. Marty Stempniak, "Don Berwick: 8 Ways to Shift the Power Back to Patients," *Hospitals and Health Networks*, December 9, 2016.

More recently, Dr. Elisabeth Rosenthal, editor-in-chief of Kaiser Health News, put the blame for America's crippled health care system squarely in the hands of for-profit entities like hospitals and pharmaceutical manufacturers in her book *An American Sickness: How Healthcare Became Big Business and How You Can Take It Back*. In it, she rightfully declares that the system stands to gain more from ongoing treatment than from curing disease. She offers a way out of this conundrum, resting with—you guessed it—consumers.

Rosenthal said in a 2017 interview with NPR, "We're not getting what we should get from a really competitive market where we, the consumers, are making those choices" (rather than drug makers, hospitals, or doctors setting prices on treatments and medicines). She urges patients to inquire about fees before accepting procedures, to make sure any referrals are in their network, and to ask any doctor who may appear at their bedside in a hospital to find out, "Who are you?" "Who called you?" and "Am I going to be billed for this?" Know what you're paying for, she cautions consumers, and never accept charges blindly without questioning whether they are valid or could be reduced.[3]

> "We're not getting what we should get from a really competitive market where we, the consumers, are making those choices."
>
> —Dr. Elisabeth Rosenthal

Some Potential Ways Forward

Looking ahead, it's up to us to embrace our jobs as leaders, experts, and innovators to make our benefits ecosystem work more harmoniously with consumer involvement. An ecosystem where doctors and providers carry out their healing missions with autonomy *and* accountability. An ecosystem where insurers do business profitably while improving their ability to service and communicate with consumers. An ecosystem where insurers and hospitals co-create common-sense pricing models (such as the recent example of Oscar and the Cleveland Clinic, see Chapter 8, "Insurers Find New Ways to Move Product"). An ecosystem where the best programmers and designers create tools that educate people in managing benefits as part of their overall financial portfolio.

> ...it's up to us to embrace our jobs as leaders, experts, and innovators to make our benefits ecosystem work more harmoniously with consumer involvement.

3. Terry Gross, "How U.S. Healthcare Became Big Business," *Fresh Air*, April 10, 2017, www.npr.org/sections/health-shots/2017/04/10/523005353/how-u-s-health-care-became-big-business.

The following are some of the promising policies and practices guiding us toward this future:

- Tax-protected savings accounts

- Employer funding for individual insurance

- Consumer-centric provider networks

- Data and digital tools for patients and consumers

- Patient-empowered healing

Tax-Protected Savings Accounts

The vast majority (96%) of employers using Liazon exchanges offer health savings accounts (HSAs), which are tax-protected vehicles for helping employees pay for their health care expenses.[4] (See more about HSAs, FSAs, and HRAs in Appendix B, "Making Sense of Benefits Terms.") The federal rules for these accounts can be improved, and their limits can be expanded, but as they stand today, they are foundational to most consumer-driven health care practices for good reason. The accounts orient users to the connection between health and wealth by encouraging actual savings and providing transparency into how benefits dollars are spent. If you have X dollars, then you need to decide how you will allocate those dollars, and by doing so, you are more conscious of costs and more likely to work to protect your own money.

4. Private Exchange Research Council (PERC) analysis, 2017, www.percinsights.com. Information here based on groups enrolling in benefits on Liazon exchanges with a benefits effective date of January 1, 2017.

Tax-protected accounts are key to helping people think about health in relation to wealth. The balance that needs to be struck is how much to invest in things that will *protect* our financial well-being versus *grow* our financial well-being. And that balance is different for each person and depends on a variety of factors, including age, health status, degree of utilization of care, income status, risk tolerance, and personal lifestyle.

> The balance that needs to be struck is how much to invest in things that will *protect* our financial well-being versus *grow* our financial well-being.

To that end, both the House-passed and Senate-proposed versions of the American Health Care Act (AHCA) and Better Care Relief Act (BCRA), respectively, included noteworthy changes. Among these were allowing tax-free contributions to an HSA to equal the out-of-pocket maximum limits under the existing HSA rules; expanding qualified medical expenses to include over-the-counter medications; and also allowing individuals to establish an HSA and pay for expenses incurred 60 days prior to setting up the account.

Another smart change: loosening up the rules around what health services can be paid for before the deductible of a high-deductible health plan (HDHP) is met, especially in cases of people with chronic illnesses, while still allowing the HDHP policyholder to maintain his or her eligibility to contribute to an HSA. Health care policy expert Chris Condeluci told NPR in early 2017, "Allowing first-dollar coverage would recognize that there are individuals who are high medical utilizers and HDHPs just are not appealing to them, unless you can change the definition to make them more appealing, while also allowing them to contribute to an HSA."[5]

There is no doubt that many people are intimidated or confused by these accounts and therefore do not utilize them effectively. We as an industry need to move beyond videos, white papers, Q&As, and other educational materials to empower consumers to take advantage of the tools these accounts provide—but that is just one part of the solution.

Employer Funding for Individual Insurance

President Obama signed the 21st Century Cures Act into law on December 13, 2016. This bill, discussed in Chapter 10, "The 'Law of the Land', Insurance Tax Reform and the November Surprise", was one of the most pro-consumer laws to become reality in a long time. The bipartisan bill includes a provision known as the Small Business Healthcare Relief Act (SBHRA), which allows small businesses with

---

5. Julia Appleby, "Health Savings Accounts Are Back in the Policy Spotlight," February 2, 2107, www.npr.org/sections/health-shots/2017/02/02/513060189/health-savings-accounts-are-back-in-the-policy-spotlight.

fewer than 50 employees that don't sponsor a health plan to fund health reimbursement arrangements (HRAs) for their employees. These financial vehicles allow employees to buy individual policies through the ACA's public exchanges or directly from insurance carriers. It puts these important decisions squarely in the hands of consumers by saying, *here's your money, now go by your health insurance.* Primarily, these vehicles have been utilized in the retiree market, where the government-operated "exchanges" known as Medicare provide the products, and this type of expansion into the group market is an experiment that merits close watching.

> *...here's your money, now go by your health insurance.*

More specifically, the SBHRA created a new type of HRA—the qualified small employer health reimbursement arrangement (QSEHRA). The QSEHRA has specific rules such as insuring all employees under the same terms, adhering to maximum benefit caps, and requiring the employer to fully fund the HRA. This can result in solid wins for employers (predictable costs and satisfied employees) and employees (choosing their own health plans). "This change provides small employers greater flexibility in terms of benefit offerings and allows eligible employers to use HRAs to help employees purchase an affordable health insurance plan that fits their individual budget and health care needs,"[6] noted Chatrane Birbal, the Society for Human Resource Management's (SHRM's) senior advisor for government relations.

6. Stephen Miller, "New Law Lets Small Employers Use Stand-Alone Health Reimbursement Arrangements," December 13, 2016, www.shrm.org/resourcesandtools/hr-topics/benefits/pages/21st-century-cures-act-stand-alone-hras.aspx.

Consumer-Centric Provider Networks

One area in health care that has been closely scrutinized over the past few years has been the trend toward narrow networks—limiting the choices of providers and facilities that are covered within a certain plan but keeping premium rates lower in exchange for these restrictions.

It's not enough to call for narrow networks and be done with it. Instead, what if every "network" could be tailored to become a personal health group for each consumer? We could manage costs by curating providers to reflect consumer habits and quality ratings, as is done in conventional networks, but we could take it a step further and give consumers the opportunity to, in effect, choose their own network, as discussed in Chapter 9, "Innovation in Benefits (Yes, Benefits)."

As an interim step toward this utopian vision, let's take the hospital systems in Pittsburgh as an example. Pittsburgh has two major health systems: the University of Pittsburgh Medical Center and West Penn Allegheny. The type of access I'm calling for is one in which a person in Pittsburgh could align herself solely with one system or the other, for one set of costs, or choose to include both systems and pay a higher premium. This kind of choice is easily integrated within an exchange-type mechanism in which the consumer can click through to find performance data and specializations about each health care system. (This rationale also harkens back to the HMO "vertical" care model during the 1980s and 1990s and discussed in Chapter 2, "Benefits: The Accidental Entitlement.")

Some analysts express concern about consumers trading off lower costs for reduced choice without knowing what they're giving up. That's where the exchange environment is so helpful. We're all accustomed to drilling down through online links to further information and using comparison tools to help make decisions before we purchase. An exchange interface offers this type of decision support and is poised to adapt to new technologies and innovations for comparing and contrasting data on quality ratings, price points, and more as it accumulates over time.

> An exchange interface... is poised to adapt to new technologies and innovations for comparing and contrasting data on quality ratings, price points, and more as it accumulates over time.

In an analysis published by the National Bureau of Economic Research in September 2014, economists Jon Gruber and Robin McKnight found that limited-choice plans can reduce patient spending by as much as one-third while maintaining access to the best hospitals. According to Sarah Kliff's reporting on Vox:

> Using a natural experiment from Massachusetts, Gruber and McKnight find that patients who switched to narrow network plans had access to a smaller set of equally good hospitals. They used more primary care but went to the emergency room less. And these patients, along with

their employers, ended up saving a whole bunch of money…The drivers of this change were twofold. Patients on the narrow plans used less medical care…And when they did go to the doctor, it was usually with a provider who charged lower prices. This is a hallmark of narrow networks: to keep premiums down, they tend to only contract with physicians who will give them a good deal.[7]

Data and Digital Tools for Patients and Consumers

While hospitals are still largely for-profit businesses, and most doctors still charge on a "fee for service" scale, the economies around benefits could be tilted toward the consumer if we trusted them to manage the wealth of information that could be made available to them. Smart innovators are getting big money to do things like measure provider performance and results to create "high-performance" health networks.

> Smart innovators are getting big money to do things like measure provider performance and results to create "high-performance" health networks.

Credit: GP Kidd/Cultura/Getty Images

Just as Liazon studies user data to improve site navigation and plan offerings (see Chapter 1, "Building a Better Benefits System"), hospital systems are using analytics to improve cost management and care utilization. Massachusetts General Hospital is one facility that is ahead of this curve, using "insightful performance data to drive continuous quality improvement." Clinicians and staff benchmark themselves against "national quality and safety standards," using rich visual displays on interactive, actionable dashboards.[8]

7. Sarah Kliff, "Limited Doctor Choice Plans Don't Mean Worse Care," September 8, 2014, www.vox.com/2014/9/8/6119669/narrow-networks-quality-care-jon-gruber.

8. "Massachusetts General Hospital: Enabling Continuous Quality Improvement with Data," www.healthdatamanagement.com/web-seminars/massachusetts-general-hospital-enabling-continuous-quality-improvement-with-data.

Similar tools are helping implement value-based health care and pricing across the country. In value-based care, hospitals and doctors work with insurance plans to jointly determine pricing schedules based on health outcomes and lower spending instead of typical hospital fee-for-service models—otherwise known as *this is what it costs because I said so.*

We know how much doctors and surgeons love having insurers looking over their shoulders when it comes to how they are treating their patients, so it's going to take some time and careful incentives to make value-based care more widely accepted. But as a step in the right direction, the federal Medicare and CHIP Reauthorization Act of 2015 (MACRA) included new incentives for physicians, adjusting their reimbursement rates based on provider performance data. As noted in a Deloitte report, "that's a very important and broad-based driver for physicians, because almost all physicians are paid by Medicare, with very few exceptions."[9]

Coordination of care is also key. As we move toward a more ordered system of health care, providers and insurers will reap more profit by learning to work together on behalf of the patient rather than at their ultimate expense. The system is chaotic and characterized by waste and inefficiency without coordination of care.

> ...providers and insurers will reap more profit by learning to work together on behalf of the patient rather than at their ultimate expense.

Modernizing the industry in this way will continue and is critical. But we won't achieve a world-class benefits system if consumers are always running two decades behind.

THE NEXT FRONTIERS IN EMPOWERING CONSUMERS

The entire business of "health and wealth" needs to accelerate game-changing innovations beyond gadgets. The following are some areas ripe with potential.

Telemedicine (Telehealth)

Telemedicine, or receiving care via telephone or video conferencing, is offered by 78% of employers today, according to research by Willis Towers Watson. This rate is projected to increase to 94% by 2019.[10]

9. Deloitte, "Aligning Health Plans and Providers: Working Together to Control Costs," 2017, www2.deloitte.com/content/dam/Deloitte/us/Documents/life-sciences-health-care/us-lshc-deloitte-aligning-health-plans-and-providers-v1.pdf.

According to Brian Marcotte, president and CEO of the National Business Group on Health, "Employers' focus in 2017 is shifting away from plan design to optimizing how health care is accessed and delivered. That translates into expanded telehealth services, more Centers of Excellence options and optional selective network choices that focus on providing higher quality health care."[11]

But overall, a tiny percentage of the population actually makes use of accessing doctors' guidance online or via phone call. As with HSA usage, discussed earlier, the advantages of telemedicine for controlling health care costs is simple: If a consumer pays $50 a year for a telemedicine plan and receives one prescription via the plan to help heal a sore throat and another to get rid of a rash—two doctor visits that could each cost hundreds of dollars—the savings are evident. Once the advantages are made clearer to employees, usage of, and not just enrollment in, these service should increase.

Monitoring High-Risk, Long-Term Conditions

Interacting via technology with doctors and nurses early in the symptom cycle has preventive and psychological benefits, as well as cost-saving benefits, particularly for high-risk or long-term conditions.

Health plans are piloting programs that use data to provide additional lifestyle behavior, such as coaching and counseling, to patients with recurring or high-risk conditions, including chronic pain and depression. For example, plans are implementing short-term tele-counseling sessions with patients battling long-term depression, chronic pain, and similar issues. These measures hold great promise as long as patients understand why they're being offered the treatment, and the potential long range benefits of receiving it.

Transparency

Providing patients with information on quality, costs, and safety of treatment options can enable them to make better medical decisions while lowering the cost of care—and this information, too, can be provided online in an exchange environment. Chapter 8, "Insurers Find a New Way to Move Product," discusses the encouraging role of mobile applications (such as Health4Me for iPhone and Android devices) to put crucial health

---

10. Willis Towers Watson, "2017 22nd Annual Best Practices in Health Care Employer Survey," https://www.willistowerswatson.com/en/press/2017/08/us-employers-expect-health-care-costs-to-rise-in-2018.

11. National Business Group on Health, "Large U.S. Employers Project Health Benefit Cost Increases to Hold Steady at 6% in 2017, National Business Group on Health Survey Finds," August 9, 2016, www.businessgrouphealth.org/news/nbgh-news/press-releases/press-release-details/?ID=281.

and plan information at consumers' fingertips. Most notably, this includes the ability to comparison shop for health care services based on both quality and cost. Plenty of evidence, including the Serigraph reforms under John Torinus (see Chapter 9, "Innovation in Benefits [Yes, Benefits])" and insurance industry studies, points to consumer success in making smart decisions about health care providers when given quality information and cost estimates.[12]

12. UnitedHealthcare, "Study: People Using myHealthcare Cost Estimator Are More Likely to Select High-Quality Physicians," September 16, 2014, www.stage-app.uhc.com/news-room/2014-news-release-archive/cost-estimator-leads-to-quality-physicians.

Patient-Empowered Healing

Academic studies on patient empowerment have generally been encouraging, finding that "health care professionals across many disciplines are experiencing the benefit of empowered patients who take a more active role in the management of their disease,"[13] "by giving patients the opportunity to expand their role—and equipping them to do so—fundamentally new models of care are possible,"[14] and "increased patient involvement and shared decision-making do produce beneficial results."[15]

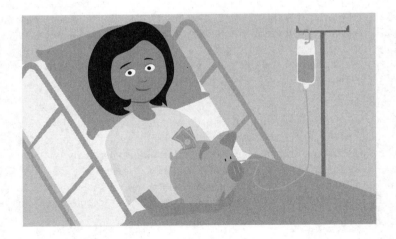

13. Jorgo Chatzimarkakis, "Why Patients Should Be More Empowered: A European Perspective on Lessons Learned in the Management of Diabetes," *Journal of Diabetes Science Technology*, 4(6):1570–1573, November 2010.

14. Jonty Roland et al., "Patient Empowerment: For Better Quality, More Sustainable Health Services Globally," All Party Parliamentary Group on Global Health, May 2014.

15. Adrian Edwards & Glyn Elwyn, *Shared Decision-Making in Health Care: Achieving Evidence-Based Patient Choice*, Oxford University Press, 2016.

Don Berwick and other leaders in the United States, the United Kingdom, and elsewhere around the world cite proven and tested examples of hospitals and other providers empowering patients and saving millions in the process:

> Don Berwick and other leaders...cite proven and tested examples of hospitals and other providers empowering patients and saving millions in the process.

- At Massachusetts General Hospital, doctors can "prescribe" a decision aid tool for patients through their electronic medical records. The patient can access the tool after a visit to better understand his or her health condition and possible courses of treatment.[16]

- Parkland Memorial Hospital in Dallas launched a program that allowed patients to administer their own long-term antibiotics at home rather than having to spend weeks in the hospital. Over a four-year period, the pilot program saved nearly 28,000 patient days along with almost $40 million.[17]

- Bellin Health in Wisconsin has helped launch a partnership among the health system, the local school district, community agencies, employers, and the government to fund education and coaching projects for high school and younger students.

- The All-Party Parliamentary Health Group has reported that "In Uganda, a large proportion of HIV/AIDs care is delivered by groups of patients working to help their peers understand and manage their condition."[18] Peer education and support is as critical in health care as in education and business.

- Mothers' firsthand experiences are at the heart of a global initiative called Respectful Maternity Care, acknowledged as "a universal human right due to every childbearing woman in every health system around the world." The initiative collects and shares first-person interviews about childbirth to inform midwives and help improve the experience of childbirth for thousands.[19]

Closer to home, organizations from General Electric to the City of Louisville have introduced trainings delivered by new companies such as Whil, grounded in neuroscience to help employees reduce stress and improve business outcomes through

16. Jonty Roland et al., "Patient Empowerment: For Better Quality, More Sustainable Health Services Globally," *All Party Parliamentary Group on Global Health*, May 2014.

17. Marty Stempniak, "Don Berwick: 8 Ways to Shift the Power Back to Patients," *Hospitals and Health Networks*, December 9, 2016.

18. Jonty Roland et al., "Patient Empowerment: For Better Quality, More Sustainable Health Services Globally," All Party Parliamentary Group on Global Health, May 2014.

19. Ibid.

workplace meditation and mindfulness. These techniques, if performed regularly, have scientifically validated success in reducing anxiety, stress, and other debilitating effects. Stress is linked to six leading causes of death, and advanced nations must do more to tackle this issue in the workplace.

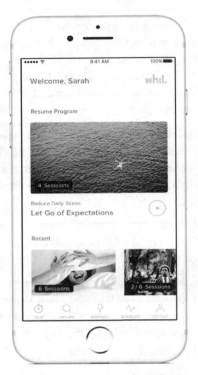

Image courtesy of Whil.com

The Utopian Vision

The convergence of health and wealth is already occurring within the benefits ecosystem. Insurance—be it health, dental, vision, disability, or something else—is a financial protection vehicle rather than anything actually having to do with the care you receive from a doctor. Insurance was designed to help people ward off financial difficulty in the event of something unpredictable happening. Everyone seems to understand this concept when it comes to retirement accounts, college savings accounts, and even mortgage insurance, but time and again when we talk about employer-sponsored insurance, we get sucked into the conversation about health care.

...time and again when we talk about employer-sponsored insurance, we get sucked into the conversation about health care.

We need to be working toward the day when people can make decisions about 401(k) investments, 529 plans, health insurance, and all the other financial protection vehicles available—together. The allocation of one's costs of protection can no longer be considered in silos and must be weighed against the desire to build prosperity in the long run. How much protection is too much? How much savings is too little? The answers to these questions vary for each person and may change over time.

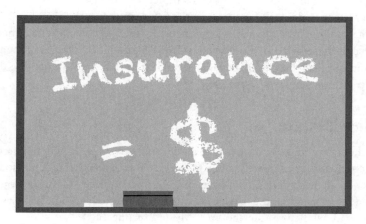

With all due respect to the politicians in Washington who talk about everything from "affordable care;" to "repeal and replace;" to "Medicare for all," that is, a single payer system with universal vouchers; you can't solve just one part of the equation. If it means the end of group insurance, the end of Medicare as we know it, or a complete overhaul of the tax system, doing what's right for the country means looking at employer-sponsored insurance in tandem with our country's burgeoning retiree population, people working for small employers, as well as those who are unemployed and those who are uninsured.

Rather than universal vouchers for all, one step along the way could be to have vouchers for a baseline purchase of "catastrophic" insurance, with employers then providing their own form of a subsidy (through an HRA or a defined contribution added to paychecks) and employees making their own decisions—whether through a Liazon-powered exchange or another marketplace, a public exchange, or directly with insurers. The bottom line would be that employees could choose the level at which to "enhance" their catastrophic coverage, based on the balance of risk/savings/protection concerns highlighted earlier. Traditionally, no one has had the impetus to improve the system—not brokers, not insurers, and certainly not employers. This needs to change, and we are having discussions now that are quite encouraging compared to where we were just 5 or 10 years ago.

While I stand by the idea that the ultimate outcome of the ACA/AHCA/BCRA discussions will likely have little impact on how we receive insurance and other benefits from our employers, the opportunity the debate has fostered is worth repeating. These developments, combined with the inroads made by the 21st Century Cures Act, give us a chance to recast the conversation: The idea of tax-free dollars given to employees of small firms to purchase insurance for the first time in history bodes well for a time in the future in which everyone can purchase their own benefits using tax-free dollars. What's more, the purchase of those benefits should be just that—a purchase. Something the person owns and can keep over time. Benefits should be portable, not something that jumps from one employer to the next.

> Benefits should be portable, not something that jumps from one employer to the next.

Shopping for Care

Throughout this book, we have talked about using private exchanges to purchase health coverage and, ultimately, a full 360-degree financial protection portfolio. Now, let's take the defining property of a true benefits marketplace—elasticity—one step further. (See more about the need for elasticity in a marketplace in Chapter 6, "Six Questions to Ask Before You Choose a Private Exchange.")

Using a Marketplace to Purchase Non-Emergent Health Care on an As-Needed Basis

A utopian vision for "shopping for care" could look like one of the following vignettes:

- Your son twists his ankle playing basketball. Rather than go to the nearest emergency room or urgent care center, you log on to your marketplace, search clinics in your area, compare prices and quality ratings, and book an appointment through the system at your convenience.

- You are admitted to the hospital for a serious back injury. Once the injury is stabilized, you need to go to a rehab center for physical therapy. Rather than wait for the resident to make her rounds (potentially causing you to spend another costly night in the hospital) and refer you to the first available facility (regardless of whether it is in your network or near your home), you take action from your hospital bed. You (or a family member or advocate) log on to your marketplace and assess rehab centers based on the same three factors in the above scenario: price, quality, and convenience (that is, location). When the resident finally appears, you assert where you would like to be treated and let her know you have already booked the facility. All you need at that point is the referral.

In both of these scenarios, the care that is appropriate for one person may not be the same for another—just as in the case of coverage. One person may have a cost issue, while another may be more concerned with doctor ratings or using a known provider, and still a third may just want something nearby, regardless of the cost. Timing in terms of the deductible cycle may affect these decisions as well. For one consumer, needing care at the beginning of the year before his deductible is met means a higher cost to him, whereas if the patient has already reached his deductible, the choice to pay the coinsurance for a pricier procedure becomes more palatable. A smart marketplace system will take all these factors into account and recommend the best solution based on each person's unique needs, just as it does for coverage.

Opponents of this type of shopping mechanism for health care talk about medical needs for serious accidents or life-threatening diseases not being suited to commoditization, and they are right. However, when we think about care, our minds tend to gravitate toward the catastrophic kind, when the reality is, most of the care we need is suited to a marketplace environment. According to data from the CDC's National Health Interview Survey in 2015, 94% of the under-65 population did not need an overnight hospital stay, and only 4.5% needed hospitalization for one night over the previous 12 months.[20] Indeed, sometimes people need highly specialized care, but most of the time, "care" means we need to go to a doctor or clinic, take a diagnostic test, or fill a prescription. Transparent, accessible pricing, along with accurate measures of quality, can make all the difference in how we make these decisions.

> Transparent, accessible pricing, along with accurate measures of quality, can make all the difference in how we make [health care] decisions.

WHEN SHOPPING FOR HEALTH CARE MATTERS MOST

Shopping for procedures such as a routine MRI or X-ray or a planned surgery makes sense. A person should be able to compare the service, costs, and quality and then decide where to have the procedure. Many common (and expensive) surgeries and treatments could be purchased through online shopping and possibly even bidding for services—all enabled within the exchange model. The benefits marketplace creates free market purchasing leverage across a range of consumer needs.

But what about when the stakes are higher for health matters?

Debra Sherman was a health care reporter for Reuters when she was diagnosed with Stage 4 lung cancer and started the blog "Cancer in Context" to document her personal experience finding the right care. A September 2013 post titled "Finding the Best Hospitals to Treat Your Cancer"[21] underscores the importance of being able to shop for care based on your own particular concerns—and sometimes that means quality over price as an evaluation measure.

Sherman was in the admittedly enviable position of having more than a decade of reporting experience behind her and access to colleagues in the field who could point her in the right direction for making important decisions about her care. Her blog questioned how people without access to these resources could know where to go and what to do in terms of researching their own options—and how they could be assured that their best interests

20. U.S. Centers for Disease Control and Prevention, "Summary Health Statistics: National Health Interview Survey, 2015," Table P-10a, Age-adjusted percent distribution (with standard errors) of number of overnight hospital stays during the past 12 months, by selected characteristics: United States, 2015, https://ftp.cdc.gov/pub/Health_Statistics/NCHS/NHIS/SHS/2015_SHS_Table_P-10.pdf.

were being addressed over the financial interests of providers and facilities that would be offering care.

What if there were a way to seek out the specialized care that Sherman wrote about on one's own and make judgments based on success rates rather than price or provider network? What if a patient could identify specialized facilities for her condition, treatment regimens, quality ratings, and patient reviews, and compare options, all within one container? The exchanges of the future could be built to address and counter some of the "financial incentives" driving providers that Sherman cautioned against when more patients are enabled and empowered to take health care matters into their own hands.

21. Deborah Sherman, "Finding the Best Hospitals to Treat Your Cancer," September, 13, 2013, http://blogs.reuters.com/cancer-in-context/2013/09/13/finding-the-best-hospitals-to-treat-your-cancer/.

Certain types of care can be commoditized, and the sooner we start thinking about it that way, the sooner competition will set in, prices will come down, and the consumer will be fully in charge. In this vision, not only will doctors and facilities compete on quality as well as price, but as every good commodity will seek to outsell its competitors, so too will health care providers differentiate by offering discounts and promotions. They can take a lesson from the airline industry and adjust prices based on demand throughout the day, or, like online hotel bookings, offer a discount for advance payment. Some chiropractic and vision facilities, such as Manhattan Total Wellness and Sterling Optical, are already offering Groupons for massage treatments and vision exams, respectively, to attract new customers; they realize that consumers are already choosing these kinds of services based on price, quality, and convenience and so are using technology to attract those consumers while they are otherwise living their lives online.

> Some chiropractic and vision facilities... [are]offering Groupons... to attract new customers; they realize that consumers are already choosing these kinds of services based on price, quality, and convenience...

Today we can visit 10 different pharmacies within a 10-block radius and get 10 different quotes for a medication. But with commoditized care, we'll be able to get quotes instantly through our marketplaces and save ourselves the nuisance of door-to-door surveying. CVS and Walgreens can then check each other's rates for a monthly prescription for Humira and adjust their prices in real time to remain competitive.

A market-driven environment grounded in transparency on price, quality, and convenience measures will ultimately lead to higher quality and reduced cost. But there is one more factor to consider: What will insurers think of this?

An "In-Network" Conundrum?

Another factor that consumers can measure when they shop is whether a provider is in their network. For some people, this is a priority; for others, quality or convenience may rank above cost. Insurers will want people to shop around if it results in their choosing a physical therapy program that takes 7 weeks instead of 10 weeks, or if they are willing to cough up the funds to go out-of-network rather than have the insurer fund the cost of a network provider. To insurers, the cost is the cost. It's who is paying that cost that is of primary concern to them.

When we realize the utopian vision for price transparency along with accessible quality measures in shopping for care, the model for government-provided insurance won't matter as much. Buying coverage will become less important than buying care. And Washington can get on with other pressing matters facing our country.

> When we realize the utopian vision…, the model for government-provided insurance won't matter as much. …And Washington can get on with other pressing matters facing our country.

Final Thoughts

As stated in this book's Introduction, we never set out to solve the health care crisis in America. Rather, my colleagues and I got together 10 years ago to address the issue of insurance and benefits products that companies were buying for their employees typically not being the choices people would make themselves if they were spending their own money. We set out to create an environment in which people feel like they are spending their own money, and the conditions surrounding such purchases need to be deeply rooted in consumerism.

The rate of technological advance enables this utopian vision of full financial protection, which can expand to include new innovations in products and vehicles, as well as more tools, knowledge, and education, all in the name of customization and self-service. Companies are not in the business of providing benefits to their employees, nor should they be. Group insurance needs to be reformed because costs are rising higher than what most employers can bear, and employees shouldn't be put in the position of changing plans (and associated providers and facilities) every year simply because their employer opted for a lower-cost medical plan.

> We set out to create an environment in which people feel like they are spending their own money, and the conditions surrounding such purchases need to be deeply rooted in consumerism.

Laws may evolve, pricing models may evolve, and we all know our country's political situation is a moving target right now. But my colleagues and I still stand by the same message that led us to develop our company, Liazon: As employers continue to feel the strain to attract and retain employees, they will be looking to do so in a more cost-effective manner. Everything else flows through this central premise.

Part IV

Appendixes:
A Practical Guide to
Private Exchanges

Appendix A

Private Exchanges 101

This book explains why it's so important to put the benefits consumer, or employee, first when it comes to fixing our country's broken health care system. Looking specifically at the group insurance market, this starts with how benefits are delivered and managed by employers. In this Appendix and the two that follow, we move from the philosophical to the practical in terms of how to bring choice and consumerism to America's workforce, starting with a brief tutorial on private exchanges.

What are the key features of a successful private exchange?

Funding for coverage

Money contributed by the employer and allocated to each employee to shop for the benefits that best suit their needs

Inventory of Medical plans

A meaningful selection of Medical plans with varying plan designs and a wide spread of price points

Comprehensive services

Assistance throughout the purchasing process as well as the necessary integration, reporting, and customer service to ensure everything runs smoothly on an ongoing basis

Non-medical products

Products such as Dental, Vision, Pet, and Disability insurance as well as Legal, Identity Theft, and other forms of coverage that give employees a wider range of choice and greater protection for their unique risks

Decision support

Technology to help employees determine the benefits package that is right for them, including education and plan recommendation tools

Price transparency

Exposure to real relative market prices, allowing employees to make smarter financial decisions and better understand the value of their benefits dollars

How does a private exchange work?

1 Employers fill an online "store" with a variety of benefits including multiple medical, vision, and dental plans as well as a variety of additional ancillary products.

2 Employers allocate money towards their employees' benefits which employees can use to shop for the benefits they want.

3 Employees access an online portal where transparent pricing, coupled with education and decision support, helps them make choices.

4 Employees choose the benefits that make sense for their unique needs, creating a personal portfolio of coverage. They use the money allocated by their employer and can add their own if they choose.

5 Ongoing information and support gives employees a year-round destination for engaging with their benefits (updating life events, learning about plans and products, etc.)

What are the key differentiators of a private exchange vs. a public exchange?

Both put consumers in control of purchasing their benefits, but they are otherwise two completely different entities.

	Private Exchange	Public Exchange
Users	Active and retired employees of companies that provide benefits	Individuals purchasing insurance on their own for themselves and their families
Operators	Private companies	Government bodies— individual states or the federal government
Products	A large variety of benefits that may include Medical, Dental, Vision, Life, Disability, Critical Illness, Wellness, Legal, Pet insurance, and Telemedicine, among others	Medical, Dental, and Vision
Government Subsidies	No	Yes

What are the key differentiators of a private exchange vs. a benefits administration platform?

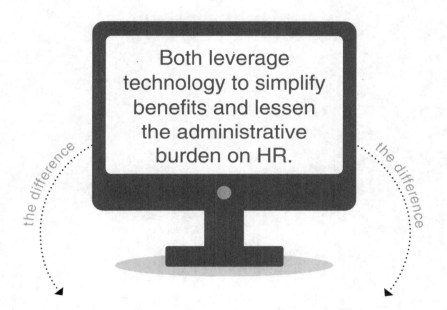

Both leverage technology to simplify benefits and lessen the administrative burden on HR.

Benefits Administration Platform:

Paperless enrollment

Private Exchange:

Provides meaningful choice through multiple product and plan offerings and aids in making good choices through decision support tools.

Appendix B

Making Sense of Benefits Terms

Who knew benefits could be so complicated? We did.

In the benefits industry, terms used to describe health care, health insurance, insurance marketplaces, private exchanges, and employee benefits are sometimes used interchangeably, and this has led to a great deal of confusion in the industry. For clarity, this Appendix explains a number of terms used to describe frequently referenced concepts in three key areas: benefits, health care consumerism, and private exchanges. We also include a guide to common benefits products and offerings available through Liazon exchanges.

On the pages that follow, words in **bold** are frequently referenced throughout this book; words in *italics* are industry terms that often allude to the same or similar concepts as the bolded terms. We do not profess to be the ultimate authority on benefits terminology, but because we believe education is a key component of a successful benefits experience, we provide a glimpse into the lexicon that has helped to inform our work over the years.

Terms Related to Benefits

Employee benefits—When people think of employee benefits, they typically think of insurance offered through group plans—meaning at discounted, prenegotiated rates by insurers for a number of people, such as employees of a particular firm. But really an employee benefit is anything extra that an employer gives to employees in addition to salary, as part of their total compensation. Taken broadly, this could mean a collection of traditional health and nonmedical products, but it could also mean incentives for health or well-being, such as wellness programs, ergonomic furniture, on-site yoga classes, and employee discounts at gyms; help with career development, such as tuition assistance

or occupational training; and
even discounts for local entertainment, such as movies or
shows. The more creative ways
employers can think of to keep
employees engaged, the more
expansive the term "employee
benefits" can become.

> The more creative ways
> employers can think of to keep
> employees engaged, the more
> expansive the term "employee
> benefits" can become.

Employer-sponsored benefits—Employer-sponsored benefits are
insurance and other products and programs offered to employees by
their employer as a means of attracting and retaining them. These may
be paid for completely or in part by employers or, as in the case of
private exchanges, offered in a marketplace or benefits store in which
employees may use money given to them by their employers, known
as **defined contribution**, to purchase the benefits that best suit their
needs.

Nonmedical benefits—Also be referred to as *supplemental, voluntary, ancillary,* or *specialty* benefits, nonmedical benefits include
benefits that help fill the gaps left by traditional medical insurance.
These typically include dental, vision, accident, critical illness, and
hospital indemnity insurance. Nonmedical benefits may also include
non-insurance products, such as telemedicine and health coaching,
which also help fill gaps left by medical insurance but are not traditional insurance products. These offerings are sometimes considered
"supplemental" because they supplement traditional health insurance, "voluntary" because employees can decide whether they want
to purchase them, and "ancillary" because they are offered separate
from and in addition to medical benefits. In effect, all these terms
are misnomers due to the fact that they make some benefits seem
more important than others, and the industry does not appear to
have consensus on when exactly to use which term. We feel that it's
important for a set of benefits—both medical and nonmedical—to
work together.

Benefits products—Benefits products may take the form of traditional insurance, such as health, life, and disability; nontraditional
options such as telemedicine and health coaching; **money accounts**
or **spending accounts** such as HSAs and FSAs; and other forms of
protection, such as legal plans or identity theft protection. Benefits
such as 401(k) plans, home and auto insurance, wellness programs,
paid time off (PTO) buy-up, tuition assistance and a company

stock purchase plan may also be purchased or enabled through an exchange's technology. (See explanations for the various benefits products and offerings available on Liazon exchanges in the "Guide to Common Benefits Products on a Private Exchange" section at the end of this appendix.)

Medical insurance—Medical insurance is a benefit product that provides financial protection against the costs of treatment and prevention of disease. Medical insurance may also be called *health insurance* or *coverage,* because certain conditions and treatments are "covered" under a specified plan.

Health plan—A health plan, also referred to as a *medical plan,* an *insurance plan,* or a *health insurance plan,* is a specific package of services with a predefined provider network and cost structure offered by an insurer. Different types of health plans, or *plan types,* include HMOs (health maintenance organizations), PPOs (preferred provider organizations), POS (point-of-service) plans, and HDHPs (high-deductible health plans). New hybrid arrangements combining different elements of these plan types are emerging to create an even greater range of health plan choices.

> Different types of health plans, or *plan types*, include HMOs (health maintenance organizations), PPOs (preferred provider organizations), POS (point-of-service) plans, and HDHPs (high-deductible health plans).

Insurers—An insurer—also called a *carrier* or *payer*—is a company that provides health plans or nonmedical insurance, along with administrative services in processing claims for people (individual plans) or companies (group plans). In some cases, the insurer may bear the risk associated with claims from an employee population (fully-insured employers); in other cases, they act solely as the administrator (self-insured employers). Well-known medical insurers include Aetna, Blue Cross Blue Shield, UnitedHealthcare, and Cigna; some insurers that provide nonmedical products are MetLife, Humana, Allstate, and Guardian. With **individual insurance**, a person buys coverage from an insurer (or through a broker or a public exchange) on his or her own; with **group insurance**, a person obtains coverage as one of a number of people collectively covered through an employer or association, a trade group, a society, and so on.

Terms Related to Health Care Consumerism

Health care—Sometimes the terms health care and health insurance are inadvertently used interchangeably; however, they are not the same thing. Health care refers to the treatment and prevention of illness and disease, including medical procedures or interventions that create or sustain life (e.g., obstetrics). *Health insurance* is a financial instrument, as described earlier in this appendix in the section on **Medical insurance**.

Health care consumerism—Health care consumerism is a movement to educate and engage individuals so that they become more involved in their own health care by becoming better, more informed shoppers—or consumers—when it comes to their options for buying coverage, receiving care, and obtaining and understanding their health insurance.

Consumer-driven health care—Sometimes referred to as *consumer-directed health care* or *health care consumerism*, consumer-driven health care is a movement to keep the rising costs of health care in check by better engaging the health care consumer in managing his or her utilization of services. The thinking behind it is that helping people become more educated and engaged consumers of health care will enable them to spend their dollars more wisely and better manage their overall care.

> ...consumer-driven health care is a movement to keep the rising costs of health care in check by better engaging the health care consumer in managing his or her utilization of services.

Consumer-driven health plan (CDHP)—A CDHP is the hallmark of the consumer-driven health care movement and typically refers to medical plans that have higher deductibles (known as high deductible health plans [HDHPs]) and lower premiums than traditional plans, along with a savings or reimbursement vehicle such as a **health savings account (HSA)**, **medical flexible spending account (FSA)**, or **health reimbursement arrangement (HRA)**. The thinking here is that consumers can save money on lower premiums and won't be wasteful in terms of spending money on unnecessary treatments or tests if they will have to pay for them (before their deductible is met).

High-deductible health plan (HDHP)—An HDHP is a medical plan that features a higher deductible (the portion of payment for medical services a person must contribute before the insurer will pay, excluding preventive care) than traditional plans. An HDHP is considered

"HSA-qualified" or "HSA-eligible" if the purchaser of the plan can open a health savings account to set aside tax-free money to help pay for eligible medical expenses.

Money account—A money account—also referred to as a *spending account* or *savings account*— is a financial vehicle (such as an HSA or a medical FSA established through a bank or an HRA entered into with an employer), in which tax-free funds accrue for an employee to put toward eligible health care expenses, including deductibles, copays, and coinsurance, but not premiums.

- **Health savings accounts (HSAs)** are only offered with high deductible health plans. They are considered triple tax-free because the money is put into the account before taxes, accrues interest tax free, and can be withdrawn tax free when used for eligible medical expenses, even through retirement. Money in an HSA rolls over from year to year and stays with an employee after he or she leaves their job. HSAs are gaining favor as a long-term health care savings vehicle and also as a way to help offset high deductibles in the near term.

> HSAs...are considered triple tax-free because the money is put into the account before taxes, accrues interest tax free, and can be withdrawn tax-free when used for eligible medical expenses...

- **Flexible spending accounts (FSAs)** also accrue money tax-free, but, in general, the money must be used within the coverage year. There are three types of **FSAs**: medical, dependent/child care, and commuting (parking, transit).

- **Health reimbursement arrangements (HRAs)** provide money to employees from a fund established by the employer as reimbursement for money spent on allowable medical expenses and post-retirement health insurance premiums.

Benefits consumers—Benefits consumers are individuals who are more involved in their own health care decisions and therefore act as "consumers" by becoming shoppers (or purchases, or buyers) of benefits, much as consumers operate in a retail environment.

Terms Related to Private Exchanges

Private exchange—A private exchange may also be referred to as a *private benefits exchange*, a *private insurance exchange*, a *private health insurance exchange*, or a *benefits marketplace*. A private exchange is an online marketplace for purchasing insurance products and other benefits offered to employees by their employer and administered by a broker, a consulting firm, a financial services company, an insurance carrier, or a "pure play" technology company.

> A private exchange is an online marketplace for purchasing insurance products and other benefits offered to employees by their employer...

Public exchanges—Public exchanges were created under the Affordable Care Act (ACA), a U.S. federal statute enacted by President Barack Obama in 2010. Public exchanges are operated and administered by the U.S. government on a federal or state level as vehicles for providing health coverage to individuals and administering government subsidies for people who cannot otherwise afford care.

Benefits store—A benefits store contains the merchandise offered within an online benefits marketplace or exchange. When referring to the choices employees can make in Liazon stores, we generally use the terms "products" (for example, medical insurance, life insurance, identity theft protection, legal plans) and "plan types" (for example, HMOs, PPOs or HDHPs for medical insurance) to distinguish between the various benefits they can choose from as well as the "plans" available to them within those products or plan types.

Decision support system—A decision support system helps an employee sort through the available merchandise in a benefits store to determine what combination of products and plans is best for him or her to purchase. Liazon's decision support includes a recommendation engine, online educational resources, plan comparison tools, and plan summaries.

> A decision support system helps an employee sort through the available merchandise in a benefits store to determine what combination of products and plans is best for him or her to purchase.

Recommendation engine—A recommendation engine, also known as *recommendation logic*, is a more sophisticated form of decision support (as it relates to Liazon exchanges), in which an employee is asked a series of questions related to his or her expectations of care utilization (such as health status, chronic illnesses, and expectations for pregnancy or prescription drug use), along with the employee's risk tolerance, financial position (income and savings), and lifestyle preferences. The answers employees provide are used to create a set of recommendations for products that best fit their needs.

Benefits portfolio—Liazon's *decision support* system considers the answers to key profile questions to provide a recommended benefits portfolio, or *customized portfolio*, of benefits, including a medical plan and other products, that best fits an employee's needs. As in the case of a 401(k) portfolio of various assets to provide financial protection in retirement, a benefits portfolio contains *a combination of products and plans* that work together to achieve complete financial protection against the uncertainties in life.

Defined contribution—A defined contribution (for benefits) is an amount of money that an employer gives to each of their employees to purchase products and plans in a benefits marketplace. Similar to 401(k) investments, a defined contribution strategy is used in lieu of a traditional, one-size-fits-all "defined benefit" strategy, in which the employer chooses a limited number of options to offer employees rather than giving them money with which to purchase what they want. Liazon believes employers should give their employees money to let them spend as they choose in a benefits store; this is made possible through defined contribution. However, some employers would rather not disclose this amount and instead show employees the true cost of their share of the premium (total plan cost minus the employer's contribution); this is the "net cost" of benefits.

> A defined contribution is an amount of money that an employer gives to each of their employees to purchase products and plans in a benefits marketplace.

Private exchange operator—A private exchange operator, also referred to as a *service provider* or *sponsor*, can be a company that develops a private exchange operating mechanism or technology platform and offers it as a solution to private industry under its own name or—in the case of a brokerage, a consultancy, or an insurer—as its own branded private exchange powered by a technology *service provider*. An insurer, a brokerage, or a consultancy is considered a *sponsor* of a private exchange if is uses another company's technology to power the system.

Guide to Common Benefits Products on a Private Exchange

Products Commonly Found in Liazon Benefits Marketplaces

Accident insurance
Accident insurance provides you with a lump-sum cash payment if you're hurt in an accident. The money can be used to cover any expenses you may have, including out-of-pocket costs from your Medical insurance (such as copays, deductibles, and/or coinsurance) for emergency treatments and hospital stays; travel, transportation and lodging fees, including costs for flying in loved ones; over-the-counter medicines; physical therapy; child or pet care; and help around the house.

Critical Illness insurance (or Cancer insurance)
Critical Illness Insurance pays you cash if you're diagnosed with a covered illness (such as cancer, heart attack, stroke, or Alzheimer's) and you can use that money for any expenses if you develop one of the conditions covered in the plan. While most Medical plans will generally cover the costs of your doctor and hospital visits, there are a host of expenses you could put this extra money toward, such as additional bills like transportation and lodging for family members, daily living expenses like rent, mortgage, food, and much more.

In some cases, you'll be able to purchase Cancer insurance instead of Critical Illness insurance. This is a very specific type of Critical Illness insurance which only provides a benefit for a cancer diagnosis; it does not cover any other illnesses.

Dental insurance
Dental insurance can cover a range of services to help keep your mouth and gums healthy, from routine exams to root canals and braces. Plans differ in how much they pay, what doctors you can see, and what services they cover. Most Dental plans will cover preventive care, such as scheduled Dental exams, X-rays, and cleanings. You might want to consider a higher level of coverage if you think you'll be in need of fillings, tooth extractions, services to restore damaged teeth, braces, and more.

Dependent Care FSA
If you pay for outside care for a child or disabled adult, you may want to consider a Dependent Care FSA which lets you set aside pre-tax dollars to pay for these costs. With this type of FSA, you file your receipts and are reimbursed tax-free by your FSA vendor, or can arrange to have a provider paid directly through your account. There are annual limits as to how much you can contribute to this type of FSA, and you can arrange to have deductions from your paycheck go directly into your account.

Disability insurance
Disability insurance replaces a portion of your income when you can't work due to an illness or injury over a certain period of time. Consider your savings and expenses, your spouse's income, and your likelihood to be absent from work for an extended or prolonged period of time when deciding if this benefit is right for you.

Employee Life insurance
Employee Life insurance is a group policy that has pre-determined levels of coverage and may or may not include a provision for "Accidental Death and Dismemberment" (AD&D). An AD&D benefit covers death, loss of a limb, or loss of sight as a result of an accident. Depending on your own financial situation, Employee Life insurance may provide enough coverage for your dependents in the event something happens to you. This type of policy is only available to you as long as you remain with the company.

Flexible Spending Account (FSA)
Similar to an HSA, an FSA is a tax-advantaged money account that can help you pay for certain expenses. There are different types of FSAs such as Medical, Dependent Care, and Parking or Transit. There are annual limits as to how much you can contribute to your FSA and this money will be deducted from your paycheck each pay period, tax free.

Health Coaching
Health coaching provides you with an individualized wellness program to help you meet your health goals, such as tobacco cessation, weight loss, stress management, and more. With the option to have your own personal health coach – a registered nurse or other practitioner trained in behavior modification science – you can have a skilled professional work with you regularly to explain risks and provide valuable health planning assistance.

Health Savings Account (HSA)
An HSA is a money account typically available in conjunction with an eligible High Deductible Health Plan (HDHP). Through your HSA, you set aside pre-tax funds to spend on qualified Medical expenses such as copays and deductibles, immunizations, lab fees, and much more. The interest on this money grows tax-free.

Hospital Indemnity insurance
Hospital Indemnity insurance pays you a set amount of money in the event that you're hospitalized. Depending on the plan, the amount of money may be per day, week, or month spent in the hospital or may just be one amount per visit, regardless of how long the hospital stay lasts. This money can help you cover any expenses you may have if you're hospitalized – such as home and family expenses, insurance deductibles, and copayments – that Medical insurance won't cover.

Identity Theft Protection
Identity Theft Protection monitors your credit report and thousands of other records to detect changes fast. When theft occurs, the service helps to correct bad data, reverse fraudulent charges, and restore your good name.

Legal plans
A Legal plan enables you to access a large network of qualified attorneys to manage everything from parking tickets, to wills, to the purchase of a new home – all at a flat monthly rate. Most Legal plans offer no deductibles or copays, no waiting periods, and no claim forms when you use a participating attorney.

Life insurance
A Life insurance policy can help your family maintain its standard of living, pay off any debt, secure education for children, and supplement retirement savings, should anything happen to you. This money can also be put toward final medical expenses, funeral and burial costs, mortgage, housing, and other bills related to daily life. We offer Life insurance through a group plan (referred to as Employee Life in the marketplace). If you feel you need additional coverage, you can choose to purchase an individual life insurance policy as a supplement or alternative to the group plan.

Long Term Care insurance
Long Term Care insurance is a way to offset the costs of Medically necessary, ongoing care in addition to that which is covered by your Medical insurance. This may include activities of daily living (bathing, eating, dressing, toileting, etc.) whether provided by a nursing home or assisted living facility, or accessed through home health care or hospice care. Long Term Care may apply to anyone in need of hands-on assistance, not just the elderly.

Medical FSA
A Medical FSA allows you to save pre-tax funds to spend on qualified medical expenses including Dental and Vision care, as well as prescription drugs, co-pays, co-insurance, and more. You receive a debit card from your FSA vendor that you can use to pay for these expenses.

Medical insurance
From annual physicals to ear infections to visits to the emergency room, Medical insurance helps pay for the costs of planned and unplanned visits to the doctor, lab work, and procedures. You may have a range of Medical plan options available to you. It's important to not only understand how each type of plan works and what your cost of care will be with each plan, but what you should consider in choosing one.

Parking or Transit FSA
A Parking FSA allows you to save pre-tax funds to spend on costs associated with parking near work or near public transportation that brings you to work. Similarly, if you commute to work using mass transit or a commuter highway vehicle, you can reduce your expenses by using a Transit FSA. Oftentimes, you'll receive a debit card which can be used to pay for covered transportation expenses.

Personal Life insurance
While pricing for Employee Life insurance is based on the full employee population of our company, Personal Life insurance is priced at the individual level, considering your age, health, and other factors. Personal Life insurance typically offers higher levels of coverage than Employee Life insurance plans. Personal Life insurance is portable, meaning that you can take the coverage with you if you leave the company.

Personal Time Off (PTO) Buy-up
Personal Time Off (PTO) Buy-up allows you to set aside money through payroll deductions or apply part of the defined contribution we're offering through the marketplace for purchasing additional time off from work.

Pet insurance
Pet insurance helps you pay for the Medical care your pet needs, including accidents, illnesses, and preventive care. Pet insurance usually provides coverage for dogs and cats, so check your plan if you have another type of animal you may wish to cover, as this may require an additional level of coverage. Also, you may want to check to make sure your breed is covered, if there are any age limits for coverage, and if any genetic or hereditary conditions are excluded.

Telemedicine
Telemedicine plans allow you to communicate with a doctor over the phone or by email so he or she can help diagnose and prescribe medication for a range of ailments. With a telemedicine benefit, you can request a phone or video consult with a doctor or health professional without ever leaving your home.

Vision insurance
Vision insurance covers regular eye exams to catch eye problems early and may help you pay for glasses or contacts. Like Dental plans, Vision plans may vary by what doctors are covered, what you will have to pay out-of-pocket, and what, if any, discounts are available on services not covered, such as laser eye surgery.

Appendix C

Real-World Data and Applications

As discussed often throughout this book, a benefits marketplace offers "aisles" and "shelves" that are stocked with products that benefits consumers can choose to buy, just as they would choose products in any other retail environment. This appendix looks at data on real-world usage of private exchanges.

This appendix also includes a walk through the process of choosing benefits on a Liazon exchange. We conclude our examination of the current benefits landscape with a visual journey through the history of health care (courtesy of Annenberg-classroom.org) which as we all know, is still being made with each passing day.

What Really Happens on Private Exchanges?

This section looks at the data on real-world usage of private exchanges, from the Private Exchange Research Council (PERC) as well as Liazon's own surveys of employers and employees who use our exchanges.

Data from the 2017 Private Exchange Research Council (PERC) Analysis

Early in 2015, together with leading brokers, consultants, and private exchange experts, Liazon began a major industry initiative called the Private Exchange Research Council (PERC). The goal of the initiative is to assemble an analytic storehouse based on Liazon's user preference and satisfaction data over time to further the industry at large. PERC data provides insights into how people are making decisions when shopping for their benefits on a private exchange.

The pages that follow provide highlights from PERC's 2017 analysis. For ongoing PERC reports based on collective data from employees who use Liazon-powered exchanges, see www.percinsights.com.

Product Offerings on Liazon Exchanges, 2015 to 2017*

Percentage of exchanges offering a plan in that product category

Product category	2015 (%)	2016 (%)	2017 (%)	% Change 2015 to 2017
Medical Flexible Spending Account	27.3	28.6	46.6	70.5
Dependent Care Flexible Spending	26.1	27.3	43.5	66.7
Critical Illness Insurance	38.5	50.3	60.2	56.5
Hospital Indemnity	14.9	13.7	21.1	41.7
Accident Insurance	46.6	55.3	63.4	36.0
Health Savings Account	95.7	96.3	97.5	1.9
Dental Insurance	97.5	98.8	97.5	0.0
Vision Insurance	98.1	99.4	98.1	0.0
Employee Life Insurance*	88.8	88.2	85.1	−4.2
Child Life Insurance*	88.2	87.6	83.9	−4.9
Spouse Life Insurance*	88.2	87.6	83.9	−4.9
Short-Term Disability*	72.0	72.7	67.7	−6.0
Long-Term Disability*	70.2	65.8	63.4	−9.7
Identity Theft Protection	70.8	72.7	63.4	−10.5
Transit Flexible Spending Account	4.3	3.1	3.7	−14.3
Legal Plans	81.4	82.0	67.1	−17.6
Pet Insurance	65.8	58.4	46.6	−29.2
Parking Flexible Spending Account	3.7	3.1	2.5	−33.3
Telemedicine	69.6	57.8	38.5	−44.6
Health Coaching	65.2	49.1	34.8	−46.7

Source: Private Exchange Research Council (PERC) analysis, 2017. Based on groups enrolling in benefits on Liazon exchanges with a benefits effective date of January 1, 2017. www.percinsights.com
Sample: Companies in the study sample in 2015, 2016, and 2017.
N=161 firms in all years.
Among companies who offered each product in 2015, 2016, and 2017.
**Excludes employer-paid products.
Note: The changes may not equal due to rounding up.

Product Purchases on Liazon Exchanges, 2013 to 2017*

Percentage of employees who purchased a plan in each product category when offered

Product category	2013 (%)	2014 (%)	2015 (%)	2016 (%)	2017 (%)	% change 2013 to 2017
Legal Plans	2	4	6	6	6	190
Hospital Indemnity Insurance	9	13	16	20	21	141
Telemedicine	8	8	15	17	19	123
Critical Illness Insurance	12	11	18	19	21	74
Identity Theft Protection	7***	7	12	13	11	60
Child Life Insurance**	11	12	16	17	17	53
Pet Insurance	7	6	9	11	10	39
Health Savings Account	19	18	21	24	26	32
Vision Insurance	48	51	55	58	60	26
Short-Term Disability**	36	38	40	41	45	24
Long-Term Disability**	32	36	43	52	40	23
Spouse Life Insurance**	14	14	16	16	17	21
Employee Life Insurance**	40	41	43	45	45	13
Accident Insurance	18	16	17	19	20	8
Dental Insurance	72	72	71	73	74	2
Health Coaching	1	1	1	1	1	0
Medical Insurance	83	82	76	77	76	-9

Source: Private Exchange Research Council (PERC) analysis, 2017. Based on groups enrolling in benefits on Liazon exchanges with a benefits effective date of January 1, 2017. www.percinsights.com
Sample: Employee study sample with at least one plan purchase.
*Based on employees who were offered the product and purchased at least one product in 2013 to 2017.
**Net employer-paid products.
***Based on 2014 to reflect the first full year the product category was offered on the exchange.

What percentage of employees purchased an HSA-qualified plan when offered?

Percentage buying an HSA-qualified plan

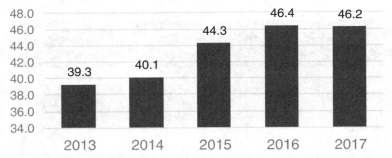

Source: Private Exchange Research Council (PERC) analysis, 2017. Based on groups enrolling in benefits on Liazon exchanges with a benefits effective date of January 1, 2017. www.percinsights.com
Sample: Data representative of all employees in the study sample who purchased a Medical plan and were offered an HSA-qualified plan.

What percentage of employees purchased an HSA-qualified plan when offered?

Percentage buying an HSA-qualified plan

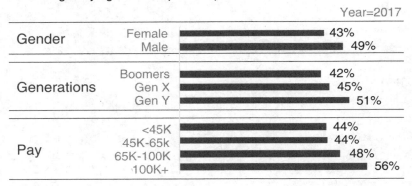

Source: Private Exchange Research Council (PERC) analysis, 2017. Based on groups enrolling in benefits on Liazon exchanges with a benefits effective date of January 1, 2017. www.percinsights.com
Sample: Data representative of all employees in the study sample who were at a company and eligible to purchase an HSA-qualified plan. N=96,061

PERC
Private Exchange Research Council

What Do Employers and Employees Really Think About Liazon Exchanges?

To find out what people really think about the benefits marketplace experience, Liazon conducts an annual survey of employers and employees who use our exchanges to provide and purchase employee benefits.

Data from the Liazon 2017 Employer and Employee Surveys

After moving to a Liazon-powered Private Exchange to shop for their benefits, employees report that they appreciate the unique features offered
to them. Specifically, they like:

Decision
support

96%
find the education
and decision
support tools
important[1]

The array
of choice

96%
like the expanded
product offering[1]

To see
true cost

97%
find exposure to
the true price of
benefits important[1]

To be in the
driver's seat

96%
prefer to choose
their own benefits[1]

[1] 2017 Liazon Employee Survey

And employees become savvier benefits consumers as a result

85% of employees are **more engaged** in their health care decisions[1]

85% of employees are **more aware** of the cost of medical care[1]

83% of employees **better understand** what their health insurance and other benefits cover[1]

82% of employees are **more confident** in their health care decisions[1]

Employers love what the Exchange has done for their company atmosphere

89% say the Exchange has positively impacted their company culture[2]

Employees take notice, too

75% say they're more likely to stay with their employer because of the Exchange[1]

[1] 2017 Liazon Employee Survey
[2] 2017 Liazon Employer Survey

Breathing a sigh of relief

For employees:

While only **16%** of employees were originally excited about using an Exchange...

79% are now glad their employer made the switch [1]

For employers:

 90%
say their company's benefits administration has been simplified [2]

86%
think the Exchange has helped them control benefits costs [2]

→**95%**
are glad they switched to an Exchange [2]

Satisfaction all around

97% of employers [2], and **94%** of employees are satisfied with the Exchange experience [1]

1 year later—**92%** of employees are satisfied with the benefits they purchased [1]

[1] 2017 Liazon Employee Survey
[2] 2017 Liazon Employer Survey

The Exchange Experience: A Look at How Benefits Are Selected on Liazon Exchanges

This section provides a glimpse into how someone actually goes about choosing benefits on a Liazon exchange.

To start, a user completes a profile questionnaire that looks for the user's preferences based on health, wealth, protection, and lifestyle concerns that may impact the choice of benefits.

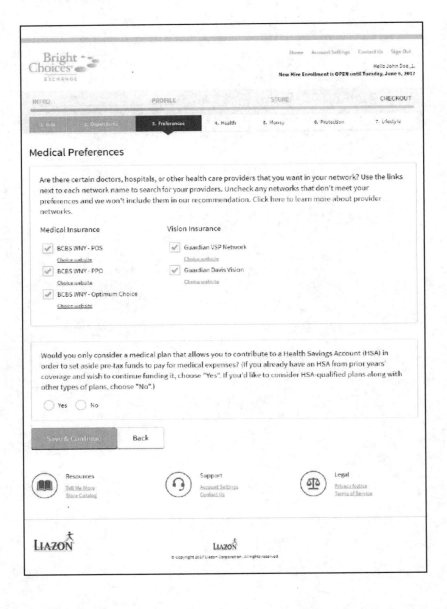

The employee gets a recommendation for the products and plans that best meet his or her needs, based on the answers to the profile questionnaire.

Health

Medical Insurance

Lighthouse OA EPO $0/10%/$5000 HSA
Lighthouse Health Insurance

We recommended this plan because it's the Lowest Expected Cost Plan that Matches Your Preferences. Our recommendation is based on the premium costs plus what you can expect to pay for medical expenses in the coming year.

Dental Insurance

Premier Dental Plan
Dental Insurance Services

We've recommended this plan since you're concerned about major dental procedures, such as bridges, crowns, dentures, and/or orthodontic care for you and/or your dependents. This level of dental insurance affords you the extra protection you need to manage the cost of care for you and/or your family.

Vision Insurance

Vision One Low Vision
Vision One

We've recommended this plan since you have expenses related to vision care, such as eye exams, glasses, or contacts. This plan gives you the extra protection you need to manage the cost of this care.

Accident Insurance

Enhanced Accident Insurance
Accredo Accident & Critical Illness

We've recommended this plan to complement our recommendation of a Consumer Driven Health plan. When paired with a Consumer Driven Health plan, critical illness insurance is a good way to cover your deductible, should you or a family member be diagnosed with cancer, heart disease, or other critical illnesses. Remember to check your plan for qualifying illnesses.

Critical Illness Insurance

Critical Illness Insurance
Accredo Accident & Critical Illness

We've recommended this plan because it can help pay for costs associated with treatment of your illness, replace some of your lost income, and even supply funds for a change in lifestyle, should anything happen to you. Remember to check your plan for qualifying illnesses.

Employees can click to learn more about particular plans and why they were recommended.

Employee Life Insurance
(Vitalis Life Insurance)

Vitalis Life Insurance

Plan Year:	Jan 1, 2018 – Dec 31, 2018
Effective Date:	Jan 1, 2018

Carrier Information
- Benefit Summary
- Vitalis Life Insurance website ⬀

Life insurance protects your loved ones, paying benefits should something happen to you. Buy the amount you need in increments of $25,000 up to five times your annual salary ($500,000 limit). For amounts up to $100,000 you do not need to prove your spouse's good health.

Why We Recommend This Plan

We've recommended the Vitalis Life Insurance Employee Life Insurance plan since family members rely on your income.

Show Amounts Per   [Month ▾]

Basic Information   ⌃

Guaranteed Issue Amount	$100,000.00	**Maximum Benefit Amount**	5x Salary
Accidental Death and Dismemberment (AD&D) Benefits	Yes	**Other Benefits**	Free will preparation

Cost & Coverage   ⌃

$25,000 Benefit	$2.15 /MO	$50,000 Benefit	$4.30 /MO
$75,000 Benefit	$6.45 /MO	$100,000 Benefit	$8.60 /MO
$125,000 Benefit	$10.75 /MO	$150,000 Benefit	$12.90 /MO
$175,000 Benefit	$15.05 /MO	$200,000 Benefit	$17.20 /MO
$225,000 Benefit	$19.35 /MO	$250,000 Benefit	$21.50 /MO

ⓘ You're currently ineligible for coverage from $275,000 to $500,000 based on your annual salary.

After employees review their recommendations and learn what they need to know about the products and plans recommended for them, they can shop for their benefits in four different categories.

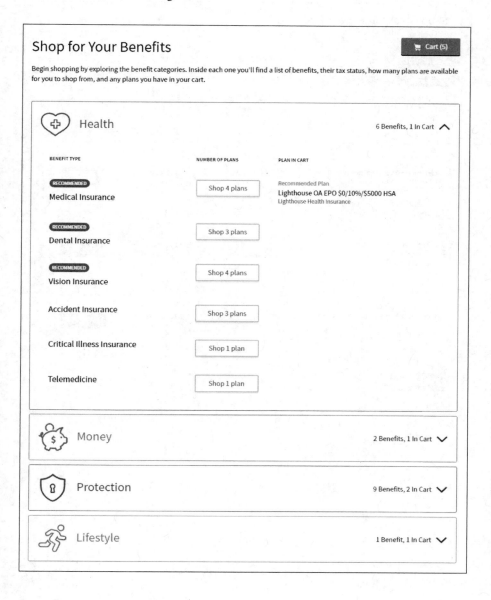

Shop for Your Benefits

🛒 Cart (5)

Begin shopping by exploring the benefit categories. Inside each one you'll find a list of benefits, their tax status, how many plans are available for you to shop from, and any plans you have in your cart.

✚ Health   6 Benefits, 1 In Cart ∧

BENEFIT TYPE	NUMBER OF PLANS	PLAN IN CART
RECOMMENDED Medical Insurance	Shop 4 plans	Recommended Plan **Lighthouse OA EPO $0/10%/$5000 HSA** Lighthouse Health Insurance
RECOMMENDED Dental Insurance	Shop 3 plans	
RECOMMENDED Vision Insurance	Shop 4 plans	
Accident Insurance	Shop 3 plans	
Critical Illness Insurance	Shop 1 plan	
Telemedicine	Shop 1 plan	

🐷 Money   2 Benefits, 1 In Cart ∨

🛡 Protection   9 Benefits, 2 In Cart ∨

🏃 Lifestyle   1 Benefit, 1 In Cart ∨

They can also explore different plans within any of the categories.

With a defined contribution strategy for benefits, employees can see the true costs of the benefits they've chosen to purchase, including how much their employers are contributing and how much they are paying.

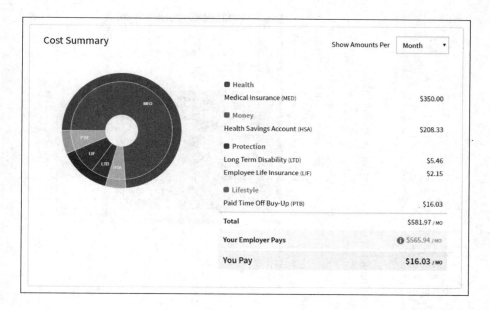

Cost Summary   Show Amounts Per   [Month ▼]

● Health	
Medical Insurance (MED)	$350.00
● Money	
Health Savings Account (HSA)	$208.33
● Protection	
Long Term Disability (LTD)	$5.46
Employee Life Insurance (LIF)	$2.15
● Lifestyle	
Paid Time Off Buy-Up (PTB)	$16.03
Total	$581.97 /MO
Your Employer Pays	ⓘ $565.94 /MO
You Pay	**$16.03** /MO

For the Benefits Geeks: A Health Care Timeline

Health Care TIMELINE

Organized Medicine Takes Shape
→ 1900s

This period marks the beginning of organized medicine. The American Medical Association gains powerful influence as the national organization of state and local associations. Unlike European countries, U.S. policy-makers find little value in health insurance.

N.Y. Health Board supervising care of babies in hot weather, c. 1900-1908.
Photo: Wikimedia Commons

Concept of Health Insurance Promoted
→ 1912

Social insurance, including health insurance, gains public attention when Teddy Roosevelt and his Progressive Party campaign on the issue. The American Association for Labor Legislation also publishes and promotes a draft bill for compulsory health insurance, but the effort is derailed when the U.S. enters World War I.

A Model for Health Insurance
→ 1929

Baylor Hospital in Dallas, Texas, starts a prepaid hospital insurance program with a local teachers union and creates what is thought to be the nation's first example of modern health insurance.

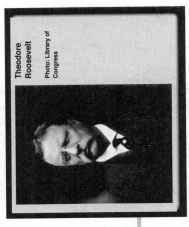

Theodore Roosevelt
Photo: Library of Congress

Source: AnnenbergClassroom.org.

Health Care TIMELINE

New Focus With Hard Economic Times
→ 1934

The Depression shifts attention to unemployment insurance and "old age" benefits. President Franklin Roosevelt creates the Committee on Economic Security to address these issues as well as medical care and insurance. But when the Social Security Act is passed, health insurance is omitted. The American Medical Association strongly opposes a national health insurance program, saying it would increase bureaucracy, limit doctors' freedom and interfere with the doctor-patient relationship.

A family affected by the Depression, 1936.
Photo: Wikimedia Commons

FDR Proposes 'Economic Bill of Rights'
→ 1944

In his State of the Union address, President Franklin Roosevelt outlines an "economic bill of rights" that includes the right to adequate medical care and the opportunity to achieve and enjoy good health. During World War II, U.S. businesses begin to offer health benefits as they compete for workers, giving rise to the employer-based system in place today.

National Health Insurance Condemned
→ 1945

Shortly after becoming president, Harry Truman proposes a broad health care restructuring that includes mandatory coverage, more hospitals, and double the number of nurses and doctors. Denounced by the American Medical Association and other critics as "socialized medicine," his plan goes nowhere in Congress.

Harry Truman
Photo: Wikimedia Commons

Source: AnnenbergClassroom.org.

Health Care TIMELINE

Discrimination Barred in Hospital Care

→ **1946**

The Hill-Burton Act (Hospital Survey and Construction Act) pays for the construction of hospitals, especially in rural areas, to close the gap in access to medical care. It also prohibits discrimination on the basis of race, religion, or national origin in the provision of hospital services, but allows for "separate but equal" facilities. Hospitals are required to provide a "reasonable volume" of charitable care.

Medicare and Medicaid Become Law

→ **1965**

President Lyndon Johnson signs into law the most significant health reform of the century: Medicare, which provides comprehensive health care coverage for people 65 and older, and Medicaid, which helps states cover long-term care for the poor and disabled.

President Lyndon B. Johnson signs Medicare Bill
Photo: Wikimedia Commons

Health Care in Crisis

→ **1970s**

Medical costs rapidly escalate now that millions more are insured after the passage of Medicare and Medicaid. In 1972, President Richard Nixon signs the Health Maintenance Organization Act as part of his national health strategy to reduce costs. HMOs are prepaid, managed-care group plans. But further action is stymied by the Watergate scandal. For the next several decades, presidents and lawmakers try, and fail, to overhaul the health care system.

Source: AnnenbergClassroom.org.

Health Care TIMELINE

Corporations Take Greater Control
→ 1980s

There is a shift toward privatization of health care as corporations begin to integrate the hospital system (previously a decentralized structure) and enter many other health-care-related businesses and consolidate control. In 1987, the Census Bureau's annual estimate of health insurance coverage in the United States finds 31 million uninsured (13 percent of the population).

States Enact Reform Laws
→ 2006

Massachusetts implements laws to provide health care coverage to nearly all state residents and calls for shared responsibility among individuals, employers and the government in financing the expanded coverage. Within two years, the state's uninsured rate is cut in half. Vermont also passes comprehensive health care reform aiming for near-universal coverage. The law creates a health plan for uninsured residents and focuses on improving overall quality of care.

Major Health Care Reform Signed
→ 2010

President Barack Obama signs landmark health care legislation. The Patient Protection and Affordable Care Act requires that all individuals have health insurance beginning in 2014. Those with low and middle incomes who do not have access to affordable coverage through their jobs will be able to buy coverage with federal subsidies. Health plans cannot deny coverage for any reason, including a person's health status, nor can they charge more because of a person's health or sex.

President Obama reacts to the passage of the health-care bill.

Photo: Wikimedia Commons

Source: AnnenbergClassroom.org.

Index

C

Cadillac tax, 186

Cancer in Context blog, 210

CareMount Medical Practice, 165–166

carriers. *See* insurers

Castlight, 161

catastrophic insurance, 207–208

CDHP (Consumer-Driven Health Plan), 52, 83, 226

choice, 1, 10, 18, 48, 52
  advantages of, 24–25, 40
  employee satisfaction and, 25–27
  meaningful, 57–59
  misconceptions about, 128–129
  private exchange differentiators
    benefits administration features, 120
    decision support systems, 114–115
    elasticity, 113–114
    minimum requirements, 109–111
    price transparency, 116–117
    "value added" tools and services, 118
    year-round customer support, 119
  products, 89–92, 102–106
  provider networks, 200

Cigna, 80, 139

The Cleveland Clinic, 158

commoditized care, 211–212

commodity exchanges, 39

The Company That Solved Health Care (Torinus), 166–167

compensation, employer-sponsored benefits as total, 41–45

Comprehensive Addiction and Recovery Act, 191

Conduent, 80–81

Condeluci, Chris, 169–172, 177–178, 182–185, 188–189, 198

consumer involvement
  benefits consumers defined, 5, 225, 227
  CDHP (Consumer-Driven Health Plan), 52, 226, 226
  consumer-centric provider networks, 165–168, 200–201
  consumer-driven innovation, 193–196
    benefits portfolios, 163–164
    customized networks, 165–168, 200–201
    market opportunities, 157–162
  consumerism, 9, 44, 70–73, 148, 194
    definition of, 226
    terminology, 226–227
  data and digital tools for consumers, 201–204
  employer funding for individual insurance, 198–199
  patient-empowered healing, 204–206
  utopian vision
    shopping for care, 208–213
    universal vouchers, 206–208

consumer-centric provider networks, 165–168, 200–201

consumer-driven health plan. *See* CDHP (consumer-driven health plan)

consumerism, 9, 44, 70–73, 148, 194
  definition of, 226
  terminology, 226–227

costs
  cost control, 19–21
  cost shifting, 129
  misconceptions about, 129
  price transparency
    advantages of, 59–67, 203–204
    in private exchanges, 23–24, 116–117
    tools for, 71
    with traditional benefits offerings, 22–23
    value pricing, 166–168

Covered California, 76–77

cultural fit for benefits, 33

customer support, 95

customized networks, 165–168, 200–201

D

data and digital tools for consumers, 201–204

Davis, Tyler, 105

decision support systems, 24, 27–29, 48, 58, 68–70, 79, 95, 103, 114–115, 127, 141, 200, 228

defined contribution model, 19–21, 59–67, 86, 116, 184
  definition of, 224, 229
  misconceptions about, 129

G

Gallagher Marketplace, 85, 127

Geisinger Health System, 157

Gniewek, Barbara, 73, 109, 111, 115–116, 118

Graham, Thomas J., 158

Grassley, Chuck, 172, 188

group insurance, 225

Gruber, Jon, 200

guidance. *See* decision support systems

H

Hall, Mark, 21

Hallmark, 10

Hamby, Blake, 105–106

Harkins, Rob, 130–135, 146

HDHPs (High-Deductible Health Plans), 25, 90, 93, 187, 198, 225, 226–227

health care, definition of, 226

health care consumerism, 9, 44, 70–73, 148, 194
  definition of, 226
  terminology, 226–227

health care timeline, 246

health insurance, definition of, 225. *See also* benefits

health insurance exchanges, 113

Health Maintenance Organizations (HMOs), 43–45

health plans. *See also* benefits
  CDHP (Consumer-Driven Health Plan), 226
  definition of, 225
  HDHP (High-Deductible Health Plan), 226–227
  indemnity plans, 43
  innovation, 157–162
    benefits portfolios, 163–164
    Castlight, 161
    customized networks, 165–168
    FitBit, 160–161
    Healthcare Bluebook, 160
    HealthPatch, 160–161
    national individual insurance market, 169–173
    RedBrick Health, 160
  managed care plans, 43–45

Health Reimbursement Arrangements (HRAs). *See* HRAs

Health Savings Accounts (HSAs), 25, 52, 95, 119, 187, 197–198, 227

Healthcare Bluebook, 160

HealthCare.gov, 76–77

HealthPatch, 160–161

Heitkamp, Heidi, 172, 188

Herzlinger, Regina, 1, 20, 44–45, 57, 190

Hewitt, Aon, 64

High-Deductible Health Plans (HDHPs), 25, 93, 198, 226–227

high-risk conditions, monitoring, 203

Hill, Kevin, 150–151

history of health insurance benefits, 42

HMOs (health maintenance organizations), 43–45

Holland, medieval commodity markets in, 38

Holler, Kevin, 59, 66

Horizon, 143

HR (human resources), role of, 51, 72, 80, 133

HRA bill. *See* Small Business Health Care Relief Act

HRAs (Health Reimbursement Arrangements), 52, 171
  definition of, 227
  QSEHRA (Qualified Small Employer Health Reimbursement Arrangement), 199

HSAs (Health Savings Accounts), 52, 164, 187, 197–198, 227

human resources (HR), role of, 133

Humana, 139

I

identity theft protection, 152–153

indemnity plans, 43

individual insurance, 225

innovation
  in benefits
    benefits portfolios, 163–164
    Castlight, 161
    customized networks, 165–168
    FitBit, 160–161
    Healthcare Bluebook, 160
    HealthPatch, 160–161

J-K

L

live advisors, 27–28

long-term conditions, monitoring, 203

Lytle, Tamara, 77

M

MACRA (Medicare and CHIP
Reauthorization Act), 202

managed care plans, 43–45

Manhattan Total Wellness, 211

Marcotte, Brian, 203

Marcucci, Rhonda, 82–83, 95, 109, 114–120

market opportunities, 157–162

marketplaces. *See* exchanges

Massachusetts General Hospital, 205

McConnell, Mitch, 175, 180–183

McKnight, Robin, 200

meaningful choice. *See* choice

medical insurance, definition of, 225. *See also*
benefits

medical plans. *See* health plans

Medicare
enrollment numbers, 88
Medicare and CHIP Reauthorization Act
(MACRA), 202
as model, 187
Part D, 47

Medicare and CHIP Reauthorization Act
(MACRA), 202

Mercer, 80–81

mergers of insurers, 138

MetLife, 143, 144, 148–150

misconceptions, overcoming,
128–130

money accounts, 224–225, 227

Moser, Jessica, 148–150

multi-carrier exchanges, 83

Murphy, Brian, 126

N

Natalie, Amy, 104–107

national individual insurance market,
169–173

Nazemi, Kevin, 141

net cost, 86

non-emergent health care, purchasing on
as-needed basis, 209–212

nonmedical benefits, 58, 60, 64, 90, 93, 106,
144, 146, 224

O

Obama, Barack, 16, 175, 228. *See also* ACA
(Affordable Care Act)

Obamacare. *See* ACA (Affordable Care Act)

operators of private exchanges
benefits advisors, 80–81
benefits providers, 80
pure-play providers, 79
traditional benefits administration
companies, 81–82

opioid addiction crisis, 191

optimized user experience, 29

organizational fit, 33

Oxford Health Plans, 143, 150–151

Oscar, 141–142

P

Parkland Memorial Hospital, 205

patient involvement. *See* consumer
involvement

Patient Protection and Affordable Care Act
(PPACA). *See* ACA (Affordable Care Act)
patient-empowered healing, 204–206

Payers. *See* insurers

PERC (Private Exchange Research Council),
33–34, 93, 146, 234

personalization, 67–70

pet insurance, 72, 153

plan comparison tools, 28, 63

point-of-service (POS) plans, 43–45

policy for national individual insurance
market, 171–172

portfolios
advantages of, 17, 59, 67
decision support, 27–28, 67, 69, 92
definition of, 5–6, 229
private exchanges, 149, 162, 164

public exchanges, 36
  challenges for, 169–173
  compared to private exchanges, 75–79
  creation of, 8
  definition of, 228
  enrollment numbers, 87–88
  stability of, 184
pure-play providers, 79

Q-R

QSEHRA (Qualified Small Employer Health Reimbursement Arrangement), 199
Raman-Tangella, Vidya, 148
recommendation engines, 24, 28, 58, 68, 90–92, 228–229
recommendation logic. *See* recommendation engines
RedBrick Health, 160
Regeneron Pharmaceuticals Inc., 157
Reinhardt, Uwe, 59–60
Respectful Maternity Care, 205
retaining employees, 3–5
retirement
  401(k), 60, 164, 229
  retiree exchanges, 76, 77–79, 88, 163, 199
Revelas, T. J., 55, 68, 70, 126–127
Richman, Barak, 20–21, 190
RightOpt, 80–81
Rockwell International, 77
Roman marketplaces, 37
Rosenthal, Elisabeth, 196
Ryan, Paul, 175, 178–179

S

Sandestin Golf and Beach Resort case study, 104–107
SBHCRA. *See* Small Business Health Care Relief Act
Schlosser, Mario, 141–142
Sears, 72–73
Section 1332 Waivers, 184
self-insured models for health insurance, 84–85

Serigraph, Inc., 166–168
service providers. *See* private exchange operators
Sherman, Debra, 210–211
shopping experience, 208–213. *See also* private exchanges
  in-network issues, 212–214
  non-emergent health care, purchasing on as-needed basis, 209–212
  optimizing, 29
Shulman, Kevin, 20
single-carrier exchanges, 83
Small Business Health Care Relief Act (SBHCRA), 171, 188
specialty benefits. *See* nonmedical benefits
spending accounts, 224–225
sponsors. *See* private exchange operators
Sqord, 157
stability of individual markets, 184
Starbucks, 10
Sterling Optical, 211 stores. *See* benefits stores
Strater, Rick, 85, 127–129
Subramanian, Ashok, 12, 48–49, 144, 147
Sumerian civilization, marketplaces in, 37
supplemental benefits. *See* nonmedical benefits
supply-side economics, 38–40
surveys
  Liazon employee surveys
    2017 Employer Survey Report: Employer Satisfaction with Private Exchanges, 20, 67
    2017 Employee Survey Report: Health Care Consumerism in a Marketplace Environment, 10, 25, 60, 67, 92, 115, 125, 129, 130, 146, 171
    Data from the Liazon 2017 Employer and Employee Surveys, 237
    Employer and Employee Survey Results, October 2015, 171
  Willis Towers Watson Surveys
    2015/2016 Global Benefit Attitudes Survey, 4
    2016 21st Annual Best Practices in Health Care Employer Survey 52, 77, 88, 185